The Tonawanda Senecas' Heroic Battle Against Removal

The Tonawanda Senecas' Heroic Battle Against Removal

Conservative Activist Indians

Laurence M. Hauptman

excelsior editions

State University of New York Press
Albany, New York

Cover image: Ernest Smith's WPA Seneca Arts Project painting *The Story of Bare Hill*

Published by State University of New York Press, Albany
© 2011 State University of New York

Excelsior Editions is an imprint of State University of New York Press

For information, contact State University of New York Press, Albany, NY
www.sunypress.edu

Production by Diane Ganeles
Marketing by Anne M. Valentine

Library of Congress Cataloging-in-Publication Data

Hauptman, Laurence M.
   The Tonawanda Senecas' heroic battle against removal : conservative activist Indians / Laurence M. Hauptman.
        p. cm.
   Includes bibliographical references and index.
   ISBN 978-1-4384-3577-0 (hardcover : alk. paper)
   ISBN 978-1-4384-3578-7 (pbk. : alk. paper)
   1. Tonawanda Band of Seneca Indians of New York—History.   2. Tonawanda Band of Seneca Indians of New York—Politics and government.   3. Seneca Indians—New York (State)—History.   4. Seneca Indians—New York (State)—Politics and government.   I. Title.

E99.S3H38 2011
974.7004'975546—dc22   2010025995

10 9 8 7 6 5 4 3 2 1

To the memory of "Mrs. C.," Ramona Charles, a Tonawanda Seneca and proud of it, who introduced me to her remarkable people

Contents

Charts

Maps

Abbreviations

APS	American Philosophical Society
BECHS	Buffalo and Erie County Historical Society, Buffalo, New York
BIA	Bureau of Indian Affairs
Coll.	Collection
CorU	Cornell University, Carl Kroch Library
CU	Columbia University, Butler Library, New York, New York
DHI	Francis Jennings et al., eds., *Iroquois Indians: A Documentary History of the Six Nations and Their League*, 50 microfilm reels. Woodbridge, Connecticut: Research Publications, 1985.
ESP	Ely S. Parker
HC	Hamilton College, Clinton, New York
HRS	Henry Rowe Schoolcraft
JR	*Jesuit Relations and Allied Documents*, Reuben G. Thwaites, ed., 73 volumes. Cleveland: Burrows Bros., 1896–1901.
LC	Library of Congress
LHM	Lewis Henry Morgan
M	Microcopy
MR	Microfilm reel

MSS.   Manuscript collection

NA   National Archives, Washington, D.C.

NYHS   New-York Historical Society, New York, New York

NYSA   New York State Archives, Albany, New York

NYSL   New York State Library, Manuscript Division, Albany

OIA   Office of Indian Affairs

RBW   Reuben B. Warren

RG   Record Group

SAR   Records of the Seneca Agency in New York

SNAR   Six Nations Agency Records

SNI   Seneca Nation of Indians

Stat.   *United States Statutes at Large*

UR   University of Rochester, Rush Rhees Library

VC   Vassar College, Poughkeepsie, New York

Whipple   New York State Legislature. Assembly. Doc. no. 51,
Report   *Report of the Special Committee to Investigate the Indian*
            Problem of the State of New York. Appointed by the
            Assembly of 1888. 2 vols. Albany, New York: Troy Press,
            1889.

WHS   Wisconsin Historical Society

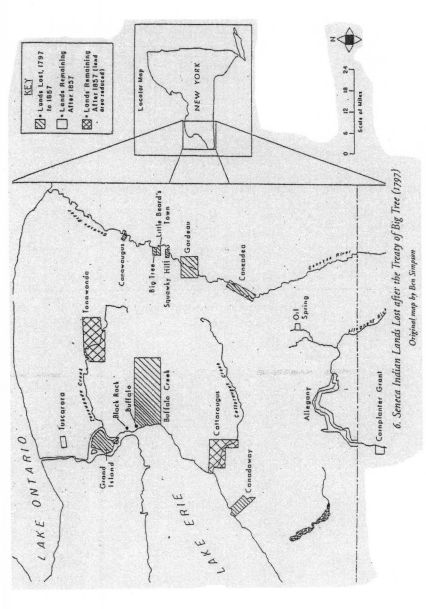

KEY

- Lands Lost, 1797 to 1857
- Lands Remaining After 1857
- Lands Remaining After 1857 (land area reduced)

Locator Map

NEW YORK

N

Scale of Miles
0   6   12   18   24

LAKE ONTARIO

Tuscarora

Genesee Creek

Grand Island

Black Rock

Buffalo

Buffalo Creek

LAKE ERIE

Canadaway

Cattaraugus

Cattaraugus Creek

Tonawanda

Genesee River

Canawaugus

Big Tree

Squawky Hill

Little Beard's Town

Gardeau

Caneadea

Genesee River

Oil Spring

Allegany

Allegheny River

Conplanter Grant

6. Seneca Indian Lands lost after the Treaty of Big Tree (1797)

Original map by Ben Simpson

Map 1. Seneca Indian Lands Lost After the Treaty of Big Treaty (1797)

Eastern Iroquoia Today

Map 2. Eastern Iroquoia Today
(map by Joe Stoll)

Tonawanda Reservation
and Environs Today

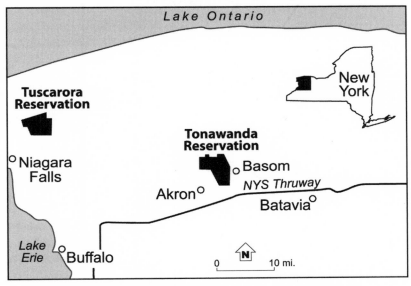

Map 3. Tonawanda Reservation and Environs Today
(map by Joe Stoll)

Preface

In their nation's oral tradition, the Senecas emerged from a hole in the top of a great hill—"Ge-non-de-wah-ga"—at the head of Canandaigua Lake in western New York. On their emergence, the Senecas soon found themselves faced with the ever-present threat of a huge poisonous snake with an insatiable appetite. The monstrous snake confined the Senecas to a small territory and killed and swallowed all tribal members except for two orphaned children. Coming to the children's rescue, the Creator instructed them on how to make a willow bow and tip their arrows with poison. Subsequently, the two brave children confronted the snake and fired their poison arrows at it. The wounded snake violently rolled down the hill, carved a cleft in the hillside, regurgitated the skulls of the deceased Senecas, and fell into the water. According to this tradition, the "Seneca Indians sprang from these two heroic children."[1]

This version of Seneca origins was told by Chief John Blacksmith, a Tonawanda sachem, in 1838 during a time of great troubles for his people.[2] Instead of a monstrous serpent drinking the lifeblood of the Senecas, the enemies were land speculators, allied with powerful friends in Albany and Washington, D.C. Instead of two orphaned children fighting alone against the gigantic snake, a remarkable alliance of chiefs, including Blacksmith, clan mothers, and a young "runner-envoy" aided by an extraordinary white attorney fought relentlessly to prevent Tonawanda removal to Kansas. As in the epic, the process of survival left a swath of victims that changed Seneca existence forever. Today two Seneca identities—the Tonawanda Seneca Band of Indians and the Seneca Nation of Indians—exist in New York State as a result of their Herculean fight against the serpent that largely took the form of the Ogden Land Company. The emergence of this separate Tonawanda Seneca world is the focus of this book.

The Tonawanda Senecas' struggle was an intense contest, resolved only after six decades of unrelenting pressures. While the Seneca settlement along Tonawanda Creek could be traced to before the American Revolution, the federal government first acknowledged the existence of a Tonawanda Indian Reservation—seventy square miles in size—at the Treaty of Big Tree in 1797. In 1826, as a result of lobbying by the trustees of the Ogden Land Company, a federal treaty at Buffalo Creek—one never ratified by the United States Senate—reduced the reservation to 12,800 acres. As a result of further machinations by the Ogden Land Company, state and local interests, and federal officials in Washington, D.C. and on the ground in western New York, the Tonawandas were dispossessed of all their lands in another treaty at Buffalo Creek in 1838, one not ratified by the required two-thirds vote of the United States Senate. This land loss was confirmed by a third federal treaty at Buffalo Creek in 1842, one formally ratified by the Senate and proclaimed by President John Tyler.[3] Only in 1857 did the Tonawandas achieve a major victory.

The United States–Tonawanda Seneca Treaty signed on November 5, 1857, ratified by the Senate on June 4, 1858, and proclaimed by President James Buchanan on March 31, 1859, is one of the more important federal-Indian accords in American history.[4] By its terms, the Tonawanda Senecas were "allowed" to repurchase 7,549 acres of their 12,800-acre reservation at $20 per acre from the Ogden Land Company, their adversary. Arthur C. Parker, the noted anthropologist of Seneca ancestry, has dubbed the 1857 treaty as "blood money," a reward to the Ogden Land Company for its shenanigans and fraudulent actions over the decades.[5] Although Parker's assessment is basically correct, the Treaty of 1857 and what followed through 1863, nevertheless, brought three positive results for these Indians: (1) federal recognition for the first time as a separate Seneca entity, namely, the Tonawanda Band of Senecas, governed by a council of chiefs, set apart from the Seneca Nation of Indians, an elected system of governance; (2) the continued existence, however reduced, of the Tonawanda Indian Reservation; and (3) the beginning of the end of the Ogden Land Company's interference in Tonawanda affairs and its incessant efforts to dispossess these Indians.

From the earliest two decades of reservation life, 1797 to 1819, Tonawandas had begun to establish a separate path from the other communities and territories that made up the Seneca Nation: Allegany, Big Tree, Buffalo Creek, Canadaway, Caneadea, Canawaugus,

Cattaraugus, Gardeau, Little Beardstown, Oil Spring, and Squawky Hill. In the 1820s, under the controversial tutelage of Red Jacket, the reservation became the center of resistance to the Ogden Land Company's efforts to force all Senecas off their lands. In the three-decade period after the Seneca prophet Handsome Lake's death in 1815, Chief Jemmy Johnson and other followers of the *Gaiwiio*, the Code of Handsome Lake, inspired a religious revitalization that gave these Indians hope in times of desperation. Through the brilliance of activist sachem John Blacksmith, supported by eight clan mothers, the Tonawanda Council of Chiefs developed strategies of resistance, employed the youthful Ely S. Parker as a runner, and hired one of the ablest attorneys in mid-nineteenth-century New York State, John H. Martindale, to advocate for their cause.

Most histories of the removal era merely treat Indian communities as victims, nobly fighting a losing battle against the inevitable, Manifest Destiny. In contrast, the present book views the Tonawandas as most able strategists and actors who succeeded, albeit at a high price. The author believes that the Tonawandas' struggle against all odds is one of the most significant but neglected stories in Native American history. Although certain aspects of their heroic battle have been told before, the present study attempts to provide a more complete explanation of why the Tonawanda Seneca Reservation still exists today in western New York State.

Historian William Armstrong previously recounted Ely S. Parker's prominent role in lobbying for justice for the Tonawandas from the mid-1840s to the ratification of the treaty. However, Parker was not alone; he was one of several individuals pushing the Tonawandas' cause.[6] Other studies, such as a dissertation written by Mary Conable, largely focus on the machinations of the Ogden Land Company, do not examine the inner workings of the Tonawanda Council of Chiefs, and overemphasize the roles of Lewis Henry Morgan and Henry Rowe Schoolcraft as well as the pro-Indian white citizens of Genesee County.[7] Moreover, still other scholars have largely concentrated on other aspects of Tonawanda history in the period prior to the American Civil War, including the important development of the Handsome Lake religion or how these Senecas influenced the origins of the discipline of anthropology.[8]

In a doctoral dissertation written in 1996, the late Deborah Doxtator examined the history of clans in three Iroquoian communities: Tyendinaga, Grand River, and Tonawanda.[9] In an accurate but all-too-brief assessment of Tonawanda society from 1797 to 1857, Doxtator concluded: "The collective experience in fighting the American government, the Ogden Land Company and other Senecas who seemed willing to allow the Tonawanda lands to be lost, created a great solidarity within the community and a unified expression of their separate identity."[10] She stressed that the Indians were strengthened in their determination to resist by the formal establishment of the Handsome Lake religion whose center was at Tonawanda. Moreover, according to Doxtator, the emergence of "a single consolidated reserve identity," namely a community-nation, in response to outside threats, came to subsume many of the functions of clans.[11]

While Doxtator was right, that is that this "culturally conservative community, predominantly Longhouse, and fiercely nationalistic" formed a "reservation community-nation identity" in fighting back against the Ogden Land Company, she restricted her analyses to social organization, not exploring the political acumen of the Tonawandas.[12] Unfortunately, she ignored the brilliant tactics and legal defense of the Tonawandas' struggle largely drawn up by these Senecas themselves and implemented by their attorney, John H. Martindale. Their carefully worked out strategies led directly to a major victory in the United States Supreme Court, to the federal-Tonawanda Treaty of 1857, and ultimately to the repurchase of 7,549 acres of their reservation.[13]

Unlike Doxtator's perceptive dissertation or other previous writings, *The Tonawanda Senecas' Heroic Battle Against Removal: Conservative Activist Indians* examines the strategies employed by the Tonawanda Council of Chiefs, with the support of eight clan mothers, in their efforts to resist tribal dispossession and tribal dissolution. They were faced with all of the following: pressures of the Holland and later the Ogden Land Company; rapid settlement and urbanization occurring as a result of the transportation revolution after the War of 1812; local, state, and federal officials' intent and policies to acquire tribal lands and remove the Indians by legal as well as by illegal methods; paternalistic, misguided Quakers who believed they knew what was best for the Indians; sharp divisions within the Seneca polity; and even the actions of self-serving Indian leaders from other communities willing to take bribes or sell out the Tonawandas. The Tonawandas' numerous strategies, including a conscious effort at delay, and events transpiring 1,500 miles away in eastern Kansas were major reasons why their reservation still exists today and why there are two Seneca governments and identities in New York State today. Because circumstances in Kansas changed rapidly during the decade of the 1850s, the Tonawandas' strategies were effective.

The Tonawanda Senecas' Heroic Battle Against Removal: Conservative Activist Indians is based on nearly forty years of archival research, but also on thirty-five years of fieldwork at Tonawanda. I have been strongly influenced by anthropologists as well as Civil War historians who have long understood the need to undertake systematic fieldwork. Benjamin Cohn of the University of Chicago once wrote about the need to do fieldwork: "It is not just the idea of the exotic, but the sense one gets that other systems work, that there are such things as cultural logics, that there is as much rationality in other societies as in our own, even though they flow from other principles."[14]

In 1974, at the encouragement of Dr. William N. Fenton and at the invitation of Cephas Hill, a Seneca elder, I was invited to the Tonawanda Indian Reservation. Realizing that the Great Depression's generation was rapidly dying off, I hoped to combine interviews with my archival research on the 1930s. Eventually this work was to lead to the publication of my book *The Iroquois and the New Deal* in 1981.[15] Hill, a septuagenarian who had worked with anthropologists Fenton and Arthur C. Parker in the 1930s, greeted me and took me to visit his friend, ninety-two-year-old Harrison Ground. Both Indian men had worked on the WPA Seneca Arts Project from 1935 to 1941. Ground had been one of the leading woodcarvers of False Face masks, while Hill, also known as a carver, served as an assistant and timekeeper to Parker on the project as well as a very accomplished Indian trickster. Since then I have visited this community once or twice a year, spending time with elders at the Peter Doctor Indian Education Memorial Foundation awards dinner, making presentations about my research to community groups at the Tonawanda Indian Community House, and teaching classes of Seneca children at the Akron High School. I have had the privilege of learning from Tonawanda Senecas themselves.

I have attempted to overcome several problems affecting my research. First, during the first half of the nineteenth century, most Tonawandas were fluent in the Iroquoian languages but could not read or write English. In the 1840s, they depended on Ely S. Parker, their runner and young sachem-in-waiting, as their scribe and interpreter.

Consequently, because of Parker's very important role and his own substantial personal correspondence that has survived, later historians have examined the Tonawanda struggle merely through his eyes or those of his remarkable family. Ely, his father William, his uncle Samuel, and his great-uncle Jemmy Johnson all served as chiefs during the fight to restore Tonawanda lands. Secondly, at this time missionary presence at Tonawanda was far less than at the other major Seneca reservations at Allegany, Buffalo Creek, and Cattaraugus. Although the Baptist church was founded on the reservation and had an influence there, Quaker and Presbyterian presence was nonexistent. Hence, with a few exceptions, missionary writings are limited in describing Tonawanda Seneca history from 1797 to 1861. Consequently, in order to overcome these two research problems and uncover information, I had to understand what responsibilities came with the position of chief or sachem as well as clan mother; examine court decisions, federal agency reports, military records of the War of 1812; survey newspaper accounts for bias; scrutinize firsthand observations and notes made by travelers passing through western New York; and analyze the numerous petitions sent by the Tonawanda Senecas to Washington or Albany to determine clues about tribal leadership.

I would like to thank the members of the Peter Doctor Indian Education Memorial Foundation, especially Ramona Charles, for their encouragement. The late "Mrs. C.," the longtime superintendent of the Tonawanda Indian Community House, first introduced me to the Tonawanda Senecas. I have dedicated this book to her memory since her knowledge of her community's history strongly shaped this book. Besides Ramona Charles and the late Cephas Hill and Harrison Ground, I should like to acknowledge the following Senecas for their help in understanding the Tonawandas: the late Chief Corbett Sundown, Chief Darwin Hill, Terry Abrams, Gi Gi Ground, Al Parker, and Paul Winney. Nya:weh!

Other non-Senecas have contributed to this project: George Hamell, formerly senior curator at the New York State Museum; Andrew Arpy, James Folts, William Gorman, and Chris Karpiak, archivists at the New York State Museum; Adele DeRosa, collections curator at the Rochester Museum and Science Center; Paul Mercer, Nancy Horan, Christine Beauregard, and Vicki Weiss, manuscript librarians at the New York State Library; Garret Livermore, vice president for education at the New York State Historical Association; Jaré

Cardinal, director of the Seneca-Iroquois National Museum; Susan Stevens, reference librarian at the Stevens-German Library at Hartwick College; Nancy Martin at the Rush Rhees Library at the University of Rochester; Susan Conklin, director of the Genesee County Archives; Donald Reid, Genesee county clerk; and Patrick Weissend, director of the Holland Land Company Museum. The librarians and staff at SUNY New Paltz' Sojourner Truth Library—Susan Kraat, Stephen Macaluso, Valerie Mittenberg, Corrine Nyquist, Joseph Stoeckert, and Heather Whalen-Smith—have also aided me significantly throughout the years in my research on the Senecas. The New York State Historical Association also allowed me to reprint a preliminary version of chapter 4 of this book that appeared in *New York History* in January 1997.

Several longtime friends have aided me in my work: David Jaman, who has taught me more than computer skills; and Dr. Airy Dixon, who has traveled with me and aided me in my fieldwork. My friend and coauthor/coeditor on many Oneida history projects, L. Gordon McLester III, taught me that Iroquois tribal politics were and are not simply carbon copies of the political behavior found in Albany, New York, Madison, Wisconsin, or Washington, D.C. I thank him for his wise tutelage.

Dr. Gary Dunham, former director of State University of New York Press, encouraged this project from its inception, and although I had resolved not to do another book, his personal visits to New Paltz prompted me to finish this project started thirty-five years ago. Above all, I must thank my wife Ruth for realizing that I had a long-standing commitment to write Seneca history and that I had one more book to complete before I ride into the sunset.

Laurence M. Hauptman
State University of New York at New Paltz

1

The Tonawanda Community

Early History

The exact date of the founding of a permanent Seneca community at Tonawanda is unknown; however, Seneca settlement there was no accidental occurrence. In the seventeenth century, Tonawanda and its environs had been in the vicinity of Neutral, Erie, and Wenro territory, three nations conquered and absorbed by the Senecas from 1638 to 1680.[1] In June, 1788, Reverend Samuel Kirkland, Presbyterian missionary to the Oneidas, who was traveling from the Seneca territory along the Genesee River to Buffalo Creek, noted when passing through Tonawanda that ruins of three ancient fortifications were visible.[2] Indeed, Arthur C. Parker, the noted anthropologist of Seneca ancestry, later suggested that some of the Senecas who settled at Tonawanda had Neutral ancestry.[3] Although it is difficult for archaeologists to separate exactly Neutral from later Seneca sites, some scholars maintain that the Senecas were establishing fishing camps and hunting in the vicinity of Tonawanda and trading with the French (and later English) at Fort Niagara by the mid-eighteenth century.[4]

Migrations to Tonawanda continued to occur from the American Revolution well into the 1830s. In the summer of 1779, George Washington's army in the Sullivan-Clinton campaign devastated the Iroquois villages in the Genesee River Valley and sent the Indians fleeing westward. One group of Seneca refugees settled along the Tonawanda Creek.[5] Other Senecas later came to Tonawanda after the land cession of the entire Little Beardstown Reservation in a federally ratified treaty in 1802.[6] Still others arrived at Tonawanda with Handsome Lake (Ganiodayo), the Seneca prophet, after he was ostracized from the Allegany Reservation and went into exile before the

War of 1812.[7] Another major Indian migration to Tonawanda from the Genesee Valley occurred after the federal treaty of 1826 when a large number of Canawaugus Seneca were forced off their Genesee Valley lands. Indeed, out of the 583 Indians at Tonawanda in 1830, 117 were listed by the federal Indian agent as "Cannewaugus" Senecas. Other Iroquois who were settled there by 1830 included sixteen Cayugas, twelve Onondagas, and seven Oneidas.[8]

By that time, descendants of other Indian nations, including Cherokee, Shawnee, and Catawba, also resided there along with descendants of Senecas who had intermarried with French, English, and American traders and military personnel.[9] Today, one of the more prominent family names among the Tonawandas is Poodry, a name that can be traced back to a descendant of a French officer who served in General Montcalm's army during the French and Indian War.[10] Despite the multiethnic makeup of Tonawanda society and its highly conservative nature, this community was to establish a remarkable degree of unity in their fight to retain or regain their lands.

Tonawanda, or Ta-na-wun-da, meaning "swift water" or "the rapids are there," was clearly selected as a settlement site by the Senecas based on geographical realities.[11] The location of the village, later moved upstream from the rapids, provided Senecas access to the Niagara River, approximately thirty miles away. There, the Senecas fished, hunted duck and other wild fowl and game, and, according to Arthur C. Parker, watched over the graves of their Neutral ancestors located on Grand Island and other islands in the Niagara River.[12] Besides access to a water route and rich lands and forests, the location of Tonawanda was apparently chosen by the Senecas for another important reason. Two Indian trails came through Tonawanda—one being the nearly 300-mile Seneca Trail, later known as the Genesee or Great Western Turnpike, today's New York State Route 5; and the other, connecting the seventy-eight-mile Ridge Road from Big Tree, today's Geneseo, the heart of the Senecas' Genesee Country, to Fort Niagara. In the vicinity of Tonawanda the trails met and split.[13]

Arthur C. Parker also observed that at the time of Tonawanda's founding, this area of western New York was rich in horticultural potential and contained thick forests of basswood, hemlock, oak, and pine.[14] In 1788, Kirkland described the fine tract of land in the vicinity of Tonawanda Creek and surrounding heavily wooded areas filled with ash, basswood, beech, elm, maple, and walnut trees. He noted that there were fourteen cabins at Tonawanda.[15]

By this time the Senecas were shifting away from large communal multi-room longhouses and had adapted and modified the log house "made with hewn logs and Moravian dovetail notches."[16] In the next half century, this type of dwelling was to be the norm in Seneca Country, accepted as a traditional style of Iroquoian architecture. According to Dorcas R. Brown, a specialist on Iroquoian dwellings, the "reservation Log House" was symbolic of the defeat, the defiance and the evolution of the Iroquoian people."[17] The Tonawanda Senecas did not simply borrow the idea; they also modified it, reflecting "Moravian construction techniques, combined with an interior plan derived from the English single-pen house and from the single-family unit inside a Longhouse."[18] Brown noted the carryover from longhouse design in the log house construction:

> Before and after the American Revolution there were log houses with bark roofs, central fire hearths, and built-in double berths along the sides. Bark roofs became shingle roofs. The central fire hearth was moved to one end, but it remained inside the house. Full wall-length berths were broken up by the front and back doors but remnants of this structure can be found in the built-in beds often found in the log houses. The loft was used for storage and/or sleeping space like the upper berths in the Longhouse.[19]

The historical record confirms Brown's interpretation. An anonymous traveler's account described the Tonawanda community in 1792 as being comprised of "many hundreds of the savages, who live in very tolerable houses, which they make of timber and cover with bark." The traveler added: "By signs I made them understand me, and for a little money they cut me limbs and bushes sufficient to erect a booth under which I slept very quietly, on the grass."[20] The account, albeit brief and tinged with racism, clearly indicates that less than ten years after the American Revolution, the Senecas had already substantially established themselves within the region, were living in log cabins, and were part of the white man's monetary economy, no longer simply employing barter exchange.

In the same year, the diverse Seneca communities, fearing further reprisals and land loss because of their alliance with the British in the American Revolution, began formal negotiations with officials in Philadelphia. In 1792, a Tonawanda chief, Gun Cleaner, was one of forty-six Iroquois chiefs and warriors who met with Pennsylvania and federal officials at Independence Hall in an effort to repair the damage caused by the bitterness of the American Revolution. With British-occupied military installations, including Fort Niagara, still on American soil, American officials, realizing the proximity of these forts to Iroquois settlements and facing a major Indian war in the Ohio Country, realized the importance of the Six Nations, especially the large Seneca population. Two years later at Canandaigua, New York, representatives of all the Seneca communities met with President Washington's federal commissioner, Timothy Pickering, and negotiated and signed a treaty of alliance and friendship.[21] In this historic agreement, the federal government returned a portion of land taken from the Senecas in the Treaty of Fort Stanwix in 1784; the treaty also gave assurances of federal protection to all of the Six Nations and a commitment to respect the territorial integrity of these Indians.[22]

By 1797, the Tonawanda community had about 150 people. According to Jacob Lindley, a Quaker passing through the area, the community was composed of a dozen "Indian houses and huts. Surrounding Tonawanda were rich forests of poplars, bass-woods, cherry, red oak. . . ." The hospitable Indians there, including a Frenchman married to a Seneca woman, were willing to sell corn and milk.[23]

Despite the transition from longhouse, with its extended family structure, to log cabin with a nuclear family structure, the Tonawandas maintained much of their pre-Revolutionary War social organization well into the nineteenth century. In her study of three Haudenosaunee communities, Deborah Doxtator described Tonawanda as retaining much of the gender roles of the past:

> Women accessed the resources of the home community, while men used the hinterland resources. In Buffalo, thirty miles from Tonawanda, in the first two decades of the nineteenth century, women sold corn, chickens and eggs that they had produced within the Tonawanda settlement,

and men sold venison and wood taken from the hinterland
areas surrounding the community.[24]

The clan mothers continued to nominate the chiefs, and children
were members of the community through descent from a Tonawanda mother. To Doxtator, these clan mothers, eight in number at
any one time, were the actual power center, choosing "clearing leaders," namely, the fourteen to sixteen civil chiefs who administered
the public affairs and daily requirements of the Tonawandas. In this
matrilineal society, these women provided a structural basis as well
as the cultural continuity of local government, designating certain
men to speak for them and their interests in council, a carryover
from the Great Law, the pre-Handsome Lake religion of the Iroquois.
Clan mothers had to be consulted when the cession of lands became
an issue.[25] Doxtator added that even when the *Gaiwiio*, the Handsome Lake religion, became centered at Tonawanda by the 1840s,
the theology focused around venerating traditional women's rituals
in the clearing: "women's agricultural activities, planting, strawberry
festival, green corn, bean festival and others."[26] Unfortunately we
know virtually nothing about individual Tonawanda Seneca women
until the mid-1840s. Only then did Caroline Parker (Ga-ha-no), the
college-educated teacher and woman of letters, begin to express herself
in detailed correspondence with her extraordinary family and Lewis
Henry Morgan.[27]

The role of Seneca women was especially noticeable in the negotiations that took place at Big Tree in 1797. There, despite assurances
of protection at the Treaty of Canandaigua in 1794, federal officials
failed to intervene in 1797 to protect the Iroquois from the clutches
of land speculators such as Robert Morris and state and local officials
intent on Indian land acquisition. When Red Jacket rejected Morris'
proposals and covered the council fire, apparently ending all further
negotiations, Thomas Morris, informed by Farmer's Brother that Red
Jacket had exceeded his authority, then presented his father's proposals
to a council of Seneca warriors and clan mothers. Like a smooth-talk-
ing flimflam man, Thomas Morris appealed to the women, whom he
insisted truly understood the desperate conditions that the Senecas
faced at the time, telling them that the "money that would proceed
from the sale of their lands, would relieve the women from all the

hardships that they then endured."[28] Faced with social disintegration caused by alcoholism and the increasing violence that resulted, the Seneca women declared themselves willing to cede land, and they did so at the treaty consummated at the Seneca village of Big Tree in 1797. Alcohol, cash payments, and promises of annuities were then made to win support for the treaty. Red Jacket received the largest payment of $600 and a $100 annuity, whereas Cornplanter received $300 and a $250 annuity. Farmer's Brother, Young King, Little Billy, Little Billy's mother, and Pollard were also "awarded" annuities. Even though under the Treaty of Big Tree, the Senecas reserved some 310 square miles—approximately 200,000 acres—and their right to hunt and fish on the lands they ceded, the Indians, nevertheless, had surrendered most of their lands west of the Genesee River, a vast empire of millions of acres. In return, the Senecas were to receive $100,000, money which was to be invested and the interest distributed as an annuity.[29] In effect, the Treaty of Big Tree reduced Seneca Country to eleven parcels.

One of the parcels was Tonawanda, seventy square miles on both sides of the Tonawanda Creek. In the treaty, however, the Senecas agreed to give Morris the preemption rights to the eleven reservations. Morris later sold this right to the Holland Land Company, a consortium of four Dutch banks. Consequently, the Holland Land Company acquired the first right to purchase all of the Seneca lands if and when the Indians were convinced to sell any or all of their territory. By the next year, Joseph Ellicott, the company's chief agent, had already initiated a survey of Tonawanda lands with the hope of some future acquisition of these Seneca lands. Thus, the reservation era began and pressures to get at the remaining Seneca estate intensified.[30]

Despite federal guarantees of a large reservation in 1797, the Tonawandas faced an insecure future in western New York. In 1802, the Seneca chiefs ceded the Little Beardstown Reservation in the Genesee Valley. The son of Chief Little Beard, also known as Chief Little Beard, and some of his small community went to live at Tonawanda.[31] In the same year, New York State began negotiations with the Senecas over the purchase of the Indian-owned islands in the Niagara River, including its largest possession, the 17,000-acre Grand Island.[32]

In the fall of 1805, Julian Ursyn Niemcewicz, a Polish aristocrat traveling to Niagara, visited the area around the Tonawanda reservation. On the road west from Batavia, the seat of the Holland

Land Company's three-and-a-half-million-acre empire, he complained about the bad road, a "torturous track full of tree trunks and rocks and holes filled with water." Referring to the region around Tonawanda as a vast but beautiful wasteland, he expressed his views about the Indians there, and the lands "still left to the poor savage." Many Tonawandas walked briskly with guns draped on their shoulders while their "poor *squaws* or women carry all the burdens." These Indian women carried their "clothes, tomahawks, or Indian weapons, along with one or two *papooses* . . . attached by a band that they pass around the forehead. It is on this that all the weight rests." Niemcewicz added that many of the Indians were eating pumpkins raw or cooked. "Their shelters have roofs of linden bark attached to four poles, built usually on the banks of streams."[33] The Polish traveler expressed disappointment that, unlike the Holland Land Company's efforts further east, the lands west of Batavia had not been sold to and settled by more non-Indians, which he equated with "civilization."

With the outbreak of the War of 1812, the Tonawanda Senecas found themselves in a most difficult position. By that time the Seneca prophet Handsome Lake was living and preaching at Tonawanda and insisting that the Indians reject the calls by Americans to enter into another white man's war.[34] A rumor spread that the Seneca prophet was rallying troops on behalf of the British Crown. Consequently, the Senecas, because of their lingering memories of their past alliance with the British that led some Senecas to flee with Joseph Brant to Canada at the end of the war, were increasingly seen as a "fifth column" by whites in western New York. Added to this was a second rumor, namely, that Senecas were with the Shawnee prophet's forces at the Battle of Tippecanoe in November 1811. In order to dispel accusations of disloyalty, the Tonawanda chiefs and warriors held an open forum with the non-Indian residents of Batavia in the first days of spring in 1812.[35]

Chief John Sky was the Tonawandas' spokesman at the meeting. He immediately rejected the idea that the Senecas at Tonawanda were pro-British, insisting that "we do not thirst for blood." He added that the Tonawandas were "a small part of the Seneca Nation" and that there was "nothing . . . to be gained by spilling the blood of our fellow creature. Our children are as dear to us as your children are to you. We value our little property—by war we know we shall lose it."[36]

Chief Sky carefully spelled out other concerns to his largely white audience at Batavia. Although a convert to the new Longhouse religion, but distancing himself from Handsome Lake for his Christian onlookers, he, nevertheless, frankly expressed his opposition to missionary proselytizing among his people. He fervently expressed the view that these missionaries shook "that faith which the Great Spirit has breathed into us; which is our greatest comfort and consolation in this world." Sky saw these clerics' presence as totally disruptive, tending "to destroy the foundation of our hopes of a future life; but to throw us into religious parties and confusion."[37]

Sky also pointed out differences with other Seneca communities based on moral grounds. He asserted that the "principal chiefs and warriors of Buffaloe [Creek] regard themselves as the great leaders of the Seneca Indians. But in point of sobriety and good order they are not our leaders." Trying to curry favor with his audience, he emphasized that the Tonawandas were temperate, law-abiding peoples.[38]

In his remarkable speech, Chief Sky brought up other troubling issues. He accused certain whites of theft of Tonawanda resources, insisting that many "bad people among our white brethren" have cut down and carried way the Senecas' finest timber. Calling this "a very great grievance," the chief maintained that if a Seneca "cut a flick" of the white man's timber for a fire in a hunting camp, he might be murdered "for this small transgression." He urged his audience to help the Tonawandas by enforcing the laws of trespass.[39]

Despite the preaching of the Seneca prophet Handsome Lake to avoid joining in a "white man's war," numerous Tonawandas did enlist in the War of 1812 and fought in every major campaign on both sides of the Niagara River, fighting at Black Rock, Chippawa, Lundy's Lane, and Queenston Heights. They were under the command of Chief Little Beard, the son of the well-known chief of the same name who had been killed in 1806.[40] Approximately ninety Tonawandas served in the American army in the War of 1812, an extraordinarily high number that was approximately half of all the males in the community.[41] Chief Sky encouraged enlistments and his own son served in the war. Besides combat on the Niagara frontier, the Tonawandas gathered intelligence and served as couriers between Buffalo, the Genesee Country, and Albany.[43]

Despite their high enlistments and their commitment to the American cause, when the British forces that included Indians from the Six Nations Reserve in southern Ontario crossed the Niagara River and marched on Black Rock and Buffalo in 1813, the Tonawanda community found itself in the path of a retreating American army. According to historian Carl Benn, these fleeing American troops "stopped long enough to take advantage of the confusion to rob the Senecas at Tonawanda before continuing their withdrawal from the border region. Although their homes had been looted, the Tonawandas' food supply was saved since much of it had been hidden below the floorboards of their cabins.[44]

Why did the Tonawanda Senecas, including followers of Handsome Lake, go to war in 1812 in direct conflict with the prophet's teachings against joining in another white man's war? First, with rapidly increasing non-Indian populations around them, the Tonawandas, especially Chief Sky, were well aware of the consequences if they went over to the British side. Elders' memories of the Sullivan-Clinton campaign, General Washington's retribution against the Senecas in 1779, was still in their minds. Secondly, they had signed a treaty of friendship and alliance with the United States at Canandaigua in 1794 and were committed to uphold this accord. At a council meeting at Buffalo Creek on July 25, 1813, Sky reiterated his people's friendship to the United States. Thirdly, they were promised financial remuneration for serving. Fourthly, the Senecas served under their own Indian commanders as in the days of forest warfare; for young males, service in the War of 1812 allowed them to replicate the experiences that they had heard elders speak of in council, namely, how they had earned their stripes, leadership qualities, on the warpath. Hence, war was still an avenue of social mobility in Iroquoia. Although more speculative, Arthur C. Parker suggested a fifth reason for Seneca involvement, namely a defense "of the graves of their [Neutral] forefathers" buried on Grand Island.[46]

By the end of the war, the Tonawandas were in desperate shape. Wartime inflation ravaged New York. The war also had delayed the distribution of their federal annuity payments. Contributing to the Senecas' economic distress was the collapse of a bank in which previous annuities had been deposited.[47] In September 1815, the Seneca Nation agreed to sell the islands in the Niagara River to New York State. In an accord, in which one of the signatories was Chief Sky, the Senecas ceded Grand Island. One inducement was a promise of an annuity from the state. The Senecas also hoped that by relinquishing some land, a cession might stem the hunger of land companies and state officials; however, this piecemeal cession, much like the Little

Beardstown Reservation cession in 1802, only whetted the appetite of the non-Indian world. Unlike the 1802 treaty, which was held under the auspices of the federal government and ratified by the United States Senate, the New York State–Seneca Treaty of 1815 had no formal approval from Washington. To this day, despite a recent federal court decision, the Tonawandas still claim ownership of the islands in the Niagara River and insist that they were coerced into signing over this territory.[48]

Besides the loss of Grand Island, what immediately followed the war was the "Year Without Summer" that produced famine and starvation. Because of the massive eruption of a volcano in the East Indies, global climate change resulted. In 1816, Indians in western New York lost their crops. Epidemic diseases soon followed. To compound the pressures on Indian life, New York State began to build the Erie Canal in 1817. Tonawanda Creek was to be a feeder for the canal, and a major land rush was to begin soon after the canal's completion in 1825.[49]

The pressures to survive led a troupe of Senecas to visit and tour England after the War of 1812. Among the performers was twenty-two-year-old Sta-cute or Steep Rock, a Tonawanda Seneca-Onondaga Indian. In 1818, the Senecas were cast as "Wild Indian Savages From the Borders of Lake Erie . . . The Chief and Six Warriors of the Seneca Nation." They performed their dances and songs at concert halls at Leeds, Liverpool, and Manchester. Although they were presented as exotic specimens, the English Society of Friends showed a special interest in their welfare while in Liverpool and Manchester.[50] The English press soon favorably covered their performances.[51] In a letter to the *Leeds Mercury*, one writer commented that the Senecas were "one of the most favorable specimens that Paganism could present."[52] To their English audiences, they appeared to be the epitome of the "Rousseau's wild child," the simple, unspoiled natural man of the forest world.[53]

In 1817–1818, two white visitors—Estwick Evans and Timothy Alden—came to Tonawanda and wrote down their observations about the community. Although Evans' brief account was laden with bias and overall had a limited understanding of these Indians, he did point out several realities of Tonawanda Seneca life of the times. Evans indicated that the village was "situated upon a plain, and contains about one hundred huts." The nearby creek, that ran through the center of the community, was filled with "an abundance of fish."

Evans' description of the physical setting is significant, especially since he noted the number of residences and the importance of fishing to the community. Although he referred to the Tonawandas' alleged superstitious beliefs, he made mention of the White Dog Ceremony, an ancient practice of the Iroquois that was still being performed in 1817. He pointed out funerary practices, including the burial of the deceased's clothes, pipe, dish, and spoon in the gravesite, a practice that still continues today. Evans also recounted the belief in the Spirit Journey of the deceased and the rewards for living a virtuous life.[54]

In 1818 Timothy Alden, a Presbyterian missionary sent by the Society for Propagating the Gospel who later became the founder and president of Allegheny College in Pennsylvania, visited Tonawanda. On July 16 and 17, 1818, he witnessed a council meeting and praised the Senecas for hospitality. He compared Chief Sky, who held forth at the ceremony, with the great orators of ancient Greece and Rome, but noted that his health was fading quickly. Chief Sky was to die the following year. Quite importantly, Alden noted that the Tonawandas were undergoing a spiritual revival based on the moral instructions of Handsome Lake.[55] Coming at a time of increased pressures by agents of the Ogden Land Company, it was this revival that in part helped the Tonawanda Seneca community withstand some of these very same pressures.

On March 4, 1819, the New York State Assembly issued a report on the Iroquois and their lands. The report disparaged the agricultural efforts of the Indians, work "chiefly done by the females." It indicated that because of intemperance and over-leasing, the Indians were incapable of protecting themselves and that they were being surrounded by whites "who have usurped nearly all of their possessions." The legislators had taken their cue from Congressman David A. Ogden and his associates, the trustees of the Ogden Land Company, who had for nine years pushed plans to remove the Iroquois, including the 365 Tonawandas, from the state or to concentrate them all on the Allegany Indian Reservation. The report recommended that the Indians "concentrate themselves in some suitable place" for their own protection where they could be instructed in "piety and agriculture" and gain the "benefits of civilization." The report authorized the governor to cooperate with federal officials to carry out this goal.[56]

In the aftermath of the War of 1812, state officials, interested in building New York's economic base and promoting rapid non-Indian settlement in central and western New York as well as meeting the challenge of the continued British presence in Canada, developed the Erie Canal and its extensive branch canal system. Seneca reservations stood in the way of what Albany officials defined as "progress." Two Seneca reservations were on the Erie Canal's east-west corridor— Tonawanda and Buffalo Creek—and five Seneca reservations—Big Tree, Caneadea, Canawaugus, Gardeau, and Squawky Hill—were on the Genesee Valley Canal corridor.

The Tonawandas, as well as other Seneca communities, faced a challenge that permanently changed their world. Events between 1819 to 1830 played a major role in producing a schism in the Seneca polity and furthering the formation of two Seneca governments that exist today in New York. While Chief Sky started to define a separate path for the Tonawandas from the chiefs at Buffalo Creek, Red Jacket was to widen the split with his words and actions between 1819 and 1830.

The Awakener

To many Tonawandas today, Red Jacket, Sagoyewatha, or "He who keeps them awake," is a much despised Seneca.[1] He is often depicted by Tonawanda followers of the *Gaiwiio* as a man condemned by the Creator to push a dirt-filled wheelbarrow up a hill for eternity because he signed treaties that sold Seneca lands. Even though Red Jacket was a member of the Wolf Clan, he is associated by Tonawandas with the Beaver Clan, perhaps because of adoption; and, until recently, this clan was proscribed from having a chief on the Tonawanda council.[2] Furthermore, throughout his life, Red Jacket was a rival of Cornplanter and Handsome Lake and viewed the latter as an "impostor." Thus, he was viewed by some, but not all, of Handsome Lake's followers with disdain.[3]

Red Jacket's sense of morality was questionable at best, largely because his name appears on treaties ceding Seneca lands and because of his excessive drinking. Although he received no compensation for agreeing to the Buffalo Creek Treaty of 1826, which dispossessed the Tonawandas of approximately 70 percent of their territory, Red Jacket did receive a cash payment for placing his name on the Treaty of Big Tree in 1797.[4] Thus, many contemporary Tonawandas see this great orator as a self-serving, scheming individual who betrayed the Senecas. Yet, while his actions are not to be universally lauded, Red Jacket contributed significantly to the formation of the Tonawanda identity and these Indians' separation from the Seneca Nation.

Much of the previous writings on Red Jacket focus on his legendary battles with missionaries, his outspoken defense of Indian sovereignty, namely, the right to adjudicate alleged criminal offenses by tribal members; and his assertions that the federal government under treaties had a fiduciary responsibility to the Iroquois. While

Red Jacket's role in opposing the Ogden Land Company's efforts to obtain Iroquois lands is well known, his important connections to Tonawanda in the decade before his death have never been explored before. At Buffalo Creek, he was a pine tree chief, a non-hereditary honor that was often fleeting, which was based on his superior intellect and speech-making abilities.[5] His role at Buffalo Creek clearly declined after 1819, and rivals such as Chief Young King challenged his right to serve as spokesman and ate away at his prestige. Consequently, Red Jacket shifted his focus to Tonawanda, becoming a borrowed orator, espousing the cause of the Tonawanda Council of Chiefs in the last years of his life.

Red Jacket's connection to Tonawanda did not suddenly arise after 1819. Indeed, he had relatives there. Tonawanda Chief Jemmy Johnson was the son of Red Jacket's sister. Moreover, Red Jacket would make frequent visits to the home of Johnson's niece, Elizabeth Parker, on the reservation. Ironically, while Jemmy Johnson was a disciple of Handsome Lake at Tonawanda, he nevertheless was strongly influenced by the Seneca prophet's enemy, Red Jacket.[6]

In 1810, David A. Ogden, a former Federalist congressman and Holland Land Company attorney from New York City, created a trust that later became known as the Ogden Land Company. In the same year, the Holland Land Company conveyed to this trust its preemptive rights, namely, the right of first purchase, which they had secured in 1797 at the federal Treaty at Big Tree, to the Senecas' Cattaraugus, Buffalo Creek, Allegany, Caneadea, and Tonawanda reservations. These lands totaled 196,335 acres.[7]

Among the shareholders were other members of the Ogden family—David A. Ogden, Thomas L. Ogden, Charles Le Roux Ogden, and Abraham Ogden—and Thomas and Aaron Cooper and Joshua Waddington.[8] On February 8, 1821, David A. Ogden transferred his preemptive right to his brother Thomas Ludlow Ogden, Benjamin W. Rogers, and Robert Troup as trustees. On December 19, 1829, the Ogden Land Company trustees conveyed their interests to Thomas Ludlow Ogden, Charles G. Troup, and Joseph Fellows. Even after the death of Ogden and Troup, the Ogden Land Company, largely through the direction of Joseph Fellows, continued the push to remove the Tonawandas from their lands until the late 1850s. If the company could convince the Iroquois, especially the most populous Senecas, who possessed the largest and most desirable lands, to move, either to an isolated area in the southwestern part of New York State or to the west beyond the Mississippi, the Ogdens could reap a significant profit.[9]

Well before the War of 1812, the company conspired to expand its Indian landholdings. The proprietor planned strategies to fool the Indians during negotiations in council. As early as August, 1810, Robert Troup, the trust's attorney, wrote Jasper Parrish, the federal Indian subagent who worked closely with the Ogdens in their schemes, informing him that the company's intent, that is, to purchase all the tribal lands, should be hidden from the Indians at the ensuing council in September. Troup insisted that the meeting should exclusively focus on getting the Indians to move. Troup also suggested that the reservations be sold and that all the Iroquois be concentrated on the Allegany Indian Reservation. Troup outlined a formula to achieve this goal. If the Allegany alternative was rejected, the trustees would work with the federal government or its agents to do "everything in their power . . . to induce the Indians *to accept of a grant of land in the west* [emphasis Troup]"; then make a formal proposal about land cessions to the Indians; then have the government offer a seat on the Arkansas or "locate a spot in the Northwestern Territory," but not in Ohio, Illinois, or Indiana; and, finally, to have Parrish encourage the Indians to appoint a delegation to visit Washington and meet with President Madison.[10]

Even before the War of 1812 ended, the trustees of the Ogden Land Company continued their efforts to encourage removal westward. While assuring the Indians that he would not force them off their lands, Ogden, nevertheless, lobbied for this goal with Albany and Washington officials, as well as with religious leaders. He wrote Bishop J. H. Hobart, the prominent Episcopal bishop of New York, that the Indians in the vicinity of Buffalo had become "more depraved than any others to be found in the U.S." and that their situation "has become offensive to common decency."[11]

With the plans for canal development and the construction of the Erie Canal that began in 1817, the value of Seneca lands rose exponentially.[12] Once a transportation route was in place, the Ogden Land Company proprietors soon realized that by buying out or dispossessing the Indians, they could make a financial windfall. Indeed, Seneca lands from the Genesee River to Lake Erie were right in the path of New York's transportation revolution, and land companies had an unholy alliance with the state legislature in promoting their interests. Indeed, the makeup of the New York State Board of Canal Commissioners clearly reveals this iron triangle of interests among land, transportation, and political leadership in the empire state.[13]

In the years from 1810 to 1819, the Ogdens also attempted to obfuscate their financial motives, stressing the idea of bringing civilization and enlightenment to the Indians and progress and development to all New Yorkers. By concentrating all the Indians on the Allegany Indian Reservation, which would be away from the central water route needed for a future canal, the Ogdens insisted that the Indians would have enough cultivation to survive and would be, at the same time, isolated from all white interferences and vices. Hence, removing the Indians, much like the rhetoric of the later Jackson administration, was actually presented as a way to "save" the Indians.

On May 26, 1817, David A. Ogden wrote to the sachems, chiefs, and warriors of the Seneca Nation that his "intention" was not "to press you on a sale of the lands you now occupy." He told them that the Ogden trustees had not authorized timber stripping on tribal lands, a growing problem, and insisted that all offenders would be prosecuted.[14] Despite the repeated Indian rejection of land sales after the Seneca cession of Grand Island and other islands in the Niagara River in 1815, Ogden intensified his lobbying efforts, continuing to suggest that all Iroquois be concentrated at Allegany. He won cooperation for this effort from New York State officials by March 1819. Ogden then approached Secretary of War Calhoun about holding a treaty council with a federal commissioner present to facilitate his Allegany plan. Favoring the idea, Calhoun soon appointed Judge Morris S. Miller to serve as the federal commissioner, hoping that this aim could be accomplished.[15]

At the same time, Ogden appealed directly to President Monroe, once again lobbying for the removal of the Senecas from New York State. Calling the Indians half civilized and half savage and completely debased in the vicinity of Buffalo, Ogden urged removal for the Indians' benefit and one "demanded by public sentiments." He insisted that the Indians were "becoming a heavy encumbrance, retarding the progress of cultivation and improvements and detracting from the public resources and prosperity." Despite their limited size, "little more than 2,000 souls," their extensive tract totaled "220,000 acres of rich lands capable of giving support in profuse abundance to 50,000 of our citizens"; there "not one acre in a hundred" was cultivated or improved by the Indians. Because their lands were not taxed nor do the Indians "bear any part of the burden of roads and other objects of local improvement," Ogden insisted, they were in the way of the progress of the nation and even an impediment to national security: "These extensive tracts being situated principally along our western frontier, the acquisition of lands and [a] hardy white population in that quarter would appear moreover to be an object of immense importance to the United States." Because of their allegedly degraded condition, especially those in the vicinity of Buffalo, Ogden observed the Senecas were affecting "materially the growth of that important place."[16]

Red Jacket and his allies at Tonawanda attempted to slow down the Ogden Land Company's campaign. In that year, a major council of all the Senecas was held at Buffalo Creek. Now more of an activist, Red Jacket took the lead, challenging the Ogden Land Company. Besides David A. Ogden and Judge John Greig, who represented the company, the well-attended council included all the representatives of all the Seneca communities; federal Indian treaty commissioner Judge Morris S. Miller; Massachusetts Indian commissioner Nathaniel Gorham, Jr.; United States-British Canadian boundary commissioners Peter Porter and Joseph Delafield; and council interpreters Jasper Parrish and Horatio Jones.[17] It should be noted that Parrish and Jones were in the pay of the Ogdens, Porter was heavily involved in the operations of the company, and Gorham and his family had been major land speculators in Iroquois Country.[18] While Ogden sought different ways to convince the Senecas at the meeting, even offering a $4,000 annuity for their removal if they were willing to accept his proposals, Red Jacket emerged from the meeting as the great defender of the Senecas.[19]

Red Jacket, in one of his more passionate addressees, replied to Ogden:

> If Mr. Ogden should tell us, that he had come from heaven with the flesh on his bones, as he now is, and that the Heavenly Father had given him a title, we might believe him. . . . The President [of the United States] must have been disordered in mind or he would not offer to lead us off by the arms to the Allegany Reservation.[20]

He suggested to Ogden that if he needed any more land he should secure it from the Holland Land Company, whose chief agent Joseph Ellicott was in attendance, not the Indians who were being cramped in on all sides. Red Jacket concluded:

> We will not part with any of our reservations. Do not make your application anew in any other shape. Let us hear no more of it—And let us part as we met, in friendship. You discover white people on our reservation. It is my wish, and the wish of all of us, to remove every white man. We can educate our children. Our reservation is small. The white people are near us: we can send our children to their schools. Such as wish, can do so. The Schoolmaster and the Preacher must withdraw. The distance is short, for those who wish to go to them. We wish to get rid of all the whites. Those who are now among us make disturbances. We wish our reservation clear of them.[21]

Because of Red Jacket's intractable position against future land cessions and the growing anti-white tone of the council, both agents of the Ogdens and federal and state officials began to see him as a force to be reckoned with, one that needed to be silenced.[22]

Red Jacket's growing influence with the Tonawanda Council of Chiefs is clearly seen in its insistence on maintaining Seneca sovereignty, its treatment of missionaries, its criticisms of federal Indian subagent Parrish, and its resistance to and protest over Indian land loss as well as the expropriation of Indian natural resources. In 1819, Red Jacket testified in a Batavia court, near to Tonawanda, involving an Indian who was being tried for burglary. He argued that the New York court had no jurisdiction since the Indians were American allies, not subjects of New York State.[23] In 1821, Red Jacket participated in a trial involving Tommy-Jemmy, a chief at Buffalo Creek and an adherent to the *Gaiwiio*. Tommy-Jemmy had carried out a tribal execution of Caughquautaugh, who had been convicted of witchcraft in 1821. Local Buffalo residents reacted with horror at Seneca justice and demanded that Jemmy be punished, creating tensions between Indian and white in western New York. Local Buffalonians wanted Jemmy punished as a cold-blooded killer. Yet the Senecas, especially Red Jacket, defended the action as being tribal custom and under tribal legal jurisdiction. In the trial before a state court in Buffalo, Tommy-Jemmy was defended by John C. Spencer, non-Indian attorney and later a major actor in Tonawanda history. Spencer insisted that the Senecas were an independent nation and the crime happened in Seneca Territory, and thus New York State courts had no jurisdiction to try Tommy-Jemmy. Yet Red Jacket's and Spencer's arguments were to be denied.[24] On April 22, 1822, the New York State legislature passed a law giving the state's courts sole and existing jurisdiction over punishing crimes; however, the legislature granted Tommy-Jemmy a pardon since his actions were done under what appeared to be the authority derived from the councils of the chiefs, sachems, and warriors of the Seneca Nation.[25]

In July of the same year as the Tommy-Jemmy murder trial, another Tonawanda Seneca, Joseph "Bigbag," was accused of murdering his wife. Instead of having a state or federal court decide, the Senecas themselves held a trial on the reservation. Eight chiefs from Tonawanda as well as thirty-nine chiefs from as far away as the Six Nations Reserve in Canada and from the Oneida Reservation in central New York served as a panel of judges in the case. At the end of the three-day trial, the Tonawanda was declared innocent.[26] The trial of Bigbag clearly reveals Red Jacket's influence there. It is important to note that courts composed of Seneca chiefs were to hear felony cases, including murder, until three years after Red Jacket's death.[27]

It was Red Jacket's influence at Tonawanda in other areas that set these Indians apart from the other Seneca communities. For one, the Tonawandas were less accepting of missionaries. From the 1790s onward until 1825, the Buffalo Creek Reservation, despite Red Jacket's objections, became the focal point of proselytizing efforts. Historian Alyssa Mt. Pleasant has dubbed this period an era of "gradual compliance" and has insisted that this was a conscious Iroquois policy, a survival strategy aimed at successfully navigating and winning compromises with the non-Indian world. By accepting missionaries, their churches and their schools, some of the Buffalo Creek chiefs, realizing the growing numbers and power of the white world, saw this strategy as the only hope to negotiate to ensure future survival.[28] Yet this strategy failed, with the flood tide of white settlement after the War of 1812.

After repeated complaints by Red Jacket and others about trespassing whites, annoying missionaries, thieving livestock rustlers, and timber strippers, the New York State legislature passed an "Act Respecting Intrusions on Indian Lands" on March 31, 1821, forbidding any non-Indian from "settling or residing on Indian land."[29] The act created a firestorm, especially in the reactions of the various missionary societies, and it accentuated divisions between Christian and non-Christian Senecas at Buffalo Creek. Consequently, it was hardly enforced there, despite Red Jacket's efforts to get court orders to eject missionaries. Eventually, in 1825 the law was amended, allowing "any schoolmaster, teacher, or family of teachers" to reside on a reservation at the request of a "major part" of the Indians.[30]

The setting at Tonawanda for missionary proselytizing was quite different from Buffalo Creek and much more opposed by the Council of Chiefs. Around 1819, a young Tonawanda Seneca convert to Christianity, who had been instructed by missionaries at Buffalo Creek, returned to Tonawanda "carrying with him a hymn-book in his native language." According to missionary Jabez B. Hyde at Buffalo Creek, the young Seneca preacher made inroads, converting eleven others at Tonawanda. The Council of Chiefs there complained that these converts "were filling the Tonnawanta with their doctrine" and "a council of the people was called" whereby the young men were "admonished to renounce their new religion." Eleven of the converts refused to accept this and were commanded by the chiefs to "leave the Reservation and go to Buffalo, where such things were allowed, and not remain to disturb their village with their new and wicked ways." Eventually, according to Hyde, twenty-four Tonawandas left the reservation for Buffalo Creek.[31]

Red Jacket's great influence in screening missionaries and acceding to or denying them access at Tonawanda is made clear in a journal kept by Abel Bingham from 1822 to 1828. Bingham, a Baptist missionary who was not well educated, never bothered to learn the Seneca language and was tedious in his evangelical tirades against "paganism," opened a school in 1822 without formal prior approval from the Tonawanda Council of Chiefs. Bingham's appearance there occurred after Ely Stone had established a Baptist mission just off the reservation.[32]

Red Jacket was relentless in attacking this myopic missionary. He accused the cleric of going to Tonawanda to steal Indian land. The Seneca orator tried next to get the New York State law of 1821 enforced, one that allowed the removal of unwanted missionaries from

Indian lands. Red Jacket then went to a Seneca Council of Chiefs meeting at Buffalo Creek and later sought help from the sheriff and district attorney at Batavia to legally remove the missionary. Subsequently Bingham was prevented from speaking on his own behalf before the Tonawanda Council of Chiefs, not allowed to witness certain ceremonies, and locked out of his residence with his furniture placed on the road, and ordered to leave the reservation.[33]

Only after years of tremendous frustrations and fruitless efforts did Bingham achieve a modicum of acceptance at Tonawanda. Bingham was able to baptize and preside over weddings involving fifteen Tonawandas, including three chiefs: William Parker, Ely S. Parker's father; Little Beard; and Lewis Poodry. These occurred after his lengthy theological debates with Red Jacket and the missionary's change of mind about the Seneca orator, finally realizing his "sagacity."[34]

In a revealing petition to Parrish, now the federal Indian subagent, Red Jacket, working with Tonawanda chiefs Jemmy Johnson, Bigfire, and Blue Sky, relished his new role as the defender of Tonawandas. In January, 1821, Red Jacket helped draft a memorial. He insisted that the "chain of friendship needs brightening" because of problems not dealt with by federal officials to carry out its treaty responsibilities. He noted that timber depredations continued despite repeated Indian complaints; that Indians were being "profiled," thrown into jail "for the most trifling causes"; that white hunters were stealing stored venison "from the trees where we have hung it to be reclaimed after the chase"; that leasing to whites had become extreme, leading his people to become lazy; that white-constructed dams along Tonawanda and Buffalo creeks "almost entirely deprived" the Indians of their "accustomed sustenance." Red Jacket went on to condemn the missionary presence in the Seneca communities. "Each nation has its own customs and its own religion" and that it "was not intended that they [Senecas] embrace the religion of the whites—and be destroyed by the attempt to think differently on that subject from their fathers."[35]

Despite his appeal to Parrish, Red Jacket and his Tonawanda allies and Iroquois Tadodaho Captain Cold hardly trusted the federal Indian subagent, complaining about him directly to President Monroe; however, other Senecas, including Chief Young King and Captain Pollard frequently came to Parrish's defense.[36] Hence, on March 22, 1822, Red Jacket, joined by Tonawanda chiefs Blue Sky and Jemmy Johnson and Allegany Chief Cornplanter, appealed directly to Albany.

They insisted that despite the Senecas' commitment to treaties with the state, the federal subagent and New York officials were doing little to carry out an act passed by the state legislature in 1813 that was intended to protect natural resources on Indian lands: "Many hundreds of the most valuable pine trees on the Tonnewanta reservation have been cut down and carried away" by the ineffectual law and actions of the federal Indian subagent.[37]

Red Jacket's campaign to try to remove Parrish gained momentum in 1822. By this time, Red Jacket had become a resident of the Tonawanda reservation. He and his third wife Degeny Two Guns, who lived at Buffalo Creek, had separated, allegedly for reasons related to her conversion to Christianity.[38] On August 8, 1822, the Tonawandas held a major council to air the complaints against Parrish and Jones for their failure to properly distribute treaty annuities, for both men's support of proselytizing and missionary presence on the Seneca reservations, and for their failures to stem timber stripping as well as horse stealing and cattle rustling throughout Iroquois Country.[39] Later, on May 3, 1823, Red Jacket and the Tonawanda chiefs expanded their bill of particulars by including Horatio Jones as a target of their venom; they also adamantly refused to accept a federal offer to emigrate to Green Bay.[40]

Instead of official reprimands, both Parrish and Jones continued in federal employment and, importantly, in the pay of the Ogden Land Company. They were cleared of all charges after Secretary of War Calhoun appointed Peter B. Porter to investigate and after Seneca chiefs Young King, Captain Pollard, and others came to the two men's defense. Porter, one of the most important lobbyists for the Ogden Land Company, blamed these charges on Red Jacket, the able "intriguer." Porter drew on his own bitter feelings toward Red Jacket and the so-called Pagan Party. Chief Young King, Captain Pollard, and other members of the so-called Christian Party took every opportunity to strike back at their main political rivals.[41] This split weakened the Seneca Nation and exacerbated the Tonawandas' split with the chiefs at Buffalo Creek at a time when federal officials and land company representatives were discussing the implementation of a policy of Indian emigration to the Michigan Territory.

On September 3, 1823, at Moscow, New York, in Livingston County, with Major Charles Carroll, a federal commissioner, present, Mary Jemison ceded all but two square miles (1,280 acres) to

John Greig and Henry B. Gibson. Greig, a prominent attorney from Canandaigua, was in the employ of the Ogden Land Company and had previously represented Thomas Morris, Phelps & Gorham, and the Pulteney Associates. Greig and Gibson obtained all of the Senecas' Gardeau Reservation except the reserved two square miles, then in Genesee County and now in Wyoming County near Castile, New York, for $4,286, less than $0.30 per acre. This land cession and others involving the Gardeau Reservation were never submitted to or ratified by the United States Senate.[42] Yet Gardeau was "chump change" to the Ogdens. Like the great serpent in the Seneca creation belief, they wanted more to satisfy their insatiable appetite, that is, lands in the fertile Genesee as well as the vast Seneca estate of Tonawanda, Buffalo Creek, Cattaraugus, and Allegany.

The push for Seneca lands reached a crescendo in the mid-1820s. On May 13, 1825, a House of Representatives report falsely claimed that the Senecas were ready to sign a treaty for the sale of their lands.[43] By this time, through the efforts of Horatio Jones and Jellis Clute, the Ogden Land Company began making "gifts" of $80 to $120 payments to certain chiefs to entice them to sell Seneca lands. By the summer of 1825 Thomas Ludlow Ogden had convinced the War Department to hold a treaty negotiation with the Senecas. President John Quincy Adams appointed Oliver Forward, a leading merchant and harbor promoter of Buffalo, to be the United States treaty commissioner. Forward was to cooperate at every turn with the Ogden Land Company.[44] What was to follow was a disaster for the Tonawandas, the loss of 70 percent of their land base.

On August 31, 1826, in a "treaty" held under the authority of the United States at Buffalo Creek, the chiefs and warriors of the Seneca Nation reached agreement with trustees for the Ogden Land Company—Robert Troup, Thomas L. Ogden, and Benjamin W. Rogers—who were represented by their attorney, Greig, the same fellow who had secured much of the Gardeau Reservation in the "treaty" of 1823. Nathaniel Gorham, a leading speculator in Indian lands, was appointed, once again as he had been in the Gardeau Treaty of 1823, as a superintendent on behalf of the claims of the State of Massachusetts under the terms of the Hartford agreement of December 16, 1786.[45] Besides Forward, Phelps, Greig, and Seneca representatives, others in attendance included six interpreters, including Horatio Jones, who had served for more than three decades in this capacity, and Dr. Jacob Jemison (Jimeson), Mary Jemison's grandson and a trained physician who had attended Dartmouth College. Parrish was also in attendance.[46]

At this "treaty" the Senecas ceded all of their remaining Genesee Valley lands, including Big Tree, Canawaugus, and Squawky Hill reservations in Livingston County; the remaining two square miles at the Gardeau Reservation in Wyoming County; and the sixteen-square-mile Caneadea Reservation in Allegany County. In addition, under this "treaty" the sizes of the Buffalo Creek, Tonawanda, and Cattaraugus reservations were substantially reduced: Buffalo Creek by 36,638 acres; Tonawanda by 33,409 acres; and Cattaraugus by 5,120. Thus, the Seneca land base was reduced by 86,887 acres.[47] Names of two of the Tonawanda chiefs—Blue Sky and Little Beard—as well as Red Jacket appear on the Treaty of 1826. Names of prominent Senecas from other communities also appear, including Young King, Pollard, Little Billy, Governor Blacksnake, Captain Strong, Seneca White, Big Kettle, Captain Shongo, and Henry Two Guns.[48]

Questions arise about why Red Jacket signed the Treaty of 1826 and about why, despite his name on the face of the treaty, he influenced Tonawanda protest over this "agreement." Samuel Parsons and Willet Hicks, two prominent Quakers, later indicated that federal commissioner Forward made direct threats to the Senecas in attendance. Quoting Red Jacket, the two wrote that Forward forced the signing by his threats. Forward allegedly told the Senecas: "Tis all one [of the Seneca reservations] whether you sign it or not; if you don't, your great Father the President will drive you off, and you will not get a cent for your lands; he will only show you the way to Cherokee Country." Red Jacket allegedly was offered $260 outright and an annuity of $100 for life.[49] Although he rejected the bribe, Red Jacket, nevertheless, acceded to the treaty. Despite being castigated by many Senecas for putting his name on it, what transpired after the "accord" suggests that Red Jacket never really supported the treaty.[50] Almost immediately, he led the opposition to it, trying to overturn the land cessions. A subsequent federal investigation of what had occurred at the 1826 treaty council supported Red Jacket's assessment.[51]

The legal validity of the "treaty" of 1826, which was never ratified by the United States Senate, was questioned from the first. According to Henry S. Manley, the former assistant attorney general of New York State, United States Indian Commissioner Forward "received money from Troup, the Ogden Land Company trustee, for unexplained expenses of the treaty."[52] The Ogden Land Company also had Dr. Jacob Jemison on its payroll because the physician favored Indian land sales and pushed for Seneca emigration to the West. Many of the Senecas who acceded to the treaty supported it to protect their own reservations from being lost in whole or in part and were willing to cede other Indian communities to protect their own territories; however some of the chiefs who signed this 1826 "treaty" were apparently "bought off." Forward defended the practice: "Small annuities may have been allowed the principal chiefs, but the payment of such gratuities I believe has been practiced under every treaty with Indian tribes of this state since the organization of its government."[53]

On January 30, 1827, Forward claimed that Red Jacket's opposition group included a minority of Senecas including a "number of the Tonnewanta [sic] Indians" whom the United States treaty commissioner insisted were not chiefs. He maintained that this group was outnumbered at the Buffalo Creek Treaty council in August, 1826, and that these vocal Indians were mainly "a few of the indians [sic] who are scattered over the small reservations upon the Genesee River, and a part of the Tonnewantas [sic]."[54] Because of the aged Red Jacket's unbending leadership of the opposition to the "treaty," he was deposed as a Seneca pine tree chief on September 15, 1827, by the pro-treaty group at Buffalo Creek. He was later reinstalled after a public outcry against the action.[55]

Red Jacket understood that to challenge Forward's actions and intimidation at the treaty council would be a lost cause; however, the savvy Seneca knew by not openly challenging Forward, he would have the later opportunity to try to overturn the treaty. Because of his fame and standing in the white world, he knew he could gain access to the highest circles of American government as long as he came off as a moderate critic of the treaty commissioner and the proceedings of 1826. His strategy proved correct, and for the next two years, after the 1826 treaty, he devoted all his energies to this cause. Importantly, Tonawandas including Jemmy Johnson joined in his petitions to federal officials and even accompanied Red Jacket in his lobbying efforts to the nation's capital. In effect, the Seneca orator was mentoring these conservative Indians in the ways of Washington and in the new politics of protest that the Tonawandas were to use so effectively right through the 1850s.[56]

As a result of this treaty, Tonawanda became *the* center of resistance to ceding any more Seneca land. The Tonawanda Council of Chiefs, who had traditionally deferred to the chiefs at Buffalo Creek, were determined to close ranks. Their anger over the loss of most of their tribal lands had long-term consequences, affecting their community's makeup, their strategies of survival, as well as their relationship with other Seneca communities. It is little wonder that when Canawaugus Senecas were forced off their lands in 1826, they migrated to Tonawanda, not Buffalo Creek, Allegany, or Cattaraugus. These displaced Senecas became incorporated over time as Tonawandas.

On March 15, 1827, Red Jacket and twenty-five other mostly Tonawanda Senecas, including Tonawanda Chief Jemmy Johnson, petitioned Governor DeWitt Clinton of New York State to investigate this 1826 accord. Drawing up their bill of particulars at a council at Tonawanda, they accused Forward of coercion. The petitioners alleged that Clute and Jones bribed the chiefs, while Greig offered money as well. They insisted that only 236 were in favor and 1,766 Senecas were opposed to the 1826 treaty.[57]

Two months later, Red Jacket appealed directly to President John Quincy Adams, reiterating some of the same arguments made in the March petition to Governor Clinton. Among those who signed this second memorial were leading Tonawanda Senecas such as Jemmy Johnson and John Blacksmith. In it, these anti-treaty Senecas insisted that they represented the vast majority opposed to the carrying out of the 1826 treaty. The memorial went on to describe why Forward was appointed commissioner in the first place. It claimed that Forward was merely appointed "to save expenses of travel, he being at Buffalo and could attend to it without much trouble, whereas great expense would be incurred by sending a man all the way from the city of Washington." Red Jacket, fearing a trick, took his own interpreter with him rather than relying on Dr. Jemison whom he did not trust. The chiefs also decided to inform the Senecas on the other reservations about what was sought by Forward. Greig, of the Ogden Land Company, who arrived after Forward at the treaty grounds, then "told Red Jacket that he would have the land." Forward then "arose and informed the chiefs that it would be a very sorry thing to them if they did not sell their lands and continued saying the company [Ogden Land Company] will like it all the better for you to refuse to sell, and in that case you will not get one cent for your lands as you will be driven off them by the President of the United States." Soon after Parrish added a threat of removal "that if they did not sell it would be a serious thing for them" because the president had already appointed a set of commissioners "to go to the west and look out a tract of land for them." The memorial castigated both Parrish and Jones for offering bribes to win over the acceptance of the treaty. The Seneca memorial then called for the dismissal of Parrish and Jones and the appointment of future federal commissioners "living out of our immediate vicinity." It also sought Adams' support for the retention of the Seneca lands lost in the "treaty" of 1826: "Your red children feel determined not to release their lands and possessions unless compelled to do so by our father's power which we are unable to resist, but we have every appearance that the hand of our father will not be raised against a handful of his suffering children."[58]

In early 1828, the United States Senate took up debate on the "treaty." On February 29, the Senate by a vote of twenty to twenty failed to ratify the "treaty."[59] The Senate also placed an "injunction of secrecy" over deliberations over the "treaty" of 1826 with the Seneca. On April 4, the Senate passed the following ambiguous resolution: "That by the refusal of the Senate to ratify the treaty with the Seneca Indians, it is not intended to express any disapprobation of the terms of the contract entered into by individuals who are parties to that contract, but merely to disclaim the necessity of an interference by the Senate with the subject matter."[60]

In the meantime, in March 1828, three anti-treaty Seneca chiefs, including Red Jacket, had had an audience with President Adams in Washington. They insisted that their lands should not be taken away from them nor should they be compelled to go west. They once again urged the president to remove Jasper Parrish, charging him with receiving money from the Ogden Land Company, defrauding the Indians of their annuities, and failing to protect them. They asked the president to appoint a special emissary to investigate and report on this matter.[61]

On May 9, 1828, the secretary of war appointed Richard Montgomery Livingston of Saratoga, New York, to investigate the events surrounding the 1826 "treaty." Livingston's report is both revealing and disturbing at the same time. The report was ironically sent to former Ogden Land Company proprietor Peter B. Porter, the newly appointed secretary of war. Livingston maintained that, until August of 1826, the Seneca chiefs "disputed about religion, but clung to the common object of retaining their lands." At no time from the founding of the Ogden Land Company in 1810 until ten days after the council of 1826 had been in session "were any of the chiefs . . . willing to convey any of their lands." Livingston reported that immediately after the War of 1812, the Ogdens gave $5,000 each to Parrish and Jones in order to "influence" the Senecas to extinguish their title. Until 1826 these efforts had failed. The appointment of Forward to push a land transaction was done "without the solicitation or privity of the tribe." Forward then convened a council on August 11, 1826, employing arguments "addressed to the hopes and fears of the nation," implying that removal to the West was the only other option. "The terrors of a removal enchained their minds in duress," leading them to submit "to sell a part to preserve the residue." Livingston also claimed that the Ogden Land Company proprietors and Forward had a secret rendezvous at Rochester prior to the council in which they perfected their strategy. He pointed a finger at Dr. Jacob Jemison, who had been retained by the Ogden Land Company, as well as at many of the chiefs, especially some Christian converts who resided around the Seneca Mission at Buffalo Creek, who had become dependent on federal annuities and other "rewards."[62]

Largely because of the negative findings expressed in the Livingston Report, the "treaty" of 1826 was left to stand and never resubmitted to the United States Senate for its advice and consent. After the outpouring of support by reservation residents for Red Jacket's anti-treaty stance in 1826 and the recantation by almost all of the chiefs who had agreed to the massive land sale, Red Jacket was politically rehabilitated.

Thus, the 1826 "accord," which was never rescinded by federal authorities, was a major watershed in Tonawanda history. Earlier, John Sky had first articulated his differences with chiefs at Buffalo Creek. Before his death in 1830, the controversial Red Jacket, the aging orator, had espoused the Tonawanda conservatives' position on sovereignty, missionaries, and protection of the reservation's natural resources. In the future, that is, in 1838 and after, the Tonawandas were not going to blindly follow the lead of Buffalo Creek and its chiefs. They were going to go it alone and establish their separate strategies to ensure their future in their much reduced homeland. They were slowly becoming a separate Seneca identity.

   While the Tonawanda chiefs were finally forming a united front in the face of the Ogden Land Company and its operatives, a major revitalization had been underway that shaped and still shapes these Senecas' worldview. The development of the Handsome Lake religion could be directly traced to the reservation in the period 1812 to 1860. Indeed, Tonawanda Territory was the incubator for the Code of Handsome Lake. While the Seneca prophet briefly lived in exile here, the reservation became central to the religion's development. Although Handsome Lake was born at Canawaugus, lived most of his life at Allegany where he received his visions, and died at Onondaga, his disciples, especially Jemmy Johnson, contributed immensely to the formal development of the religion in the four decades after the prophet's passing.

3

He Carries a Heavy Weight
on His Shoulders

Eight months after Red Jacket's death on January 20, 1830, Chief Jemmy Johnson, Sose-ha-wa•ʾ, or "Great Burden Strap," became the Tonawanda Senecas' major spokesman and remained so until the early 1840s. In September of that year, Johnson's role was confirmed at a "Grand Indian Council" at Tonawanda in a solemn ceremony that lasted three days. According to one report, many chiefs addressed the assembled in speeches that lasted for four or five hours each. In traditional form, women played a noticeable role in the assemblage. One newspaper reported that during the social dance that followed, women set the rules and men followed, much different than the newsman was used to seeing in the white world.[1]

Johnson's exact genealogical connection to the Seneca prophet Handsome Lake is unclear. Some have reported that he was the grandson of the prophet. According to anthropologist Elisabeth Tooker, Johnson was Handsome Lake's mother's sister's daughter's son; hence in Seneca kinship terms he was the prophet's "grandson." Whatever the case, both the prophet and Red Jacket were the greatest influences on Johnson's life and helped determine his actions until his death in 1856.[2]

Jemmy Johnson was born at Canawaugus, the birthplace of both Handsome Lake and Cornplanter, around 1774.[3] He and his family had lived through the American Revolution and witnessed the Seneca time of troubles that had followed the upheaval. His family had settled at Allegany and became influenced by the prophet and his visions.[4]

In 1799, after emerging from a catatonic state, Handsome Lake opened his eyes and began to recount a vision, a religious message that he had just received from four well-dressed messengers who had come to him with the Creator's commands. This first vision, later followed by two others, was to have a profound influence on the Iroquois who were faced with disaster in the aftermath of the American Revolution. In the following months, Handsome Lake had other visions, falling into trances and seeing many wonders and gaining insights relating to moral and social reform. He saw the punishment of wrongdoers: wife-beaters, drunkards, gamblers, witches, sinners. He traveled to the realm of the blessed, learning in this pleasant world how families among the Iroquois should live in peace in their own communities. Instructed by the sacred messenger who accompanied him on his spiritual journey, he was urged to continue to perform the Iroquois' religious ceremonial cycle.[5]

In his third vision, which took place in 1800, he was commanded to write down the *Gaiwiio*, to preserve it for all time, and to carry the message to all the peoples of the Six Nations. Handsome Lake combined his teaching with an emphasis on family values, condemning gossip, philandering, abortion, and alcohol, all of which were rampant at the time. He claimed to have received the "Good Message" from messengers of the Creator to advise his people. He strongly warned against any further alienation of Indian lands and land sales to whites, as well as proscriptions against warrior participation in another white man's war—both ignored by the Iroquois well before the prophet's death in 1815.[6]

In 1809, after being criticized for his support of executing witches and the withdrawal of an endorsement by Cornplanter, his half brother, for his preaching at Coldspring, Handsome Lake and his followers went into exile at Tonawanda. Jemmy Johnson went with him and settled at Tonawanda. Johnson's extraordinary family were to reshape the Tonawanda community and make a major mark in American history as a whole. His niece, Elizabeth Johnson, Ga-ont-gut-twus, later a Tonawanda Wolf Clan matron, was a part of the later fight against the Ogden Land Company. Elizabeth was well schooled in Seneca traditions by her uncle.[7] Lewis Henry Morgan described her as "the very picture of goodness of heart and natural kindness. . . . a very dignified, industrious and noble looking woman."[8] Laura Parker Doctor, Elizabeth's granddaughter, later told Arthur C. Parker:

> Grandmother [Elizabeth] made baskets. She made a great
> many of them and would take a wagon and team and sell

them to the stores in the neighboring towns and villages. She made all kinds of farm baskets, household baskets and fancy baskets. Once I made some little baskets and when I went with her on a trip I sold them for three cents each. But, Grandmother could make the real Indian baskets too. Some were of corn husk and were thought valuable by the Indians. She could make burden straps or tumplines of slippery elm and basswood bark fiber. She made very fine bead-work too and Aunt Carrie learned from her. My Grandmother always dressed in the old-time costume, until after awhile she had white folks' dresses. Her older clothing consisted of a beaded broadcloth skirt, an overdress covered with brooches, leggins and moccasins, but after awhile she had shoes. It was a long time until she had a hat. Her head covering was a small shawl made of a sort of wool bunting with a ribboned edge bordered with white breads. It was very pretty and I think I like such a head-throw now because my Grandmother did.[9]

Ga-ont-gut-twus married William Parker, later a pine tree chief. They had seven children: six boys—Levi, Newton, Nicholson, Solomon, Spencer, and Ely; and one girl—Caroline. The Johnson-Parker family produced two Civil War officers, an army general who later became the first Native American to become United States Commissioner of Indian Affairs, a federal Indian interpreter, as well as a remarkable educator and woman of letters.[10] By serving as Lewis Henry Morgan's informants, they helped shape the discipline of anthropology in the United States.[11]

The religious role that Jemmy Johnson played at Tonawanda in the development of the *Gaiwiio* has long been emphasized by such scholars as Anthony F. C. Wallace. Wallace has maintained that as a result of Johnson's teachings, the Tonawanda version, one that emphasized the "sacredness of the family" and condemned adultery and other vices, was "to become the standard by which other speakers' versions were judged, and it was this version that was carried from village to village in the fall of each year in the Six Nations Meetings." Wallace added that by 1850, under Johnson's "guidance," "a new renaissance of traditional Iroquois religion," the Code of Handsome Lake, was spread.[12]

According to tradition, women at Tonawanda were disturbed by the fact that community members were ignoring Handsome Lake's admonitions about abortion, adultery, family responsibilities, alcohol, gambling, and gossip, as well as the prophet's call for respect and support for elders and orphans in the community. Responding to the women, Johnson, after considerable reflection, decided to preach. After a council at Tonawanda, he decided to make his preaching an annual affair.[13] Fluent in the Iroquoian languages, he became widely recognized and respected. Johnson's reputation grew and delegations from various longhouses came to Tonawanda to hear him preach and carry back his message to their own communities. In this tradition, the Indians, on the first occasion to hear Johnson, brought wampum to Tonawanda; "the truth of the messages and the return of this wampum symbolized that this central fire of the Handsome Lake teachings was to continue to burn at Tonawanda."[14] Tooker has noted that the first record of Johnson's annual speech coinciding with a Condolence Council is in 1845. Hence, as she has brought out, Tonawanda became the epicenter of the Handsome Lake religion in New York.[15]

What most scholars have not properly understood about Chief Johnson was his political role, that is, as the spokesman of the Tonawanda Council of Chiefs after the death of Red Jacket in 1830. As is true today, politics and religion are never completely separated from Iroquois existence, and all councils begin with the invocation. Part of not fully understanding Chief Johnson's role can be placed on scholars' relying only on the picture presented by Lewis Henry Morgan. In order to understand Chief Johnson's role, it is necessary to jump forward in our narrative to the mid-1840s.

Morgan, who first met the chief along with Johnson's famous grand-uncle in a bookstore in Albany in 1844, saw the chief as the caretaker of an ancient tradition then in decline whose rituals had to be scientifically recorded for posterity. Subsequently Morgan and his fellow members of the organization "the Grand Order of the Iroquois" were invited into the community to observe the "doings" of a Grand Council held at Tonawanda on October 1, 2, and 3, 1845.[16] Indeed, this Grand Council was well advertised, indicating that the Iroquois were not trying to hold a closed ritual, but had other purposes in mind. Although confusing the Tuscaroras with the Tonawandas, the *Rochester Daily American* described the forthcoming council a few days in advance:

Grand Council of the Six Nations.—An interesting ceremony will take place on Monday next, the 29th inst., at a village of the Tuscarora [*sic*] tribe of Indians at Tonnewanda. Within the last three years, two Sachems and several Chiefs of the Seneca Nation have died. Application was consequently made soon after their demise in the manner authorized by the laws and customs of the Six Nations, to the Great Civil Chief of the Confederacy at Onondaga for a Grand Council to fill the vacancies, and his consent obtained. But owing to a variety of circumstances, the assembling of the Council has been hitherto delayed. It will occur at the time and place above mentioned.

It is about fourteen days since the sacred wampum was transmitted by the Tuscaroras [*sic*] to the other nations. Within a few days, several of the chiefs and warriors have passed this place on their way to the Council. The ceremonies, which are long and impressive, will continue several days. The Grand Sachem of the Confederacy will be present and will preside. Governor Blacksnake, from the Allegany reservation, was expected, but his great age—ninety six—it is understood will prevent. No grand council of the Six Nations has been held for the last thirteen years. All the Nations of that renowned confederacy, except the Mohawks, will be represented.[17]

The revival of the Condolence Council to coincide with the chief's address after years of neglect was extremely significant. Anthropologist William N. Fenton has noted that the Condolence Council was the "ritual paradigm that governed the proceedings [of forest diplomacy] and guided the behavior of Iroquoian and Algonquian speakers alike throughout the lower Great Lakes."[18] This council was for mourning dead chiefs, lifting up the minds of bereaved relatives, and installing their successors. The ceremony was and is essential for understanding the Iroquois as well as their relations with outsiders—Indian and non-Indians. It consists of rites known as the Welcome at the Woods' Edge, the Roll Call of the Founders, the Recitation of Laws, the Requickening Address, the Six Songs of Requiem, and the Charge to the New Chief. In this ritual, invited guests gather at the woods' edge and are welcomed into the village where the chiefs read the Roll

Call of the Founders, recounting the sacrifices of past leaders. Dead chiefs are recognized for their service to the nation, mourned, and their successors are raised and validated, "requickened in the titles of the founders so that the league may endure."[19] Then the face of the new chief is revealed and he is charged in his new duties to carry out the people's will.

The ritual of mourning and installation of chiefs is also filled with numerous metaphors that attempted to strengthen the house (nation).[20] Dispelling the clouds and restoring the sun are metaphors used to emphasize the importance of this bereavement and installation ritual. To create alliances of the gathered participants, there are references to keeping the path open by clearing rivers, rapids, and roads; polishing a chain; and maintaining a perpetual fire to bind.[21]

The Iroquois' expectation was that all guests observe and respect these Indians' traditions and learn the proper forms of the ritual. Fenton has written that, through the seriousness and religiosity of the Condolence Council, the Iroquois attempted to manipulate the foreboding white world to their new advantage. Knowing their great power had waned by the eighteenth century, the Iroquois Confederacy saw alliances as indispensable for survival. Whether weaker Indian nations such as the Munsees, Nanticokes, Saponis, Tutelos, or Tuscaroras, or more powerful Europeans such as the English or French, one thing was clear, as Fenton has observed: "Whoever came to the Iroquois came on their own terms."[22]

In the past, the hospitality and generosity of the Six Nations during this Condolence Council ceremony was exceptional. It included the "passing of wampum belts, the distribution of presents and the enormous expense of the expected feast." Besides social dancing that always followed the end of the ten-day period of the condolence council, a lacrosse match was held, which was intentionally planned as part of the rite, for lacrosse was more than a game. It was a "game that anciently discharged social tensions" by discouraging intervillage warfare, keeping the warriors fit, and cheering the depressed relatives of the deceased.[23] The ceremony, in effect, reinvigorated Iroquois existence, renewed political forms, restored society, and built or strengthened alliances. Hence, by inviting Morgan, his associates, as well as others, the chief was consciously linking them to the Iroquois in a chain of friendship that Johnson hoped to draw on for Tonawanda survival.

The first day of the 1845 council was devoted to a condolence ceremony and, during the last two days, Chief Johnson held sway in Seneca with his annual speech, recounting the life and teachings of Handsome Lake. Seventeen-year-old Ely S. Parker, Johnson's grandson, served as Morgan's translator, later providing a transcript. Morgan, the would-be anthropologist, was also able to meet with other Iroquois chiefs, including Onondagas Captain Cold (Frost), the League Tadodaho, and Abram LaFort; Cayuga chief Peter Wilson; and Seneca sachem John Blacksmith.[24] Subsequently, Parker sent Morgan a transcript of Johnson's speech at an 1848 council, not attended by Morgan; the attorney-anthropologist later interviewed both chiefs, Johnson and Blacksmith, in Rochester in June of 1849, getting from them a brief explanation of the religious system of the Iroquois.[25]

The relationship between Morgan and the Tonawandas is always seen one way, that is, through the eyes of the scholar Morgan; however, the savvy Tonawandas, especially Chief Johnson, were using Morgan for their own purposes as well. By publicizing the event widely and inviting guests such as Morgan, the "event" could also be viewed as a form of resistance to threats to remove the Tonawandas, a way to show that despite the efforts of the Ogden Land Company, Iroquois culture and religious traditions were alive and well.

As Elisabeth Tooker rightly points out, the holding of the 1845 Condolence Council at Tonawanda was motivated by the crises of the times: the loss of the Buffalo Creek Reservation in 1838 to 1842, and with it, the Onondaga council house where the meetings of the league had previously been held; the death of key sachems; and the internal squabbling about the chiefs' system of governance on the Allegany and Cattaraugus reservations that was eventually to lead to the creation of an elected system there in 1848.[26] Moving the Grand Council to Tonawanda, despite treaties aimed to dispossess these Senecas, and condoling and raising new chiefs in the ancient manner, was an Indian-directed strategy of survival. By opening up the "doings," as they were called to the general public, the Indians were hoping to win allies. Hence, the ritual of 1845 was a political event, just as much as a religious ceremony.

Chief Johnson, with Blacksmith joining in, played along with Morgan and his colleagues in the hobbyist organization, the Grand Order of the Iroquois, even after the conclusion of the Condolence Council.[27] The chiefs employed other devices, including self-deprecation and flattery, to win over their non-Indian guests. They wrote to Morgan on April 12, 1846:

> I beg leave to call your attention for a few moments to what I have to say. The Old Confederacy of Iroquois are nearly gone. A new Confederacy [Grand Order of the Iroquois] is arising in its place. You are at its head. You are desirous to save [us] if possible for the few remnants of the Old Iroquois that live. I am happy that this is so. I have been acquainted with many societies who have attempted to shield the Indians against the injustice and frauds of the whites, and who have desired to assist in saving the Indians from oppression and injustice. But none have I ever wished to succeed until I heard of your organization. I am happy that it now exists and only regret it is not older.[28]

Several months earlier, Morgan's organization had held a meeting in Ithaca, whose aim was "to prevent the execution of the treaty by which the Indians are to be driven from the Tonawanda and Buffalo Creek Reservations . . . and to work in earnest to effect the object."[29] Although their efforts were to no avail, the organization sent Morgan to Washington, helped finance Senecas to go there too, and began an effort to collect a petition of 50,000 signatures to protest Tonawanda removal.[30] Morgan's organization had devoted itself "to make a last struggle to save their [Tonawanda] homes."[31] On July 24, 1847, Morgan appealed directly to the commissioner of Indian affairs on behalf of the Tonawandas, insisting that the "very spirit of justice should penetrate American legislation and administration of our affairs of the Red Race."[32] Indeed, later Morgan became the great publicist for the Iroquois, comparing them to the Romans when he published his findings in his classic ethnography in 1851.[33] Morgan also continued to encourage and recommend the schooling and employment of Jemmy Johnson's family members right through Reconstruction. Hence, the chief's cultivation of his relationship with Morgan had benefits for his tribe as well as his own family.[34] Chief Johnson, referred to by Henry Rowe Schoolcraft as the "High Priest" of the Tonawandas, was as much a political spokesman as a religious leader.[35] In the decade and a half that followed Red Jacket's passing, Johnson's role as designated spokesman of the Tonawanda Council of Chiefs is clear, even though he shared influence with Chief John Blacksmith, after the latter was condoled as a league sachem in 1839. The fact that Canawaugus Senecas joined the Tonawanda community led by Canawaugus-born Jemmy Johnson appears to be more than a coincidence.[36]

A year after the passage of the Indian Removal Act by Congress in 1830, the Tonawanda chiefs sent a memorial drawn up in council to President Andrew Jackson. While praising their soon-to-be-fired Indian subagent Judge Justus Ingersoll for his good advice, the chiefs led by Jemmy Johnson noted the vast improvements on the reservation made by the Senecas, namely, the "comfortable houses, shoemaking and milling, [and] every thing that white men do." Because of this "progress," the chiefs hoped "that the white man will not wish us far away but will take us by the hand as friends and neighbors."[37]

Efforts to remove the Senecas and other Iroquois sped up when Ingersoll was replaced by James Stryker in late 1830, an action opposed by the Tonawandas. Once again, internal conflict erupted within the Seneca Nation, and attempts were made to dispose chiefs for suggesting sale of lands, for removal west, or for excessive intemperance.[38] In his appointment in late 1830 as the federal Indian subagent, Stryker, a loyal Jacksonian attorney from Middletown, New York, was directed by the secretary of war "to aid the expected emigration of the New York Indians to Green Bay, suggesting that he also move to Buffalo to secure this effort.[39] By November 1833, the subagent pushed for the creation of an exploring party to visit the West with the intended purpose of selecting lands in which to resettle the New York tribesmen.[40]

By February 1834, Seneca chiefs led by Big Kettle at Buffalo Creek and Jemmy Johnson of Tonawanda petitioned for Stryker's removal. They insisted that he had refused to distribute the annuity; disturbed the peace and harmony by frequently calling councils to consider emigration; bribed the Seneca interpreter; induced Senecas such as Young King and Captain Pollard to write unauthorized letters to Washington; fostered divisions and discord, failed to be honest and had no integrity; recognized the authority of nine chiefs who had been previous deposed; and finally, served as a secret employee of the Ogden Land Company.[41] Much of this criticism proved to be correct, and Stryker's nefarious role was decisive in leading up to the Treaty of Buffalo Creek on January 15, 1838, that dispossessed the Senecas of all of their reservations, except for the one-mile-square Oil Spring.

Chart 1. The Proprietors of the Ogden Land Company in 1840*

"Partition of Lands in the Indian Reservations in the Counties of Erie and Genesee in the State of New York by and among the proprietors." "Division into twenty shares of one hundred and eighty lots in the 12,800 acre tract in the Tonawanda Reservation made by Joseph Jones and Elias K. Cook."

November 20, 1840, Geneva, New York

---

1. Abraham Ogden, 503 acres
2. Robert Troup's estate, 536 acres
3. James Wadsworth, 518 acres
4. Robert Tillotson, 548 acres
5. Isaac Ogden, 522 acres
6. Robert Troup's estate, 513 acres
7. Shaw & Wilson, 504 acres
8. Shaw & Wilson, 529 acres
9. Robert Bayard, 518 acres
10. Joshua Waddington, 550 acres
11. Joshua Waddington, 509 acres
12. Joshua Waddington, 525 acres
13. Joshua Waddington, 525 acres
14. Duncan Campbell, 511 acres
15. Benjamin Rogers, 523 acres
16. Benjamin Rogers, 523 acres
17. Peter Schermerhorn, 507 acres
18. Thomas Ludlow Ogden, 557 acres
19. Thomas Ludlow Ogden, 513 acres
20. Wadsworth & Murray, 502 acres

---

*Ogden Land Company Record Book, 1811–1871: "Indian Reservations," 119–123, NYSL.

By 1837 Stryker was working directly with Thomas Ludlow Ogden and his land company. In February 1837, the federal Indian subagent and prominent Buffalonians Henan Potter and Orlando Potter contracted

> to use their best Endeavors and Exertions to dispose and induce the said Indians to adopt and pursue the advice and recommendations of the Government of the United States in respect to their removal and future location, and on the

just and fair terms to sell and release by Treaty their said
reserved Lands or such parts thereof as are not cultivated
or rendered subservient to their support.[42]

According to the contract that was to expire in May 1838, the Ogden
Land Company was to compensate the three according to the number of acres released by the treaty. If all Indian lands were to be
acquired, both Stryker and Potter would receive $10,000 and Allen
would acquire a tract of land at Buffalo Creek. The Ogden trustees
indicated that before payment would be made to these three men,
the subcontractors had to deliver a minimum of 40,000 acres to the
company, that among other tracts included 10,000 acres of Buffalo
Creek and 1,000 acres of Tonawanda. In this agreement with the three
subcontractors, the Ogden Land Company was to pay out $26,500
to individual Indians or whites to facilitate approval of land cessions.
Thus, because of the time limit set in the contract, Stryker had a
major incentive to speed up the negotiations.[43]

Well before this time, Stryker was assisted in his efforts at Indian
removal by John F. Schermerhorn, a New York clergyman and longtime Jackson supporter. Schermerhorn had been directly involved in
removal negotiations with twenty different Indian nations. Prior to his
appearance in Seneca Country, he had been directly involved in negotiating the Treaty of New Echota of 1835 that resulted in the removal
of the Cherokees.[44] Even before his official appointment by Jackson to
the post as federal commissioner to treat with the Six Nations, he had
been corresponding with members of the Seneca Indian emigration
party. By July 1836, he had calculated how many Indians he had to
remove from New York.[45] In the fall of 1836, Schermerhorn wrote
to President Jackson, noting obstacles in his way in New York where
he maintained that the majority of Indians were opposed to removal;
nevertheless, he reassured Jackson about his commitment to secure
the removal of New York tribesmen.[46] Schermerhorn also wrote to
the commissioner of Indian affairs that he had "laid the foundations
for the ultimate and speedy removal of the whole of the New York
Indians, both those who reside at Green Bay and those who are still
within this state."[47] It should be noted that Schermerhorn speculated
in Wisconsin lands while serving as a commissioner dealing with
the Indians in the West and, even well after his dismissal as treaty

commissioner, he specifically received a $2,000 payment in Article 8 of the Buffalo Treaty. Moreover, the New York cleric had family connections to the Ogden Land Company.[48]

Because of increasing criticism of Schermerhorn following an exposé of his tactics in securing the Cherokee Treaty at New Echota, the New York cleric's role in negotiating with the Six Nations was short-lived. On October 29, 1837, he was replaced by Ransom H. Gillet, a former Democrat congressman and junior law partner of the powerful New York senator Silas Wright. Born in Columbia County but a resident of Ogdensburg, the heart of the Ogden Land Company's domain, Gillet was part of the Albany Regency, the Democrat political machine founded by Martin Van Buren, who now assumed the presidency in 1837. Even before his official appointment, Gillet had advocated Indian removal from New York State.[49] Gillet was to wrap up the treaty negotiations within three months and then spend the rest of his life deflecting criticism about it, blaming the illness of the Indian interpreter, the Ogden Land Company, the arbitrariness of Schermerhorn, the corruption of Stryker, and his own lack of previous experience in negotiations with the Indians.[50]

The Tonawanda Senecas did not stand by idly and allow Stryker, Schermerhorn, or Gillet to push for removal of their Indian community. In the half decade before the Treaty of Buffalo Creek of 1838, the Tonawandas had repeatedly joined in with their anti-removal allies in other Seneca communities to neutralize these three men's efforts to force emigration. In 1834, Jemmy Johnson, described as "the principal chief of the Tonawanta Reservation," and Sachem Little Johnson of Buffalo Creek and Chief James Robinson of Allegany were chosen as delegates at a special council at Buffalo to go to Washington to meet with federal officials to "make all things straight" between the Senecas and the government of the United States.[51] While Johnson and Robinson were anti-removal chiefs, it appears that Little Johnson, who was later deposed as a League sachem, acceded to the government's wishes to organize an Iroquois "exploring party" to look at lands to resettle west of the Mississippi.[51] Later, in January 1836, pro-removal Senecas, including Little Johnson and Young King, Captain Pollard, Captain Strong, and George Jamieson, wrote that the exploring party would probably "bring back a favorable report of the country that they have gone to visit." They insisted that many Senecas at Buffalo Creek opposed removal and consequently have "exhibited a violent and hostile spirit." The pro-removal memorial urged that their anti-removal opponents should not be able to go to Washington by being funded by annuity moneys.[52]

By October 1837, the anti-removal chiefs that included Jemmy Johnson and James Robinson helped secure a memorial from the Grand Council at Buffalo Creek, condemning Schermerhorn and his efforts to promote emigration. The two chiefs were supported by prominent Senecas including Big Kettle, Governor Blacksnake, Jack Berry, as well as chiefs from other Iroquois communities such as Chief Moses Schuyler of the Oneidas. Raising their sovereign rights under the Treaty of Canandaigua, these chiefs insisted that all discussions of emigration had to be done in open council, not secret meetings, that no coercion was acceptable, that only Iroquois leadership authorized by council could speak on behalf of the community. Once again pointing out their "rapid advances"—sawmills, grain mills, large barns, good wagons, useful agriculture implements, schools, council houses, churches, and so forth, the chiefs insisted: "There is, therefore, no sufficient reason for the whole nation to be removed" on the account of a few immoral types found in all communities in America. "We have resolved to adhere to our present locations to remain and lay our bones by the side of our forefathers." They emphasized that they were at peace with their white neighbors and had already "disposed of our lands again and again until our seats are reduced" to the bare minimum for their children.[53]

Despite this protest, Gillet "found" some chiefs, head men, and warriors to sign off on a treaty, although the accord was largely not an expression of how most Iroquois and their chiefs felt. This federal "accord," the Treaty of Buffalo Creek of January 15, 1838, was largely an imposed agreement that merely satisfied the interests of Albany politicians and especially Ogden, Joseph Fellows, and the rest of the company's proprietors. Under this fraudulent treaty consummated as a result of bribery, forgery, the use of alcohol, and other nefarious methods, the Seneca "ceded" all their remaining New York lands— Allegany, Buffalo Creek, Cattaraugus, and Tonawanda—except the one-mile-square Oil Spring Reservation to the Ogden Land Company and relinquished their rights to Menominee lands in Wisconsin purchased for them by the United States. In return, the Indians "accepted" a 1,824,000-acre Kansas reservation set aside by the federal government for all the six Iroquois nations as well as the Stockbridge-

Munsees. The Indian nations had to occupy these Kansas lands within five years or forfeit this reservation. For a total of 102,069 acres in New York, the Indians were to receive $202,000, $100,000 of which was to be invested in safe stocks by the President of the United States; the income earned was to be returned to the Indians. The United States was to also provide a modest sum to facilitate removal, establish schools, and purchase farm equipment and livestock for the Indians' use.[54]

With the aid of the Society of Friends, the Senecas challenged the legality of the Buffalo Creek Treaty of 1838. For the next four years, they waged a major battle to overturn the treaty. Although they were to succeed partially by 1842, the result was to prove disastrous to the small community at Tonawanda.

4

The Compromised Treaty

Three years before the historic Condolence Council of 1845, the Tonawanda Senecas faced the greatest crisis in their history. On May 20, 1842, the federal government concluded a treaty with the Seneca Nation at Buffalo Creek. This "accord" is one of the more significant but least understood of the twenty-five federal-Iroquois agreements.[1] The treaty was one of only three accords to allow for the return or repurchase of lands by the Iroquois, specifically providing for the ceding back of the Allegany and Cattaraugus Indian reservations; however, neither Buffalo Creek nor the Tonawanda reservations were returned. The treaty was also the only one to mention the issue of taxation. Article 9 of the treaty provides an assurance by the federal government to intervene on behalf of the Senecas:

> to protect such of the lands of the Seneca Indians, within the State of New York, as may from time to time remain in their possession from all taxes and assessments for roads, highways, or any other purpose until such lands shall be sold and conveyed by the said Indians, and the possession thereof shall have been relinquished by them.[2]

Right down to the present day, this treaty strongly influences Seneca life, the interactions of the two Seneca governments in New York—the Seneca Nation of Indians and the Tonawanda Band of Seneca—as well as the Iroquois Indians' relationship to New York State government, especially in regard to Albany's power to collect sales taxes on the Iroquois reservations. Today, tribal members of the Seneca Nation of Indians refer to the treaty as the "Compromise Treaty" since two of its reservations—Allegany and Cattaraugus—were returned; however, to the Tonawandas, it is referred to as the "Compromised Treaty" since their lands were not returned and consequently, they view the accord as a "sell out" of their community.[3] Indeed, the treaty and the Seneca Nation's establishment of a republic with an elected system of government in December 1848 completed the schism that started before the War of 1812.

The "accord" was a direct response to rectify the numerous problems associated with the Buffalo Creek Treaty 1838. Besides the clear exposure of frauds perpetuated by agent Stryker in collusion with the Ogden Land Company and certain Indians themselves in "facilitating" the "accord," the previous treaty had never received the two-thirds requirement by the United States Senate in the ratification vote. Although President Van Buren had formally proclaimed the treaty in 1840, Vice President Richard Johnson of Kentucky had simply broken a tie vote when the treaty had come up for a vote in the Senate, leading to an outcry that the treaty was bogus. A major result of what had happened in 1838 was a movement to overturn the treaty. Of course, many Senecas continued to demand the return of four reservations lost in 1838.[4]

The participants in the treaty council of May 20, 1842 that dispossessed the Buffalo Creek and Tonawanda Senecas had far different perceptions of what had transpired there. Ambrose Spencer, the federal treaty negotiator, interpreted that his mission had been totally satisfactory to all concerned and that there was never a fairer one entered into by the Indians.[5] Yet, according to the Hicksite Friends' proceedings of the 1842 treaty council, as many as sixteen of the fifty-five chiefs—fifteen chiefs from Tonawanda and Israel Jemison, a chief from Cattaraugus—rejected the federal-Indian accord.[6] In the Tonawanda protests over the 1842 treaty, the memorials indicated that about forty Seneca chiefs did not sign, but all of the emigration party chiefs and "some chiefs from Allegany and Cattaraugus and a few from Buffalo" did assent to the treaty.[7] Four years later, the Tonawanda chiefs insisted: "by our national laws it was, and still is, necessary that *all* of the chiefs should be of one mind; that they must *unanimously* agree to make a treaty, otherwise it cannot be made." They concluded: "In this fundamental law of the Iroquois, and of our nation, we at Tonawanda would have found protection."[8]

In their protests over the 1842 treaty, the Tonawanda chiefs saw a great injustice. Even at the treaty council, they complained that the meeting was a farce and that the "negotiations" were predetermined long before they arrived.[9] Indeed, the chiefs were largely right in their assessment, except for their belief that the Ogden Land Company was once again behind the whole affair. The major architects of the Treaty of 1842 were two New Yorkers—John Canfield Spencer, the secretary of war, and his illustrious father, Ambrose Spencer, the United States commissioner to treat with the Seneca. The two men allied themselves in the negotiations with three prominent representatives of the Hicksite Friends—Benjamin Ferris, Griffith Cooper, and, most importantly, Philip Thomas.

Before the treaty council of May 1842, all the Seneca communities had reached agreement among themselves that called for a reduction of the size of each of the four reservations, rather than surrendering any one. This agreement would have allowed for approximately twenty acres per family use on each of the four reservations.[10] Even at the time of the treaty council in May, the Senecas believed that there would be negotiations over the retention of their lands. Instead, they were presented with a *fait accompli*. This fact was recognized by chiefs John Blacksmith and Jemmy Johnson at the treaty council in 1842: "The treaty [1838] was made before it was brought into council, and the present one [1842] was also made before it was brought here."[11]

Quite significantly, both the representatives of the Hicksite Friends and the Whigs, especially the powerful branch of the party in New York State that included Millard Fillmore, Hamilton Fish, Horace Greeley, William Seward, Thurlow Weed, and the Spencers— father and son—received much of what they desired in the treaty. By consciously working with the Hicksites, the conservative Whigs wanted to extend New York State jurisdiction over Indians, save federal moneys, continue to develop state roads, canals, and railroads, insure the future prosperity of Buffalo, and close the books on the much criticized, now discredited, and expensive Indian removal policies of the Jacksonian and Van Buren eras. In effect, Albany was to become the new "Great Father" while the Hicksites were to have the primary responsibility to lead their Seneca charges to Truth and Salvation.

Much of the Senecas' positive image of the Friends today is largely based on the benevolent work of Joseph Elkinton and his Quaker School at Tunesassa and by the noble efforts of the society in later fighting the Kinzua Dam in the late 1950s and early 1960s.[12] It is clear that despite the Seneca image of the Friends, the Hicksite negotiators in the 1840s had a Whig-like agenda. They were also hardly intent on minding their own business when it came to Seneca affairs. Both the Hicksites' and the Whigs' program was to absorb the Indians into the body politic in the most cost-efficient but most humane way. To both, the Indians were to become taxpaying citizens of the state, but protected under law. Do-gooder Hicksites and conservative Whigs both saw the Indians as a vanishing race that had to be carefully transformed for their own good. They could not be left to their own "antiquated" political systems to negotiate a treaty in 1842 or to plan for their future. To the Hicksite Friends, the Senecas could not long endure because of constant pressures by avaricious and morally corrupt whites. The Indians could not survive as separate enclaves in the dominant white world and had to learn to cope with the larger society. Thus the Hicksite strategy, which at times became policy at the federal and state levels, was designed to bring "civilization" to the Senecas in order to absorb them into American society.

In response to Jacksonian Indian removal policies, the Hicksites developed what they considered was a workable formula of assimilation. This "Americanization" process included proselytizing on reservations to stamp out "pagan" influences, however different and less coercive the Quaker style was; the white man's education, whether state or missionary directed; United States citizenship; and, eventually, much later in the process, Indian fee simple title, which had to be encouraged to instill personal initiative, allegedly required by the free enterprise system. The Hicksites understood that the Indians were not yet ripe for the last part of the formula—land in severalty—because of the nefarious activities of the Ogden Land Company and the question of their preemptive right to Seneca lands.

Among the three major Hicksites at the negotiations was Philip Thomas, the philanthropist who later founded the Thomas Asylum, later the Thomas Indian School, in the 1850s. Thomas fit the Whig profile. The politically savvy Quaker had been the president of the Merchants' Bank in Baltimore and a commissioner of the Chesapeake and Ohio Canal. He was also the founder and chairman of the Baltimore and Ohio Railroad, which by the time of the Civil War laid track to Buffalo and Rochester but also through the Allegany Indian Reservation at Salamanca.[13] By 1842, the Hicksites knew full well that the Buffalo Creek Reservation, one of their major missions, was now overrun with white squatters and timber strippers and had little chance of being returned to the Indians.[14] They also knew that, although losing this mission at Buffalo Creek, their overall "civilization" program for the Seneca was still on track. Quite significantly, the Society of Friends had no presence at Tonawanda and had little influence there. The events that transpired from 1841 to 1843 also reveal that the Hicksite representatives also had disdain for the traditional government, the Tonawanda Council of Chiefs.[15] Yet, despite this Hicksite influence, policies immediately before, during, and after the Treaty of 1842 were not set by them, but by the Whig Party, that had first come to power in Albany in 1837 and in Washington in 1841.

By 1842, the Whig Party was quite diverse. It included outspoken boosters of western New York such as Millard Fillmore, Albany leaders promoting state interests such as Seward and the two Spencers, and national party leaders such as Clay in Washington with longtime frontier racist attitudes toward Indians.[16] In Hicksite circles, there was no more heroic figure than the New England Whig secretary of state Daniel Webster. It was Webster who had earlier opposed Indian removal policies and who first advised the Friends to seek a new federal-Seneca treaty to supplement the fraudulent one of 1838; in his typical conciliatory, legalistic manner, one appealing to the "people of the Inner Light," Webster saw this new federal-Seneca accord as an alternative to a long, bitter, and costly struggle in the courts.[17]

The Whigs had taken advantage of criticisms of Jacksonian Indian policies, despite the irony that President Harrison was renown as an Indian fighter, and that John Bell, their first secretary of war, was the author of the Indian Removal Act of 1830. During the so-called Log Cabin presidential campaign of 1840, the Whigs bitterly blamed Jackson and Van Buren for the Second Seminole War, the most expensive Indian war in United States history, which claimed 1,500 American soldiers and cost the nation $60 million. Hence, by 1842, forced removal of Indians was a discredited policy. The Second Seminole War, which started in 1835, continued unabated until 1842, precisely the same year as the federal-Seneca treaty. Much time during the presidency of Tyler was devoted to trying to secure "peace with honor" and to extricate the country from its Florida morass.[18]

Importantly, Tyler's main "point man" in Washington working on securing peace in Florida in late 1841 and 1842 was John Canfield Spencer, the prominent attorney with offices in Canandaigua and Albany, who had worked as counsel for the Senecas in the early 1820s. Spencer's family owned ironworks, and invested in canal building and in land, including some financial dealings with the Holland Land Company. Although involved in land speculation himself, he and his father had little love for the crude practices of land jobbers such as the Holland and Ogden Land companies whose actions often retarded rather than promoted state economic policies. In the 1820s, he had tried to overthrow Joseph Ellicott's control of the Holland Land Company, and, in the mid-1830s, helped to challenge the company's claimed title to some of their vast landholdings. As conservatives and anti-Masons who feared social disorder, both Spencers, political opportunists to the core, knew that by their populist-styled attacks on the rich holdings of land companies, the Whigs could win votes from their Democrat enemies. By 1840, John Canfield Spencer had become one of the major leaders of the Whig Party, both in and out of New York State.[19]

John Canfield Spencer's career sheds light on his later involvement in the drafting of the Seneca Treaty of 1842. After graduating from Union College, he served as private secretary to Governor Daniel D. Tompkins, as judge advocate general in western New York during the War of 1812, as district attorney for five western counties of New York after the war, as a United States congressman from 1817 to 1819 and as a member of the New York State Assembly, serving as speaker in 1820. By the 1830s, Spencer served as the secretary of state of New York and as superintendent of the Common Schools where he promoted the use of government moneys for the Christianization of the Indians.[20] Appointed secretary of war in 1841, he advocated the building up of the Civilization Fund. He maintained that educating Indians was, in the words of historian Ronald M. Satz, "a wiser long-range investment than funds for military weapons."[21] It was these ideas which were quite attractive to his Hicksite allies in 1841–1842.

By the early 1840s, frontier folk had become vocal about the numbers of Indians who had been removed to the Trans-Mississippi West. To them, moving more Indians to Indian Territory was unacceptable. With politicians such as the powerful senator Thomas Hart Benton clamoring for American expansion in the 1840s, forcing more eastern Indians westward across the Mississippi did not make much sense. Even previously removed Indians objected to a new exodus of eastern tribes west. Later, at the treaty council of 1842, this fact was

Chart 2. The Seneca Treaty of 1842: Compromise or Compromised?
Principals: Ambrose Spencer, John Canfield Spencer

1. Returns Allegany and Cattaraugus, but not Buffalo Creek and Tonawanda reservations
2. Article 9 (re: taxation)

→ Whig Agenda	Seneca Agenda Majority View until May 1842	← Hicksite Friends Agenda
1. Follow fiscal conservatism, except for transportation agenda—promotion of canals, highways, railroads.	1. Opposes Indian removal.	1. Opposes further Indian removal.
2. Promote economic development of western New York; see Ogden Land Company and other major land jobbers as creating political backlash and restricting real development.	2. Oppose giving up any of four reservations (Buffalo Creek, Allegany, Cattaraugus, and Tonawanda); reluctantly willing to make partial land cessions of each of four reservations.	2. Favor end to Second Seminole War.
3. Oppose further Indian removal, based on fiscal restraint and frontier politics.	3. Oppose land-speculating companies; see the Ogden Land Company as their primary enemy.	3. Encourage Indian "civilization" program:
4. Try to end Second Seminole War.	4. Oppose state taxation.	a. fits religious principles
5. Encourage Indian "civilization" program:		b. fits overall goal to transfer Indians into western-educated, self-sufficient, Christian farmers and taxpayers under American law and legal guarantees
a. cheaper		4. Favor New York State jurisdiction.
b. fits conciliation		5. See economic development of western New York as "inevitable."
c. politically expedient		6. No mission at Tonawanda.
d. alternative to Jacksonian policies		7. See traditional council of chiefs as "antiquated" system that must go.
e. makes Indians into taxpaying American citizens		8. Oppose Ogden Land Company and its methods.
6. Favor New York State jurisdiction		

not lost on the participants. The Hicksite Benjamin Ferris observed that "strenuous exertions were made" to procure other lands for the Seneca in the west, "but there were so many difficulties laid in the way by the whites and Indians already located there, that the object was defeated."[23] Hence, the Friends pushed to concentrate the Seneca populations onto two reservations, rather than force removal to the trans-Mississippi West. To them, it would be more humane, but also would be politically practical, cheaper to accomplish, and would facilitate the Friends' "civilization" program.

The Whig divergence with Jacksonian–Van Buren approaches toward the Indians is easily seen in examining President Tyler's appointment of Ambrose Spencer as the federal commissioner to treat with the Seneca Indians in 1842. Spencer's appointment was no mere accident. Besides being the father of John Canfield Spencer, the secretary of war, Ambrose Spencer was literally the grand old man of New York State politics. Although a strong advocate of state jurisdiction over Indians, he was, nevertheless, a longtime opponent of forced removal and Jacksonian–Van Buren Indian policies. A man with dark, flashing eyes and the energy of two men, Spencer had significant previous experience in the adjudication of Indian matters. Ambrose Spencer, a Connecticut Yankee by birth, attended Yale University, but was graduated from Harvard in 1783 at the age of eighteen. He became an attorney, practicing law in Claverack and Hudson, New York, and soon became a major player in the politics of Columbia and Albany counties. He was elected as a Federalist candidate to the New York State Assembly in 1793 and to the New York State Senate two years later. In 1798, Spencer bolted the party and joined the Democratic Republicans of George Clinton and Thomas Jefferson. Indeed, on and off for the next three decades, Spencer was associated with and allied to the Clinton family. His second and third marriages were to DeWitt Clinton's sisters. In 1802, Spencer became the attorney general of New York State, serving in this capacity until his appointment to the New York State Supreme Court two years later. In 1819, he became the presiding justice of this three-member court. After leaving the court, he practiced law in Albany and was elected the city's mayor in 1824. He later briefly served in Congress from 1829 to 1831, becoming one of the more vocal opponents of the Indian Removal Bill of 1830. After losing election, Spencer dabbled in politics and devoted much of his time toward outfoxing Martin

Van Buren. Although first a Federalist and subsequently a Democratic Republican and Clintonian, Spencer, in the last nine years of his life until his death in 1848, served the Whigs, and, in fact, presided over the party's convention in Baltimore in 1844.[24]

Despite his advanced age in 1842—Spencer was seventy-seven years of age—the jurist had the makeup for his rough assignment in Seneca Country. A strong-willed, self-confident man, he had little to prove or gain from his assignment. His son was already enshrined in Whig Party inner circles. One would ask why he even took this low-priority assignment in the first place. Yet Spencer was the most logical appointment that could have been made. In 1822, as the presiding justice of the New York State Supreme Court, Spencer rendered the decision in *Jackson v. Goodell* involving the alienation of the lands of John Sagoharase, an Oneida Indian veteran of the American Revolution, who had been awarded bounty lands in the military tract in the Township of Junius, Seneca County, New York.[25] Spencer's opinion in this case clearly shows his views on state power over Indians. Spencer insisted that the Indians were not aliens outside of state jurisdiction. He argued that these "*Indians* are born in allegiance to the government of this state, for our jurisdiction extends to every part of the state; they receive protection from us, and are subject to our laws." The New York jurist continued: "Indeed, our legislature regulates, by law, their internal concerns, and exercises entire and perfect control over them."[26]

After passage of the Indian Removal Act of 1830, Spencer was a leader in trying to overturn the act. He even went so far as to advise the Cherokee delegation while on its visit to Washington, strongly suggesting that the Cherokees bring their case before the United States Supreme Court by hiring William Wirt, the former attorney general under presidents Monroe and Adams, as counsel to protect their rights. The Cherokee took the advice and the rest is history: *Cherokee Nation v. Georgia* (1831).[27]

Thus, Ambrose Spencer had long experience in Indian-related matters, much more than the average federal negotiator. As a practical Whig attorney, Ambrose Spencer hoped to implement a far-reaching goal: his son's John's "civilization" plan, one supported by influential Hicksites, and which also corresponded to the political and economic aims of Albany politicians. To both Spencers, there was no contradiction between advocating citizenship for Indians as well as state jurisdiction over Indians as well as taxing them, and being against forced removal. With the backdrop of the Second Seminole War, Ambrose Spencer received his formal instructions in 1842.[28]

These instructions provide a key to unlocking the mysteries surrounding the Seneca Treaty of 1842. On February 17 of that year, Commissioner of Indian Affairs T. Hartley Crawford, an "old and warm friend" of Andrew Jackson and strong supporter of the Indian Removal Act of 1830, wrote Spencer pointing out to his negotiator the Indians' strong objections to the Treaty of 1838. Crawford indicated his hope that the new negotiations would be conducted in a "conciliatory spirit on all sides," calling the "proposed arrangement" "one of compromise." The commissioner added that Washington was concerned with two overriding factors: "an already flourishing and still advancing portion of the Territory of New York from the encumbrance of Indian populations, and those Indians themselves from the temptations that surround them where there they now are." He then explained the interests of the Ogden Land Company in the negotiation. Significantly, Crawford observed: "There is much more land embraced in small reservations than the Seneca can use." He then outlined the federal position, namely that Buffalo should never be returned to the Indians, maintaining that the reservations nearest to the city [Buffalo Creek and Tonawanda] would be the "most agreeable to the Senecas to yield." The commissioner added that the Indians "would thus be furthest removed from the vicinity of the whites and there will be the least interference with the progress of improvement of that important section of the state." Among other things, Crawford warned Spencer not "to depart from the provisions" of the Treaty of 1838 "except in respect to the Senecas and in reference to them only with the modification as to quantity of land to be ceded."[29]

Spencer's instructions in February were especially important in what they did not include. Nowhere did Washington specify the surrender of the Tonawanda Indian Reservation, nor did federal officials even hint at discussions of the tax issue. Two weeks after Crawford's letter, Ambrose Spencer wrote the commissioner, clearly confirming that Tonawanda was not specified: "The principle and perhaps sole object of the [new] treaty as you represent is to enable Major Ogden and Fellows to reconvey to the Senecas all the lands ceded to them on the 15th of January, 1838, except the Buffalo and some other portions of the lands ceded, on the principles stated in your letter." Spencer added that it was "inferable [that] most [Seneca] at present . . . do not intend to emigrate or at least only a part of them" and asked for further clarifications of his mission so he "might know precisely what is expected of me."[30]

In this fiscally conservative setting, negotiator Ambrose Spencer's overall strategy was (1) to attempt to close the books on Indian removal, a policy that was too costly, politically untenable, and one that he had opposed for over a decade; (2) to cooperate with the Hicksites in order to silence their continued criticisms of Washington's Indian policies; (3) to develop inexpensive workable private arrangements such as the Friends' work with the Seneca to further the overall Indian civilization program; and (4) to maintain and extend New York State jurisdiction over the Indians. By including Article 9 in the Seneca Treaty of 1842, Spencer was not thinking that the statement would be eventually used by Senecas to challenge New York State's right to tax Indians. As a proponent of state power over the Indians, he was unwilling to give a federal commitment to overturn the state's jurisdiction over the Seneca in all areas, but acceded to tribal demands about exempting Indians from levies on road construction. Hence, it may be suggested that, in order to wrap up the negotiations as quickly as possible, Spencer included this narrowly defined assurance of federal intervention.[30]

The sentiments of the three Hicksite Friends who negotiated the treaty with the Whigs paralleled the Whiggish politics of the times. They could easily agree with the Whigs that past Indian removal policies were a costly failure, that the Second Seminole War in Florida was a stain against national honor and had to be ended, and that a conciliatory approach to domestic and foreign policies was in the overall best interests of the United States. Their fervent support for Whig Indian policies gave moral legitimacy to the overall federal government "civilization" program. Through a carefully orchestrated campaign, the Hicksites drafted pamphlets and memorials, sponsored lyceum presentations, and held strategy meetings with the secretary of war and the governors of New York and Massachusetts.[31] They promoted their interests by "encouraging" the work of Maris B. Pierce, a Dartmouth-educated Cattaraugus chief who held the position of federal interpreter and who kept the Hicksites informed about Washington as well as Seneca doings. Pierce had been educated by Joseph Elkinton, an Orthodox Friend who ran the Quaker School at Tunesassa. Pierce had signed the original Buffalo Creek Treaty of 1838, but he and others later claimed that he had reluctantly done so as a result of pressures from senior chiefs. Without question, he saw the advantages of serving as the Friends' Indian spokesman as well as the federal interpreter throughout the fight over a new Seneca treaty.[32]

Writing to federal officials including President Harrison in 1841, Pierce frequently called on the Whig administration to reappoint Griffith Cooper, a Hicksite who was serving as temporary agent in New York, to a permanent post in the Indian Service. In February 1841, Pierce reported to the Friends that the Whigs appeared to be reluctant to spend money to carry out the Treaty of 1838. By April, he wrote once again to the War Department promoting Cooper's reappointment and asking for a meeting with the secretary about a new treaty. By June, Pierce praised the Quakers' efforts in presenting the Seneca "memorials and petitions on our behalf" and for their efforts at countering the Seneca emigration party and the Ogden Land Company. In October, he repeated his request about Cooper's reappointment. By December, he attended Hicksite-sponsored meetings in Boston and Albany about the need for a new treaty. At those occasions, the Hicksites discussed the proposed treaty negotiations with Whig governors—William Seward of New York and John Davis of Massachusetts.[33]

Two memorials by the Tonawanda chiefs clarify the circumstances that transpired from December 1841 through March 1842. During the winter months, the chiefs sent a delegation to a meeting in New York City conducted by the Hicksites. Much to their surprise and anger, the Quakers had already held negotiations with United States governmental officials. At the winter meeting, the Tonawanda delegation was told to give their memorials of protest to the Friends who would present them for them in Washington. The Tonawanda delegation was also strongly urged to return home since their continued presence might threaten the negotiation; however, the Indians were also informed that two or three delegates from each reservation would soon go to Washington to meet in council. Apparently, this did not occur. The Friends also told the Indians that the secretary of war would "send a man to hold a council with us."[34]

By the time that "man," Ambrose Spencer, appeared, the final form of the treaty was already a *fait accompli*. On May 16, 1842, the principals to the treaty formally convened for "negotiations" at Buffalo Creek. Ambrose Spencer, the Hicksite delegates, and representatives from Allegany, Buffalo Creek, and Cattaraugus reservations were in attendance, along with Abram Dixon, an official emissary of the New York State Legislature who was an attorney and a farmer, as well as a New York State senator from Westfield in Chautauqua County, near the Cattaraugus Indian Reservation. Missing from the first day's deliberation were the representatives of the Tonawanda Reservation, who showed up on the next day.[35]

On the second day of the council at Buffalo Creek, Spencer proclaimed himself a New Yorker, who was "proud of the way the Indians have always been respected" in the state. To him, the Indians had always "been treated justly and humanely." Presenting the treaty as a "done deal" that had the total support of "your steadfast and benevolent friends, the Quakers," Spencer indicated it was impossible to save the Buffalo and Tonawanda reservations since it "was found impracticable and inexpedient to insist on these requests." Attempting to force agreement, he pointed out firmly that the Treaty of 1838 was still binding and remained so even if the Seneca rejected the proposed treaty.[36] State senator Dixon repeated Spencer's line nearly word for word. Undoubtedly offending most of the Senecas at the treaty council, Dixon then insisted: "You are under the protection of the laws of this state, and to a degree you are liable to their exactions and restrictions, like our own citizens." Dixon added: "Our is a government of laws, and not of force."[37]

According to the Tonawanda chiefs, instead of negotiations, "one of the Friends arose and addressed the council stating that they had come for the purpose of explaining the compromised [sic] treaty. . . . And all that resided on the Tonawanda and Buffalo Creek Reservations should emigrate to the two remaining reservations."[38] Despite a vehement reaction by Israel Jemison, a chief from Cattaraugus, and the Tonawanda chiefs, and a counterproposal "to give up a part of each reservation, reserving to each native that wished to remain twenty acres of land," the objections to the proposed treaty fell on deaf ears.[39] Jemison's proposal was one that had been agreed on by the Seneca chiefs and conveyed to the Secretary of War in early April.[40]

Even as late as the fifth day of the treaty council, Samuel Gordon, a Cattaraugus chief who later signed the treaty, clearly explained that the majority of Senecas, both the chiefs and the people, wanted a compromise, but one based on their remaining on their own reservations, however reduced in size by the terms of a new treaty. Gordon accurately predicted a bleak future if only two reservations remained: "They fear, if all are concentrated on two Reservations, there will be difficulties and jealousies among themselves. That is the main difficulty." He added: "Cannot they compromise so as to keep the same number of acres contained in the Cattaraugus and Allegany Reservations, divided among all the different Reservations?" Yet, fearing that the Hicksite Friends had been criticized to the point of leaving the negotiations, Gordon begged "them to remain and not withdraw, but go on and assist in the negotiation."[41]

The collective views of the Hicksites—Cooper, Ferris, and Thomas—were set forth in the Hicksite proceedings of the councils of April and May 1842. They saw the Indians as a vanishing race that had to be led by the hand to civilization for their own good. Importantly, they did not see the loss of Tonawanda as a great tragedy, but a Friends' opportunity to lead their charges to the "Inner Light." In language reminiscent of David A. Ogden's arguments earlier, the three men also made reference to the inevitability of Indian population decline, massive white population increases, and the corrupting influences found in Buffalo and its environs. The Friends in attendance saw the solution as simple—namely, the Senecas had to consolidate their lands, reduced to 52,000 acres (about 100 acres per family in 1842), which would be "a quantity amply sufficient for every necessary purpose." They insisted that by concentrating the Senecas on their two remaining reservations, they would be "more favorably situated for mental and moral improvement, as well as for the support of schools and other institutions for the advancement of science, and the formation of habits essential to a state of civilization." The Quakers added that this solution would make the Senecas "more accessible to their friends, and more open to the kindly influences of those who may believe it right to devote themselves to the amelioration of their condition."[42]

Despite Tonawanda calls for further negotiations, Spencer insisted he had "restricted power" and therefore had "no power to negotiate at large." He continued by calling up the names of the benevolent William Penn as well as the Quakers who had acted "in your behalf," secured the "very best terms they could possibly obtain for you," and helped prevent the necessity of forced Seneca emigration out of New York State.[43] Refusing to allow negotiations for 2,500 acres of

Tonawanda and unaware of or unwilling to accept Seneca tradition about unanimity and consensus in decision making, Spencer, on the fifth and final day of the council, insisted that majority rules and if a majority of chiefs, even pro-emigration chiefs, agreed to terms, the treaty was binding. In his defense of the treaty, Spencer urged the concentration of the Indians on the two reservations, "it will be much better for you—and your Friends, the Quakers, as I understand them intend to superintend, and offer succor, to educate you, and make you a much greater people than you are now."[44]

Thus the agenda of self-proclaimed Quaker do-gooders paralleled the objectives of Whig politicians with regard to the Tonawandas. The meddling of each also further contributed to the growing schism in the Seneca polity, whose origins as we have shown, dated as far back as the War of 1812. By December 1848, a new political entity, the Seneca Nation of Indians, an elected government without a chiefs council, was established at the Allegany and Cattaraugus reservations. The Tonawandas retained their government of chiefs and position within the Iroquois Confederacy as "keepers of the western door"; however, the Seneca Nation of Indians was now permanently separated from Tonawanda as well as from the Iroquois Grand Council at Onondaga. After the vote at the May 1842 treaty council, Chief Blacksmith, in an impassioned reaction, maintained that the fifteen Tonawanda chiefs and 615 reservation residents were unanimously opposed to the agreement since they "love their children—they love their nation."[45] For the next decade, Blacksmith, a courageous activist sachem, was to lead the fight to overturn what all Tonawandas viewed as the "sell out" of 1842. Personally threatened and physically assaulted by "goons" hired by the Ogden Land Company proprietors to drive the Tonawandas off their lands, the sachem, nevertheless, challenged the legitimacy of the Treaty of 1842 and helped prevent the scattering of his Tonawanda Seneca community. Aided by a teenage Seneca boy, Ely S. Parker, a brilliant white attorney John Martindale, the unanimity of the Tonawanda Council of Chiefs, and eight clan mothers, Blacksmith outlined the strategy that eventually succeeded in the return of 7,549 acres to the Tonawandas.

The Activist Sachem

John Blacksmith, a Tonawanda Seneca chief who in 1839 became an Iroquois League sachem, was the leading voice in council opposing removal to the West. Over the next twelve years, he led the fight against removal to the West. Blacksmith helped develop the strategies used by the Tonawandas against the Ogden Land Company and his influence shaped these Indians' responses well after the sachem's death in 1851.[1] A conservative Seneca, recognized for his great knowledge of Iroquois history, the sachem was an activist voice in dealing with the greatest crisis in Tonawanda history.

The Hotinohsyóni? (Hodenosaunee or Haudenosaunee), meaning in the Seneca language "they [who] are of the extended lodge," draw strength from the past to survive over 450 years of Euroamerican contact.[2] They have maintained a cultural as well as political presence in their homeland, which sets them apart from many other native peoples east of the Mississippi. Their ability to adapt is built into the very fabric of their ancient League of the Iroquois and its rituals. Each of the nations had league chiefs, called sachems; Blacksmith was one of these sachems. Although each nation was not equally represented in council, the league did not act as a western-styled political unit and thus was not based on majority-rule voting. Instead, all decisions were focused on achieving consensus, which often required long debate over days, months, or years, or was never achieved. Hence, until the crisis caused by the American Revolution, these nations avoided internecine conflict, since agreeing to disagree was a basic axiom accepted by the sachems. If consensus was not achievable, member nations were allowed to follow their own path.

At the core of the league's rituals was the Condolence Ceremony, the Hai Hai, where deceased chiefs were replaced by new ones; while attending to grief, the ceremony tied the exploits of great leaders of the past to the present.[3] When a sachem died, the eldest matron of his clan chose his successor, and the one chosen would assume the title and identity of the deceased. Thus, through the Condolence Ceremony, the people were reminded of past history and leadership as well as the glorious achievements of the league.[4]

The Iroquois' Great Law (Kaianerekowa) defined the duties and rights of sachems, chiefs, clans, and nations, but also evidenced flexibility. At times, if there was no suitable replacement, a chief might be borrowed from one clan or one nation to serve. Men such as Red Jacket with special abilities, but not "condoled," would be recognized with honorific titles such as pine tree or war chief. The women, clan mothers, had the inherent right to choose the new sachem or force an unworthy one out, symbolically removing his badge of honor, his antler horns, from his head.[5] Hence, sachems such as Blacksmith had to defer to the women and seek their guidance.

Asher Wright, the prominent Presbyterian missionary and authority on the Senecas in this period, recorded the minutes of a Six Nations Council held at Onondaga on July 17, 1839. At that condolence ceremony, Jáoyatigrati, Blacksmith was installed as Deonihogáhwa (Deyonihnhoiga:ʔwen), the "Doorkeeper," the fiftieth sachem of the Six Nations.[6] Blacksmith replaced Chief Little Johnson of the Buffalo Creek Reservation, who had been deposed because of his signing of the Treaty of 1838. Importantly, Blacksmith was the Wolf Clan sachem. The Wolf Clan sachem was and continues to be associated in Iroquoian tradition with clearing the path and leading his "pack" away from danger. This role was precisely Blacksmith's mission from 1839 to his death in 1851, when Ely S. Parker was installed with the same league title. Even after Blacksmith's death, his legacy lived on and inspired the Tonawandas in their struggle with the Ogden Land Company.[7]

In the colonial era, the Iroquois excelled at playing off the powerful English and French empires as well as manipulating other native communities to serve their interests. Even though they were not the most numerous of woodlands Indians, they learned how to make it appear as if they were more powerful than their numbers. They mastered forest diplomacy and projected power even long after it had waned. In the period 1838 to 1859, the Tonawanda chiefs demonstrated this very same skill. Thus, while taking an active outward stand in their struggle to fight off the Ogden Land Company,

Chart 3. Tonawanda Seneca Chiefs Whose Names Appear on Petitions, 1840–1857*

Chief's Name	Name Appears on 1857 Treaty	League Name
Babcock, George		
Bigfire, John	yes	
Blackchief		
Blacksmith, John (d. 1851)		Wolf Clan sachem of the Six Nations: Deonihogáhwa
Blinkey, Thompson	yes	
Blue Sky		
Charles, Addison	yes	
Cooper, Richard		
Cooper, Snow	yes	
Doctor, Isaac	yes	
Ground, Jabez	yes	
Hatch, John	yes	
John, Joshua	yes	
Jonas, Benjamin	yes	
Johnson, Jemmy (d. 1856)		
Kennedy, Lewis		Deer Clan sachem of the Seneca Confederacy Council: Haondyéyah
Luke, John		
Mitten, James	yes	
Moses, William	yes	
Parker, Ely S.	yes	Wolf Clan sachem of the Six Nations: Deonihogáhwa
Parker, Samuel	yes	
Parker, William	yes	
Poodry, Lewis	yes	
Printup, David	yes	
Shanks, Isaac	yes	Wolf Clan sachem of the Seneca Confederacy Council: Dagéhsadeh
Sky, George	yes	
Spring, David		
Spring, Jesse	yes	
Tiffany, Jesse		
Washington, William		
Williams, James	yes	
Wilson, John	yes	

*Headmen and warriors are also listed on these petitions, found mostly in OIA, NYAR, M234, MR583–589, RG75, NA.

the council, with the support of the eight clan mothers, was actually imitating certain features of its time-honored, traditional methods of dealing with the outside world. Hence, Chief Blacksmith, using this ancient method, was able to encourage schisms in the non-Indian world that proved beneficial to the Tonawandas.[8]

Chief John Blacksmith was born around 1781 in the waning days of the American Revolution. At that time, most of the Senecas were impoverished, huddling as refugees at Fort Niagara, living on rations supplied by their allies, the British. The postwar period was one of great suffering for the Senecas, dispossessed of millions of acres of their lands in the Treaty of Fort Stanwix in 1784.[9] Hoping for better days and believing that cooperation was the best strategy to maintain their shrinking land base, Senecas in the hundreds volunteered for service in the United States army during the War of 1812. Blacksmith was one of those warriors, serving under the command of Seneca officers and chiefs Little Beard and Farmer's Brother on the Niagara frontier in 1813.[10]

With the building of the Erie Canal and its opening in 1825 and the rapid settlement of western New York that followed, the Ogdens colluded with local and Albany politicians as well as federal agents to remove all the Indians from the central and western parts of the state, succeeding in 1826 and culminating in the Buffalo Creek Treaty of 1838. The later treaty led to major protests, including a Quaker-directed campaign to restore the Indian land base in New York, resulting in the United States Senate's ratification of the Seneca Treaty of 1842.[11] It was this 1842 treaty that mobilized the Tonawandas and their chiefs to wage a relentless campaign to avoid removal and regain their reservation in the decade and a half that followed. Although chiefs from Allegany and Cattaraugus, but not all, agreed to this 1842 arrangement, not one of the Tonawanda chiefs put his name on this treaty, and they held a long-standing resentment and distrust toward the Quakers, especially Philip Thomas, for their efforts in negotiating it.[12]

Except for his participation in the War of 1812, Chief Blacksmith's life before 1838 is not well documented. Although he could communicate and understand English, he could neither read nor write the language. As a youth he was an avid hunter and a keen student of Seneca history with "an intimate knowledge of Indian localities" in today's Livingston, Monroe, and Ontario counties. He was reputed to be an authority on the French invasion of the Seneca Country in 1687, the devastating Denonville Expedition. He and his wife Susan (Gaoyogwas), a clan matron, and their children resided along Tonawanda Creek.[13] Blacksmith, along with his household of six that included his wife Susan, occupied four plots of land, totaling 43.5 acres and valued at $415. These holdings included an 11-acre orchard, a barn, and a residence.[14] Until 1846, Blacksmith had a sawmill operation at Tonawanda, one that became the envy of Ogden Land Company proprietors.

Henry R. Schoolcraft, as did Lewis Henry Morgan, realized early in their visits to Tonawanda that Chief Jemmy Johnson, Ely S. Parker's grandfather, was the "great high priest of the Confederacy." Yet, both recognized that Blacksmith was the most politically savvy chief on the council. Schoolcraft described him as "the most influential and authoritative of the Seneca sachems . . . somewhat portly, is easy enough in his manner, and is well disposed, and even kindly towards all who convince him that they have no sinister designs in coming among his people."[15] According to Schoolcraft, Blacksmith was of the Wolf Clan, "born on the forks of the Tonawandas and is 59 years old" (he was actually sixty-five or sixty-six). Schoolcraft referred to him as an authority on Iroquois history. Blacksmith recounted to him the oral tradition that the Senecas had once lived "on the banks of the Seneca and Canandaigua Lakes" and that these Indians were called "*Dun-do-wau-ohuh,* or People of the Hill, from an eminence now called Fort Hill (Bare Hill), at the head of Canandaigua Lake."[16] He also gave Schoolcraft instruction in the Seneca language.[17]

Schoolcraft, who had been a much-maligned Indian superintendent in Michigan during Andrew Jackson's presidency, was suspect almost from the beginning.[18] Schoolcraft was appointed by Governor Silas Wright as the official census taker and authorized by the New York State Legislature to undertake the compilation of data on New York State's Indian population in 1845.[19] The Tonawanda chiefs refused to cooperate, viewing him as a spy or agent for the Ogden Land Company and the state. Blacksmith became his ardent foe:

Why, why is this census asked for, at this time, when we are in a straitened position with respect to our reservation? Or, if it is important to you or us, why was it not called for before? If you do not wish to obtain facts about our lands and cattle, to tax us, what is the object of the census? What is to be done with the information after you take it to Governor Wright, at Skenectati? [*sic*][20]

Consequently, the Tonawandas, unlike other Six Nations communities, refused to list individual households and their holdings in the Indian census of 1845, and Schoolcraft acknowledged that Blacksmith was behind the chiefs council's decision.[21]

Blacksmith's name is regularly on petitions to Albany and Washington from 1838 onward. The chief's name soon begins to appear first on these petitions, and, by the mid-1840s, Chief Jemmy Johnson's name, that was frequently first, was now second on these documents. By 1844, Blacksmith is listed as "Head Chief."[22] As early as February 1838, Blacksmith's name appears on a petition addressed to a United States senator asking him to oppose the ratification of the Treaty of Buffalo Creek. The chiefs, including delegates from the four major Seneca communities, described the Ogden Land Company's efforts to defraud the Indians of their lands and asked that "the Government ought not to sanction its proceedings." The petitioners added:

> We have already yielded much to the whites. We were the original possessors of this continent, but now we have only as it were little plots of ground; and these little pieces we do not like to dispose of. It is the duty and privilege of mankind to judge for themselves what course is most for their benefit. If any wish to emigrate, let them exercise their own judgment and set accordingly. If any wish to remain, let them also do the same.[23]

Some among the approximately 600 Tonawandas favored emigration, including Ely Parker's brother Spencer Cone; however, most Tonawandas followed the council of chiefs' united stand against removal.[24] Blacksmith and the Tonawanda chiefs sent a formal protest about the Buffalo Creek Treaty on September, 1838. They insisted that, unlike the chiefs at Buffalo Creek, Cattaraugus, and Allegany reservations, not one from their Tonawanda council favored this treaty.[25] Thus, early in 1839, the Tonawanda chiefs, with Blacksmith's name listed third, informed President Van Buren that they were sending a delegation to Washington to lobby against Senate ratification of the treaty.[26]

In December 1839, Chief Blacksmith was the Tonawanda council of chiefs' special emissary, lobbying to overturn the 1838 treaty. He met with Colonel Henry A. S. Dearborn, the representative of the governor of Massachusetts at the treaty of 1838, informing him that "white men and Indians" were offering money to the Tonawandas "to sign the treaty" and "wished to know if it was right." He urged Dearborn to investigate whether the Indian signatories to the treaty "acted freely and independently" and offered the general the opportunity to come to Tonawanda to question the Indians. The chief praised Dearborn as the Indians' friend, indicating that the chief had observed the general's behavior in a previous council with the Indians and that he was satisfied that he "had a good heart and upright mind." The general, a hero of the War of 1812 and later secretary of war, assured the chief that he "was anxious to protect" his "poor red brethren" and do what was in his "power for their good." Yet, nothing came about by the chief's appeal.[27]

Perhaps angered by the delays in Washington to overturn the Buffalo Creek Treaty of 1838 or reject it outright and President Van Buren's lack of regard for the Indians, Blacksmith and other members of his family became even more determined to fight the injustice. Immediately after the presidential election of 1840, which brought the Whigs to power, two of the Tonawanda chiefs—Blacksmith and Lewis Poodry—sent a letter to Secretary of War Joel Poinsett informing him that the Ogden Land Company was threatening to seize the sawmill on the reservation. Their agents were buying timber from white settlers on the Tonawanda lands but complaining that the Indians there had no right to sell reservation timber since the company now owned both the land and its trees. Subsequently, the council of chiefs met the Ogdens' chief surveyor and threatened his laborers when they tried to "run some lines" on the reservation. The chiefs were joined in by the clan mothers who filed their own protest against the Ogden Land Company.[28]

Blacksmith's strategy of resistance was reinforced by the actions of his wife and Tonawanda clan mothers. In a letter dated March 14, 1841, from Susan Blacksmith and seven other matrons, including Elizabeth Parker, Ely's mother, as well as the widow of Chief Little Beard, the women, "the keepers of the kettle," and by custom "the custodians of the land," backed up the arguments against the 1838 treaty previously made by the chiefs. The women insisted that they were "troubled" and felt "deep anxiety" for their children. Knowing that a memorial drafted by Indian women would have been seen as highly unusual by white officials of the time, they indicated that they were not merely eight individuals but were speaking for the 207 women residing on the Tonawanda lands. With the exposing of frauds related to the Buffalo Creek Treaty of 1838 and the fact that the United States Senate could muster only a plurality vote, not a two-thirds vote, required for approving the treaty, a Quaker-led movement to push for a new treaty council soon gained momentum. Thus, the Tonawanda women made it clear that they were *intent* on staying on their lands.[29]

In June 1841, the proprietors of the Ogden Land Company, realizing that the 1838 treaty was suspect, took the offensive. In doing so, they revealed much of their thinking and attitudes toward the Seneca Indians. In a letter to Secretary Bell, Thomas Ludlow Ogden and Joseph Fellows filed a formal complaint since their surveyors met with formidable resistance at Tonawanda. Dismissing the Tonawandas' actions as a "pretense," Ogden and Fellows indicated that the Tonawandas had merely a five-year time limit to remain on their lands and that the Ogden proprietors had successfully dealt with the Oneidas in the past in their removal. They told Secretary Bell that they believed that a separation of the races was a progressive goal since the inhabitants of Buffalo and other towns in the immediate vicinity of the Seneca reservations were "suffering under the demoralizing effects of a most licentious intercourse between the young of the two populations." In openly racist language, they concluded that this was an emergency situation, since the majority of the Indians were "ignorant and depraved."[30]

Immediately after the drafting of the 1842 treaty, the Tonawanda chiefs expressed their strong objections to it. Their complaints were all but ignored, since Secretary of War John Spencer was the son of Ambrose Spencer, the United States Indian Commissioner who along with Philip Thomas and the Society of Friends drafted the 1842 treaty. The chiefs castigated the Ogdens, Ambrose Spencer who gave them "no voice in the matter," as well as Philip Thomas whom they viewed as imposing his solution and as an unwanted meddler not representing Tonawanda interests at heart. They indicated that the Tonawanda chiefs had been in favor of saving all four Seneca reservations, but ceding some lands on each one.[31] Long before the Tonawandas had sought outside legal advice, their chiefs had come up with a strategy of survival on their own that was to eventually turn the tide in their favor. Although unanimously rejecting the Treaty of 1842, that they frequently referred to as an illegal deed, Blacksmith and the chiefs council read the document carefully and found a loophole in the fourth and fifth articles of the document. The "amount of consideration monies" to be paid to the Indians was to be determined by two arbiters, one named by the Ogden Land Company and the other by the secretary of war, who would "employ suitable surveyors to explore, examine, and report on the value of said lands and improvements." These same arbiters were to determine and award "the amount to be paid to each individual Indian"; if the arbiters disagreed on the award, they had the right to "choose an umpire whose decision thereon" would be "final and conclusive" and file a report "according to the laws of the State of New York" with the secretary of war and the Ogden Land Company. Article 5 of the treaty provided that the amount to be "ascertained and awarded" "be paid to the President of the United States, to be distributed among the owners of said improvements," adding that "the consideration for the release thereof be paid or secured to the satisfaction of the said Secretary of the War Department," the income of which was to be paid to the Senecas annually.[32]

Optimistically, the commissioner of Indian affairs wrote to the secretary of war that the work of the arbitrators "to ascertain the aggregate value of the reservations of land granted or released, confirmed or surrendered by said treaty [Treaty of 1842] and to appraise the improvements" was to be soon completed.[33] Yet, the Tonawanda chiefs had no intention of allowing this to happen and were determined to stop this by any and all means: sending their formal protests to Washington officials, disrupting the work of the surveyors, physically removing the outsiders from their lands, and even threatening violence. If they stopped the appraisal efforts, they, in their minds, would prevent the carrying out of the treaty. Thus, after Ira Cook and Thomas Love were appointed to appraise the improvements at Tonawanda, the chiefs immediately responded with a barrage of petitions to President Tyler and the War Department.[34]

The Tonawanda Council of Chiefs had previously challenged the cozy relationship between the federal Indian subagent and representatives of the Ogden Land Company as well as the company's auctioning off of tribal lands.[35] On January 9, 1843, the Tonawanda Council of Chiefs sent a detailed memorial to President Tyler, making a formal complaint and asking for the removal of Indian subagent Stephen Osborn, complaining about his lack of sympathy for their cause, suggesting that he was profiting from the distribution of annuity goods, and claiming that he was providing no protection from the daily depredations of whites moving onto Tonawanda lands.[36]

On June 19, 1843, Chief Blacksmith tried to stop the sale of Tonawanda lands at the courthouse in Batavia, as recounted in a petition to President Tyler. He took Thomas Ludlow Ogden aside and "told him that he was giving his people considerable trouble about their lands."[37] The petitioners told the President that when Blacksmith's efforts failed, they decided to once again appeal to Tyler. The chiefs, with Blacksmith's name appearing first, wrote:

> Father, we have experienced a great deal of trouble and grief with this [Ogden] Emigration and Land Company. They are practicing all kinds of frauds to obtain our land from us which your people have told us from time to time that we should enjoy those lands for ever undisturbed[.] You have been driving our people ever since the landing of Columbus till we scarcely can find a resting place[.] We wish to live in peace and enjoy our homes undisturbed. We are now just beginning to adopt the manners and customs of our white neighbors and have erected churches and school houses for the education of our children[,] and now when we are advancing to civilization[,] would you drive us from you . . . ?[38]

By December 1843, the appraisers reported that they had met with the chiefs. When the appraisers insisted that they would run their lines and do their work anyway, "this produced a violent sensation and brought every individual upon his feet." Love and Cook added that they "were taken by the arm and told that unless we retired," the Senecas would forcibly carry them out. Then they "were accompanied by most of the council to the line of their land with a chief or warrior at each arm. No personal violence was offered."[39] When Love and Cook subsequently filed their report without setting one foot on the reservation, the chiefs complained to President Tyler, questioning how the appraisers could have accomplished that miraculous feat "without obtaining our consent [and] valued our improvement while they were seated in Buffalo."[40]

While Tonawanda Council protests were sent off to Washington, Ogden was lobbying for the carrying out of the 1842 treaty, insisting that the Tonawanda were bound by the treaty and suggesting that the Indians were being stirred up by certain local whites. However, each time, the commissioner of Indian affairs indicated that his office had no legal power for enforcing the treaty and that it was entirely a court matter.[41]

To counter Ogden's arguments, the Tonawanda Council, with Blacksmith listed as "Head Chief," repeated its complaints against the company agents, sending the following protest to the secretary of war: "We have never 'voluntarily relinquished' one foot of the lands which have been sacredly pledged to our use and occupancy. But rapacious speculators have endeavored to force it from us because we are weak and they are strong."[42] The Tonawanda Council of Chiefs, once again using a strategy of delay, questioned the legitimacy of the arbiters' survey and urged President Tyler not to act until the Indians could send a delegation to Washington to meet with him.[43]

Trying to head off land sales, the Tonawanda chiefs attempted to win support from the non-Indian population in the immediate region around the reservation. On June 19, 1844, they placed an advertisement in the *Spirit of the Times*, the local Batavia newspaper. With Blacksmith's name appearing first on the list, thirteen of the chiefs urged their white neighbors not to buy reservation lands from the Ogden Land Company. Presenting themselves as peaceful, law-abiding Indians, they insisted: "We would not create any disturbance. We ask only Justice and look with confidence to the American people for it." They pointed to their long friendship with their neighbors as well as past treaties that assured the Indians their lands. The chiefs added: "Shall the Treaties which have been made be trampled in the dust? Shall we be thus driven from our homes? We raise our voices against the injustice." Offering the public the opportunity to acquire copies of the treaties, they urged the readers of the *Spirit of the Times* not to pay attention to advertisements announcing sales of reservation lands, but to support the Tonawandas in their struggle.[44] Two months later, the chiefs council once again sent Blacksmith and Johnson to Batavia to challenge the Ogdens' auction there; the two chiefs warned the people present against purchasing Tonawanda lands from the company's agents.[45] Thus, even before the Tonawandas' hiring of able legal counsel, they were taking the fight outward. The strategy proved somewhat successful, since, over the next two years, sympathetic whites held mass meetings to condemn the Ogden Land Company and support the Indians.[46]

Blacksmith's role is hard to isolate from the consensus decision making of the Tonawanda Council of Chiefs; however, at times, his voice emerges from the group. On August 20–23, 1845, in one of the last councils ever held at Buffalo Creek, representatives from the four Seneca communities assembled to listen to their chiefs. In eloquent fashion, Blacksmith presented the Tonawanda council's case for rejecting the treaties of 1838 and 1842:

> The Tonawanda chiefs told the commissioners that they did not agree to sell their lands, that they would have nothing to do with the treaty. . . . Should the laws of the State of New York seek to enforce that treaty upon the Tonawanda Indians, they will appeal to the Great Spirit who rules higher than these laws, and who is the friend of the red man as well as the white man. As it regards the lands at the west, which, it is said, were presented to the Indians at that time, I tell this council, as I told them before, they were not presented, but given in exchange for our lands at Green Bay. I told the council that consented to the treaty of '38, what this day has proven, that the Ogden company promised them sunshine, but when the time came they would get rain, and my nephew (White Seneca) who was promised by the Ogden company a large sum of money if he would consent to sell and use his influence to get others to sell the four reservations, will have to wait before he realizes any of the promises, until a thousand suns have set, or until the Great Father of the red man has called him home. . . . As to the Tonawanda chiefs, they not having agreed to sell their lands, or consented to the treaty, will not under any circumstances receive any portion of the annuity.[47]

Blacksmith's points were then seconded by Tonawanda chief Jesse Spring, who added "a powerful invective upon the conduct of the

Ogden company."[48] Less than a year later, Chief Blacksmith was assaulted by employees of the Ogden Land Company, an action that had far-reaching consequences for the sachem as well as for all the Tonawandas.[49]

From 1844 to 1847, the Tonawanda chiefs appealed to white officials in Albany and Washington, but without success. In February 1845, the council sent chiefs John Blacksmith as well as John Bigfire and Ely Parker to Albany to consult with Governor Silas Wright, who was reluctant to intervene.[50] Since few Senecas could read or write English at the time, and because Ely S. Parker had already served as the scribe for the council since 1842, the teenager was sent to Albany to translate for the chiefs. The council explained why they were sending three representatives to Albany. After recounting how their treaty rights, especially those set forth in the Treaty of 1794 at Canandaigua, were being violated by the Ogden Land Company, the chiefs described the members of their delegation: "We have sent John Blacksmith and John Bigfire, chiefs in whose integrity and ability we repose special confidence," adding that Ely S. Parker was accompanying them as their interpreter.[51] After repeated memorials to Governor Wright, the council came to realize that they were never getting anywhere with him, since they were informed that the governor, a loyal Jacksonian Democrat, had been behind the Treaty of 1838 in the first place.[52]

In 1846, Blacksmith and the chiefs advised President Polk that they were sending Ely Parker to make their appeal for protection until the Senate helped resolve the issue. Once again, they pointed out that in 1794 the United States had made solemn promises to protect them "in the peaceful possession of their home," and now they were threatened by the Ogden Land Company that was "taking possession" of their lands by force of arms.[53] In traditional terms, the teenaged Parker was a "runner," carrying messages from the Tonawanda Council of Chiefs. Despite his youth, his assignment was a carefully calculated effort by the chiefs to aid the Tonawandas' cause. Wearing the peace medal given to Red Jacket by President Washington and subsequently worn by Chief Blacksmith as his "diplomatic papers," Parker set out for Washington City.[54] Yet, at no time was the young Parker acting on his own. He was being groomed for leadership, and Blacksmith was his mentor. Indeed, Chief Blacksmith and Parker's great-uncle Chief Johnson were watching the boy's every move.[55]

1. Tonawanda Seneca Log House. Circa 1795. Courtesy: New York State Historical Association.

2. Red Jacket (d. 1830). Portrait by Robert Weir, circa 1828. The controversial Seneca orator had an extraordinary influence on Tonawanda Seneca life and politics in the last decade of his life. Courtesy: New-York Historical Society.

3. Red Jacket Peace Medal, presented to the Seneca orator by President George Washington in 1792, was worn by John Blacksmith after Red Jacket's death. At Blacksmith's death in 1851, the medal passed to Ely S. Parker. Courtesy: Buffalo and Erie County Historical Society.

4. Jemmy Johnson (d. 1857), Tonawanda Seneca chief and a disciple of Handsome Lake. His annual speeches, recounting the prophet's teachings, helped establish the *Gaiwiio*, the Code of Handsome Lake, among the Tonawanda Senecas and in other Iroquois communities. Courtesy: Rochester Museum and Science Center.

5. John Blacksmith (1781–1851), Seneca sachem, historian, and leading Tonawanda activist in the fight to retain the Tonawanda Reservation lands and resist removal. Courtesy: Rochester Museum and Science Center.

WILLIAM PARKER
Father of Ely S. Parker. (From a daguerreotype.)

ELIZABETH PARKER
Mother of Ely S. Parker. (From a daguerreotype.)

6. William and Elizabeth Parker, father and mother of Ely S. Parker. William was a pine tree chief and wounded veteran of the War of 1812. Elizabeth was a clan mother and niece of Chief Jemmy Johnson. Courtesy: Buffalo and Erie County Historical Society.

7. Ely S. Parker (1828–1895), Seneca sachem before entering Union military service. Reproduced from: Arthur C. Parker, *The Life of General Ely S. Parker, Last Grand Sachem of the Iroquois and General Grant's Military Secretary.* Courtesy: Buffalo and Erie County Historical Society.

CAROLINE G. PARKER

8. Caroline G. Parker (d. 1892), the sister of Ely S. Parker, later wife of Tuscarora chief John Mountpleasant, teacher and woman of letters. A graduate of the Albany Normal School, now University at Albany, SUNY, she was mentored by Lewis Henry Morgan. In the 1850s, Caroline Parker was honored by being bestowed with the name Jigonsasee or "Mother of Nations," the Neutral Peace Queen who first accepted the message of Deganawidah (the Peacemaker). Courtesy: Buffalo and Erie County Historical Society.

9. Lewis Henry Morgan (1818–1881), anthropologist, attorney, and advocate for justice for the Tonawanda Senecas. The founder of anthropology in America, his classic—*The League of the Ho-dé-no-sau-nee, or Iroquois* (1851)—was researched and written during the years that the Tonawanda Senecas were struggling to remain on their lands. Courtesy: University of Rochester Library.

Henry R. Schoolcraft

10. Henry Rowe Schoolcraft (1793–1864), scholar, Indian agent, and compiler of the New York State Indian Census of 1845, one resisted by the Tonawanda Senecas. Courtesy: New-York Historical Society.

McKnight Olympia

Joseph Fellows,

11. Joseph Fellows (1782–1873), attorney, chief agent, and one of the proprietors of the Ogden Land Company. Born in England, Fellows also managed the Pulteney lands, totaling 1,267,569 acres in central New York and owned lands in Indiana, Michigan, Pennsylvania, and Virginia. He was the leading proponent of Tonawanda Indian removal and opponent of the Tonawandas' claims to their lands after the Seneca Treaty of 1842. Courtesy: Geneva Historical Society.

GEN. JOHN H. MARTINDALE *1881

WEST POINT GRAD. DIST.-ATTY. 1842–44—47–50. BRIG.-GEN.
MIL. GOV. WASHINGTON 1862–64. STATE ATTY. GEN. 1866–67.

12. John H. Martindale (1815–1881), Batavia and Rochester attorney for the Tonawanda
Senecas, district attorney, Union general in the Civil War, attorney general of New York
State. Reproduced from: George C. Bragdon, *Notable Men of Rochester and Vicinity, XIX
and XX Centuries*. Rochester: D. J. Stoddard, 1902.

13. Colonel, later general, Ely S. Parker, Tonawanda Seneca Indian sachem, General Grant's military secretary, and first American Indian to be United States Commissioner of Indian Affairs. Courtesy: National Archives.

14. General John H. Martindale (1815–1881), a West Point graduate, attorney Martindale became a brigadier general in the Civil War. Courtesy: National Archives.

6

The Runner

Between 1838 and 1847, the Tonawanda Council of Chiefs repeatedly brought their plight to the attention of white officials in Albany and Washington, especially the United States Senate, but with little success to nullify the treaties of 1838 and 1842. They sent two delegations to Albany and four to Washington (and one to Canada). They spent $5,079.31 in these efforts, what they deemed to be "in defense of national rights." The impoverished Indians spent $1,077.50 alone in sending a delegation to Washington in just the year 1846, and incurred $664.31 in legal fees in the same year. Moreover, they had borrowed $1,000 from sympathetic whites to support their efforts.[1]

W. H. Angel, the federal subagent, described the Tonawanda determination to resist, reporting to the commissioner that almost all of these Indians' time "and their energies are directed towards warding off or counteracting the efforts made to remove them." He concluded:

> In these efforts are absorbed a very large portion of their annuities, so much so, that of their share of the permanent annuity for the present year no part of it was distributed to the people. In the meantime, their schools are neglected. . . . *Aside from providing for the support of their families, the one great business of their lives seems to be the adoption of means to preserve their homes and lands, and to annul or defeat the contract or treaty* [emphasis mine].[2]

Blacksmith and the Tonawanda Council of Chiefs mentored a young Seneca boy, Ely S. Parker, who played a role in their efforts to overturn the Treaty of 1842. From the age of fourteen, Parker worked as the council's scribe. He penned and brought petitions to Albany and Washington and served as a translator for the chiefs, mostly monolingual speakers of Seneca, on their official visits to the state and federal seats of power. Because of his voluminous correspondence left behind and his remarkable career in the Civil War and as the first United States commissioner of Indian affairs of Indian descent, Parker's role at Tonawanda has been misconstrued. He was never the sole leader of his people's struggles against the Ogden Land Company. Until Parker was condoled as a sachem in 1852, he served as a "runner" for the Tonawanda chiefs and clan mothers.[3]

Parker had been inculcated with a sense of *noblesse oblige*; duty to his people came first, especially at this very time of crisis. His assignment was no accident. Although his first name was given to him in honor of a local Baptist minister, Ely was also bestowed with a Seneca name at birth: Ha-sa-no-an-da, meaning "leading name." Parker's entire life—upbringing, education, and work experiences—was in two worlds. While acquiring a great knowledge of the Gaiwiio or Old Way of Handsome Lake, the Iroquoian religion, from his grandfather Jemmy Johnson, he was a Christian, educated in the new ways of his white teachers at a local Baptist school and Cayuga Academy in Aurora, New York.[4]

The importance of "runners" in Iroquois history should not be underestimated. They were not merely gifted athletes intent on "going for the gold." Iroquois runners summoned councils, conveyed intelligence from nation to nation, and warned of impending danger. Lewis Henry Morgan, in his classic *League of the Hodénosaunee, or Iroquois* (1851), observed, "Swiftness of foot was an acquirement, among the Iroquois, which brought the individual into high repute."[5] Their skill often led to later recognition as a subchief or chief. It is also important to note that the contemporary Iroquois still designate "runners," using the term to describe people who serve the council as a conduit for the conduct of essential business, and who are accorded respect as community leaders worthy of other higher positions of authority and prestige in the nation. Significantly, runners still convey official messages and carry stringed wampum to symbolize their official role, diplomatic protocol, and Truth.[6] Importantly, as a sign of authorization from the Tonawanda Council of Chiefs, the youthful Parker wore Red Jacket's Peace Medal on his mission to Washington in March, 1846.[7]

Born in 1828, Parker had been groomed for this role since child-hood. William, his father, was a pine tree chief and a veteran who had been wounded in American military service in the War of 1812.[8] His uncle, Samuel, was a key member of the Tonawanda Council of Chiefs in the struggle against the Ogden Land Company's efforts to remove these Indians from their reservation. In Iroquoian tradition, uncles such as Samuel had more to do with the proper instruction of their nephews than the child's parents. Samuel, an ally of John Blacksmith, helped inculcate a sense of duty, one that was reflected in a dogged determination by Ely to take on this great responsibility.[9] Moreover, the Parker family had to redeem themselves in the eyes of many Tonawandas. Ely's brother, Spencer Cone, had been ostracized by most Tonawandas for initially favoring the Buffalo Creek Treaty of 1838 and, with it, emigration to the West.[10]

In his extensive correspondence with Reuben B. Warren, his non-Indian childhood friend and former classmate, Parker revealed his inner thoughts in 1846 and 1847. Parker's commitment to the Tonawanda cause was unwavering even before he left for his four-month mission to Washington.[11] In January 1846, Parker urged War-ren to circulate petitions and have them signed by the local populace in western New York, which would be presented to the United States Senate, to help the Indians "who have always been oppressed by the whites."[12] The dilemma Parker faced throughout his life was also made clear in another letter to Warren in late January. After returning from Midwinter ceremonies at Onondaga, he informed his friend that he had desired to further pursue his studies but could not go at this time, undoubtedly because of the crisis at hand.[13]

In March 1846, Parker had arrived in Washington with the Tonawanda delegation and was very busy lobbying with a Seneca delegation "furthering the cause of the Indians at Tonawanda." Park-er's letters reveal that he was frequently disappointed by the absence of William Linn Brown, the Tonawandas' attorney, who was doing diplomatic duty for President Polk, although he had been hired to serve as the Indians' legal adviser before congressional committees. The excited youngster described Washington City with the nation's impressive capitol, "with a large park in front," "splendid library" with its many beautiful rooms and outstanding paintings, as well as George Washington's household furniture in the National Gallery. He was introduced briefly to "his Excellency the President of the United

States Jimmy Polk," whom Parker described as a "fine and pleasant gentleman." He then attended the Senate where he saw the "great men of the country."[14]

Significantly, Parker apologized to Warren for not stopping to see him before he had left for Washington, blaming the responsibilities he had to the chiefs for his absence. He insisted that he "was a slave to the will of the chiefs the whole time I remained at home." The youthful Parker added that he hoped "to be a free man one of these days." In the same letter, the impatient Parker openly criticized Chief Blacksmith's deliberate style, calling him a "coward." Parker claimed that nothing had transpired with regard to overturning the treaty. He accused Chief Blacksmith of "lying supinely afraid to do or say anything lest he be directed homeward," presumably by the Tonawanda Council of Chiefs and his Wolf Clan mother. He added that it took "all my skill to kick up his spirits and we may yet do something."[15]

With his youthful exuberance, the rebellious Parker failed to see the value in the conservative nature of council behavior. Blacksmith, the wise sachem, was carefully plotting a long-term strategy, one based on slowly building the Tonawandas' cause in the capital. Parker's letters to Warren indicate that the United States was heading to war with Mexico and was faced with a major crisis in the Oregon Territory. The wise old sachem knew full well that Indian affairs had less priority at this time in the halls of Congress and in the White House. He also knew that Polk's Democrat Party had masterminded the Buffalo Creek Treaty of 1838 and had long called for removal of the Iroquois to the West. Unlike the eighteen-year-old Parker, Blacksmith had the long view of Tonawanda history and was not swayed by the extraordinary buildings of Washington and powerful politicians who occupied them. After all, he was a sachem of the great Six Nations League of Peace and Power, long established before the creation of the American nation.

In a revealing letter on May 9, Parker wrote Warren that the Tonawandas were getting the runaround, caught between state and federal pulls, and he expected a difficult fight. He had sought the intercession of the commissioner of Indian affairs to set up a meeting with President Polk, but that the secretary of war had done nothing to help the Tonawanda cause. He reported that Joseph Fellows, the major lobbyist for the Ogden Land Company and its interests, had been at the Office of Indian Affairs "asking the government to order an appraisal of the Tonawanda lands (and ascertain the individual owners)" but that the officials had refused to do any such thing. Proud of his people's determination, he wrote that "Fellows has finally become aware of the fact that he can't put the Tonawanda Indians off, unless there is a legal appraisal of the lands." He labeled Fellows as a "scoundrel most outrageously" and was delighted that the Tonawandas were still united in opposing the Ogden Land Company. Angered to the point of being "raving mad" and in agony about the plight of his people, he reported to Warren that, although he had gained some encouragement from the likes of the powerful John C. Calhoun, other senators were insisting that the Treaty of 1842 had been ratified, thus making it, like other treaties, the "permanent law of the land," and thus could not be set aside simply by a congressional resolution. Parker indicated that as a result, he had written directly to President Polk to exercise his authority "to protect these Indians from the violent aggressions" of the Ogden Land Company, "these unprincipled white men."[16]

Finally, on May 18, 1846, Parker, now alone in Washington, had an audience with President Polk. He told the president that the Ogden Land Company was pushing onto Tonawanda lands "and taking possession of our improvements by force and by arms." He showed Polk a letter from his brother Nicholson that indicated that armed men, agents of the company, were invading Tonawanda and threatening the Indians while the Senate had delayed considering the matter. Appealing to the president, he reminded Polk of the Treaty of Canandaigua of 1794 and the loyalty of Tonawandas to the United States and asked him for protection for his Indian community. Unfortunately, the president referred the matter back to the commissioner of Indian affairs, who later informed Parker that he could not take any action before the Senate acted on the matter.[17]

Much of Parker's correspondence with Warren from late May to July, 1846 dealt with his frustrations in gaining a favorable hearing with the Senate Indian Affairs Committee, attorney Brown's continued absence from Washington, descriptions of congressional fights over the tariff, and sites or events in the nation's capital. After calling the Ogdens' efforts "villainous transactions," Parker indicated that the senators had agreed that the Tonawandas had legitimate grievances but refused to "propose any remedy."[18] He reported on the visit of about fifty Indians from the Texas-Mexican border who shook up city life because of their "wild" appearance and because they wore "very little clothing to cover their bodies" as well as "all kinds of brass rings and beads and shells."[19]

Growing bored during a six-week congressional recess, Parker went to Baltimore on July 4th and "had a great time" at the Independence Day celebration. He later attended a Quaker meeting and heard one of the best sermons he had ever listened to in his life.[20] Soon after, the Seneca runner returned to Washington. He described his visit to the Washington Monument, complained that attorney Brown had not returned, castigated New York's Governor Wright as a fence-straggling politico, and informed Warren that Daniel Webster was now willing to help the Tonawandas after having been "invisible" during the debate over the Buffalo Creek Treaty of 1838.[21] On July 17, he noted that Brown had returned, that Cherokee Indian difficulties were before a special commission, that an elegantly dressed chief from Kansas was visiting the city but was rebuffed by the Office of Indian Affairs, and commented on the first-rate oratory of Calhoun and Webster in the debate on the tariff bill. Without a modicum of success, Parker returned to Tonawanda in late July 1846.[22] Although he had met with President Polk, Secretary of War Medill, and the most influential and powerful senators—Henry Clay, John C. Calhoun, and Daniel Webster—the Tonawandas had little to show for Parker's efforts.[23]

When Parker was sent back to Washington in late January 1847 to continue his lobbying efforts, he was accompanied by chiefs Blacksmith and Isaac Shanks.[24] The Tonawanda Council of Chiefs, realizing that their efforts to convince the Senate was a long shot at best, wrote Parker that they were doing this so that "the blame might not rest upon him so strongly if we should happen to loose [sic] our lands." Defensively, Parker later wrote Warren that he had "not been negligent of my duties" and that what little success bringing the issue before the Senate was because of his "skillful management."[25] Fascinated with Washington, D.C., its architecture, and its seat of American power, he described the magnificent Library of Congress, its paintings depicting biblical scenes and Columbus, as well as his attendance at legal pleadings before the United States Supreme Court, Webster's grand oratorical style, and expressions of support from senators Calhoun and Crittenden.[26] Later that month, Parker reported on the approaching crisis with Mexico, an appropriations bill, and debates over slavery, but sadly noted that there was nothing to report on the Senate's consideration of the Seneca Treaty of 1842.[27]

The Tonawanda cause went down to defeat on February 19, 1847; the United States Senate refused to intervene. While acknowledging the fraud in the original treaty, the Senate refused to abrogate the 1842 "accord" since it would "open a field of interminable difficulty, embarrassment, and expense." Whatever the criticism, the treaty was still law and all parties had to abide by its terms.[28] Extremely disappointed, Parker, unlike others, saw a silver lining in his lobbying efforts. He later wrote Warren: "I am strongly of the opinion that it will operate greatly to our advantage. We shall have scratched at the eyes of the Ogden Company and they will look upon us hereafter as dangerous customers, and as lawyers and merchants say, ask to balance accounts."[29]

In 1846 and 1847, Parker had not simply focused all of his attention on the Tonawandas' lobbying efforts in Washington. He also helped gather information while, at the same time, he attempted to open federal doors. He went so far as to ingratiate himself to the likes of Henry Rowe Schoolcraft, whom Chief Blacksmith distrusted and viewed as a slimy supplicant and supporter of Jacksonian Indian removal policies.[30] Taking advantage of Schoolcraft's status as a recognized "authority" and playing on Schoolcraft's ambition in his hopes to win a new federal position, Parker posed two important questions to him in May 1846. Since Schoolcraft had come into conflict with Chief Blacksmith in the collection of data for the New York State Indian census of 1845, Parker saw an opening. Well accepted by Morgan and the Grand Order of the Iroquois, Parker was the logical Seneca to pump Schoolcraft for information that could be beneficial to the Tonawandas. Schoolcraft, a member of Morgan's Grand Order of the Iroquois, was completing his work, *Notes on the Iroquois*. Schoolcraft had not given up his efforts to collect information at Tonawanda, despite Chief Blacksmith's refusal to cooperate with him.[31]

Parker asked Schoolcraft two questions: first, whether there was enough land on the Allegany and Cattaraugus reservations to supply the needs of the entire Seneca population, including the communities dispossessed in 1838 and 1842; and secondly, did the Iroquois, most specifically the Senecas, govern "wholly by the *unanimity* principle" historically in the past or by the *majority* principle and "whether in fact, they knew anything about *majorities* and *minorities*, before the principle was introduced by the whites among them [emphasis Parker]." Parker observed that the information would "do much to further the cause of justice."[32] Replying to young Parker's two questions, Schoolcraft stated emphatically that there was not enough arable lands to support all the Senecas if they were removed to Allegany and Cattaraugus reservations; and that "the majority principle was not known" in former times. "Unanimity appears to have been necessary in the result of all important national questions."[33] Thus, Schoolcraft, recognized in white circles as an "Indian expert," had now documented two points needed by the Tonawandas to fight the 1842 treaty, namely, that all decisions affecting the Tonawandas had to be by consensus, not majority; and that the Tonawandas' only alternative to going west to Kansas was to remain on their tribal lands.

Well into 1847 Parker continued to attempt to use Schoolcraft. Hoping to draw information from Schoolcraft again in May 1847, Parker told him of the Seneca legend of the "thunderer at the falls." Then he posed another question: What was the Office of Indian Affairs doing to help the Tonawandas?[34] He did not completely trust Schoolcraft and realized that point especially when visiting a bookstore, where he accidentally found a copy of *Notes on the Iroquois* on one of the shelves. In a resentful tone, Parker wrote Schoolcraft on April 10, 1848. Schoolcraft had failed to send Parker a complimentary copy of the book, even though the young man and his family had contributed much to Schoolcraft's folkloric sections. Obviously insulted, Parker wrote that he was not sending any more information to him "when yourself is in possession of so much about us."[35] Yet, the shrewd young Tonawanda Seneca did not completely cut his ties with Schoolcraft. Knowing that Schoolcraft had been appointed by the United States Senate to collect data on Indian tribes throughout the country, Parker continued to correspond with him in an attempt to find out about federal officials' views about the Tonawandas' struggle with the Ogden Land Company. Parker's correspondence paid off. On March 11, 1849, Schoolcraft informed Parker of the machinations of James S. Wadsworth, a leading Ogden Land Company proprietor. At the time, Wadsworth, whose family were among the original white settlers of the Genesee region, was lobbying on behalf of the Ogden Land Company, urging federal officials to appoint a new appraiser of improvements on the Tonawanda reservation lands as required by the Seneca Treaty of 1842.[36]

Encouraged by W. H. Angel, the sympathetic federal Indian subagent in New York, and Angel's partner Addison G. Rice, Parker decided to read law at Angel and Rice's office in Ellicottville, New York, just off the Seneca Nation's Allegany Indian Reservation.[37] His hobnobbing in Washington, in the highest corridors of power, convinced the young Tonawanda Seneca to pursue this career path. He later wrote in his journal kept on one of his lobbying trips to the nation's capital that Henry Clay, the very symbol of the Whig Party, told him that the elder statesman would "go a great distance to hear him plead in the United States Supreme Court."[38] After his lobbying setback in Washington and false accusations by some Tonawandas about him, namely, that he was "intriguing with the [Ogden Land] Com[pany]," Parker set off for Ellicottville. He wrote his friend Warren: "I have no cares on my mind, for I have thrown aside for the Indians for the present at least, the responsibility of planning for the Indians how to defeat the Ogden Company and their agents, accomplices and in their efforts to cheat the Indians of their lands."[39] Parker had been stung by false accusations, adding that "the Indians abused me all but to death, charging me [with] intriguing with the com [Ogden Land Company] and the most barefaced treachery was laid to me."[40] Parker's abandonment of the cause was only a temporary one. Reading Blackstone's *Commentaries* and learning the ways of a lawyer was a mere respite after more than five years of intense work supervised by the Tonawanda chiefs and clan mothers.

Despite his study and enthusiasm for law, Parker was restricted from ever gaining admission to practice because of his race and for the fact that he was not a United States citizen. Instead, he turned first to engineering and then to the military. With the help of Morgan again, he was appointed assistant engineer on the Genesee Valley Canal.[41] He later served as an engineer on the Chesapeake and Albemarle Canal, and in the late 1850s worked in civil engineering in Galena, Illinois, where he first met Ulysses S. Grant. Parker also enlisted in the New York State Militia and served in it in 1853 and 1854.[42]

Parker had been groomed for leadership and now his time had come. In declining health, Chief Blacksmith died on April 14, 1851. What followed this great sachem's death was no accidental occurrence, but one planned since Ely S. Parker's first service to the Tonawanda Council of Chiefs in 1842. He was now to succeed Chief Blacksmith on the Grand Council of the Iroquois Confederacy. Blacksmith had achieved a remarkable following, internally among the Tonawandas as well as to a wider audience. The *Rochester American* carried Blacksmith's obituary, revealing much of how the chief was perceived by the white communities in western New York:

> Died, at Tonawanda Indian village on the 14th inst, John Blacksmith (Daonehogawah) veteran King of the Six Nations, and "Keeper of the Western door of the Long House,"—aged 70 years. For a long series of years this distinguished Chief exercised an almost unlimited influence over the Senecas and the other remnants of the Six Nations. A principal leader of our Indian allies in the war of 1812, he won high eulogiums for his intrepid bravery. The funeral of the venerable Chief was attended by a large concourse of people—both Whites and Indians—and was conducted with the imposing rights and solemnities always observed by the Iriquois [*sic*] on such occasions.[43]

Besides his mentoring of Parker, Blacksmith had made many other major contributions to the Tonawanda cause. He had developed six strategies: delaying efforts at removal after the Seneca Treaty of 1842; presenting a united front by holding the council together; emphasizing the federal government's moral and legal obligation to protect their Seneca allies based on the Treaty of Canandaigua of 1794; preventing surveyors from coming onto the reservation; restricting data collection by outside appraisers or by state census takers; and winning support from non-Indians in western New York.

In a Condolence Council ceremony that followed the next year, Parker, now just twenty-four years of age, was raised to the league sachemship along with the title formerly held by Blacksmith. He was also bestowed with the Red Jacket Medal, thus given full authority to serve as a spokesman and diplomat for his Tonawanda Seneca people. This responsibility as Blacksmith's successor would eventually lead Parker once again to Washington.[44]

The Tonawanda Senecas were to pursue justice in the American court system, litigation that ended up in the United States Supreme Court five years after the sachem's death. It was no coincidence that the executor of Blacksmith's estate and litigant-successor in this case was none other than Ely Parker, the boy the sachem had tutored.

Against all odds, John H. Martindale, a non-Indian attorney of immense talent, was to use the strategies that Blacksmith had developed, cooperating with Parker, the new Seneca sachem, the Tonawanda Council of Chiefs, and the clan mothers to achieve success in the highest court in the land.

7

The Whig Mouthpiece

Although Native Americans are too often presented as simply acted upon and naive victims in the inevitable march of westward expansion, the Tonawanda Senecas disprove this generalization. In the mid-1840s, the council of chiefs hired exceptional attorneys to fight for their rights in their struggle against the Ogden Land Company. First, they hired William Linn Brown, a "Philadelphia lawyer," the nationally respected attorney and lobbyist who had political connections to President Polk and worked for him and the State Department in various diplomatic efforts. Because of Brown's busy schedule and the growing tensions caused by the increasing encroachment of white settlers on the Tonawanda lands, Brown was replaced after the effort to influence the United States Senate failed.[1] The chiefs then hired John H. Martindale, a thirty-one-year-old attorney from Batavia, in Brown's place to help the Tonawandas stave off removal. From 1846 to 1861, Martindale was the lead attorney for the numerous suits brought by and against the Tonawandas, the chief counsel for the Tonawandas in treaty negotiations, and the key figure in the later repurchase of the reservation.

Martindale was born in Hudson Falls, New York on March 20, 1815. His father, Henry Clinton, was a Yankee from Massachusetts who practiced law at Sandy Hill, in Washington County, New York and who eventually was elected to Congress for four terms (1823 to 1831). Originally a Federalist, Henry Clinton Martindale became an anti-Jackson, anti-Mason Whig who was later tied politically to Governor William Seward.[2]

Henry Clinton sent his son John to the United States Military Academy in 1831, at a time when West Point was becoming a major civil engineering institution under the forceful leadership of Sylvanus Thayer. In the class of 1835 were two individuals who influenced John Martindale's life: George Meade and Montgomery Blair. Meade's and Martindale's paths were to cross in the Civil War. Blair's and Martindale's lives were to come together in the turbulent 1850s and were to have an impact on the Tonawandas' crusade for justice. Martindale was graduated third in his class at West Point and was commissioned as a second lieutenant in the 1st Dragoons. Instead of accepting his assignment, which would have undoubtedly led to his participation in the horrific Second Seminole War (1835–1842) in the Everglades in Florida, Martindale immediately took a leave of absence from the army and eventually resigned his commission in 1836. He was one of ninety-eight commissioned officers, eight in his 1835 class alone, who resigned during the Second Seminole War. This excessive number of resignations, including that of Martindale, could not be totally attributed to protest over the war, since greater financial benefits in civil engineering and in the business world were available to top graduates of West Point. Added to this was the overall disarray of the army during the Jacksonian era.[3]

In 1836, Martindale was appointed assistant engineer of the Saratoga and Washington Railroad Company. Two years later, after reading law, he moved from the east bank of the Hudson River to Batavia, a small town and headquarters of the Holland Land Company. He practiced law there in 1838, but later, in 1851, shifted his work to Rochester. Because of his acumen and his Whig political connections, he was elected district attorney of Genesee County, serving eight years in that capacity.

Martindale was a Whig through and through. As an aspiring attorney on the rise, he tied his sails to Governor Seward and the New York State Whig Party. He supported internal improvements, transportation, and the state's unique economic rise that followed the completion of the Erie Canal in 1825 and the start of massive railroad building from the 1830s onward. Martindale was against Jacksonian removal of Indians westward, but hoped to "encourage" them to eventually become tax-paying citizens under state laws.[4] Instead of becoming "vagabonds," he wanted them to remain on their lands. Martindale believed that the Senecas were intelligent human beings, capable of being transformed into productive citizens of western New York, at that time one of the fastest growing areas of the United States.

Martindale was a master in the courtroom. A highly respected popular individual, Martindale, with his hazel eyes and black curly hair, was described as "one of the most attractive and genial of men." Of medium height, he was "strongly built, erect, with a carriage betraying his military training, and with a fine head well set upon good shoulders." His face with his well-trimmed mustache "gave character" and "instantly attracted attention." Always eloquent in oratory, with "measured and well-balanced sentences," he frequently indulged in reminiscences. Although combative in court, he was described as a man "above reproach" who exuded "sincere piety."[5]

In populist fashion, the patrician Martindale had the ability to present his clients as the underdogs fighting the mean-spirited land jobbers. He roused the local liberal populace in a four-county area—Genesee, Livingston, Monroe, and Ontario. On the morning of March 21, Martindale, then the popular district attorney, presided over a rally at the Genesee County Courthouse in Batavia, called to protest the actions of the Ogden Land Company to force the Tonawandas off their lands. Along with Lewis Henry Morgan and members of his Grand Order of the Iroquois and a few concerned local citizens, including some Quakers not associated with Philip Thomas, they expressed their outrage against the dispossession of the Indians. Speakers included Chief Jemmy Johnson as well as Frederick Follett and Isaac Verplanck, local defenders of the Tonawanda cause. The conferees organized a committee, headed by Martindale, which was to prepare a memorial to be considered later that day. When the memorial was accepted, it was sent to the United States Senate on behalf of the Tonawanda cause.[6]

The March 1846 memorial categorized the 1842 treaty as "the height of folly and dishonesty." It stated that the Tonawandas had "uniformly and unanimously opposed the treaty, in every form in which it has been presented to them, and have at all times refused to receive any portion of the consideration money, to be paid by the Ogden Land Company for their lands." Insisting that there was no necessity for their removal, the memorial challenged the racist claims of the Ogdens. It claimed that there were advantages for the Tonawandas' continued presence on their lands and that between "them and us, the kindest feelings and intercourse prevail." If left on their reservation lands, "unmolested by the intrigues and avarice of a band of speculators," the Tonawandas "would soon furnish us with an example of the beneficent results which education can accomplish, in the elevation of their social, moral and intellectual condition."

Finally, the memorial called on the United States Senate to overturn the 1842 treaty and not "give their sanction to a contract procured from the Indians by gross and palpable fraud."[7] After Jemmy Johnson spoke through an interpreter about the 1838 and 1842 treaties and the Tonawanda Senecas' historic problems with the Ogden Land Company, the assembled group adopted the committee's memorial and designated Lewis Henry Morgan as their representative "to bear the proceedings of the convention to the Senate at Washington."[8]

In 1846, Chief Blacksmith and Nicholson Parker, Ely's brother, obtained the legal services of Martindale in a court case.[9] This case was the turning point in the Tonawanda struggle to retain their lands. The Tonawandas—Chief Blacksmith and several other Senecas—had constructed a sawmill on the reservation in the 1820s. They later leased it and its operations to a white entrepreneur. After the treaty of 1842, the Ogden Land Company bought out the non-Indian lease-holder. In July 1846, Joseph Fellows, accompanied by Robert Kendle, entered the Tonawanda Reservation and attempted to take possession of the sawmill and the surrounding parcel of land, claiming ownership. In the process of securing this property, Fellows threatened Blacksmith and then assaulted him, driving the chief and his family away.[10] Immediately, Martindale filed a civil suit against Fellows. In a jury trial at Batavia in 1846, Blacksmith was awarded $825 in damages. Yet this court action was just the beginning of an eleven-year court battle that played into the Tonawanda chiefs' strategy of delay.[11] Conable has perceptively observed: "Whenever it appeared that the federal government might be moving to enforce the treaty, they [council of chiefs and Martindale] asked for a delay pending a final verdict in the case."[12] The historic and complex case involved Martindale's suits of ejectment against the Ogdens and those who purchased lands from the company.

In countersuits, Fellows insisted in his letters to Washington officials that they had the requirement to enforce the provisions of the treaty of 1842. He falsely suggested that many Tonawandas had applied for their "improvement moneys"; that Tonawandas were beggars and thieves stealing "his" or white settlers' crops on the former reservation and stripping "his" timber resources; that the Indians were impediments to the progress of the county, not taking advantage of the fertile land and water power potential; and that the Indians were violent people. Fellows and his attorneys argued for the enforcement of the treaty of 1842. They maintained that they had been rebuffed in their attempt to take possession of their newly acquired lands, and that Chief Blacksmith and his family were trespassers on Ogden Land Company property. Although rebuffed by the Indians, they insisted that they had properly tried to survey and appraise these lands under Article 4 and Article 5 of the treaty, that the appraisers had assessed the improvements made by the Indians as being worth $15,082, and that the company had subsequently deposited moneys in the United States Treasury, which held the sum in trust for the Tonawandas.[13] W. P. Angel, the federal subagent in New York, clearly outlined the contentious issue to the commissioner of Indian affairs after the case first reached the courts:

> The company claim the right to enter upon any portion of these lands which they find vacant, by virtue of their purchase; and the Indians insist that no purchase of the lands have been made that is binding upon them, and that their possession of a part is possession of the whole.[14]

The subagent then described the Indians' overriding commitment to retain their lands: "They express a willingness to have the whole question tested in a court of justice, and to abide [by] the decision of any competent legal tribunal." Yet Angel warned that the Tonawandas informed him "that they will not be driven off by the company by force in the matter attempted [by Fellows], and will defend their possessions to the shedding of blood."[15]

In 1846 to 1848 alone, Martindale initiated eviction proceedings against thirty white families who had bought reservation lands from the Ogdens.[16] The Tonawanda Senecas, at the advice of Martindale, brought so many cases that by 1852 they had to limit these time-consuming efforts, fearing that they might affect other court efforts.[17] They sued for ejectment based on two state laws. In 1813, a state law had compelled local county judges to issue warrants for removal of unwanted whites on Indian lands. Another state law passed in 1821 also restricted white intruders on Indian lands.[18]

One such case involved Ichabod Waldron, a man who had been driven off the Tonawanda Reservation two years earlier but had been allowed to return because of actions by the "High Sheriff."[19] On January 29, 1848, Waldron, in the process of illegal timber stripping, assaulted Ely Parker "with force and arms." While serving as the Genesee County district attorney in Batavia, Martindale then prosecuted Waldron. The jury found Waldron guilty and fined him fifteen dollars.[20] The Waldron incident was not the only one that occurred. As early as 1846, the company began settling their enforcers on Tonawanda. In response, according to Parker, the Senecas ordered "these white rascals off" and started putting "their crops into the ground." The Indians frequently went to court filing trespass suits. Parker proudly insisted: "Thus you see how we at Tonawanda are yet fighting for our lands."[21] Yet, in 1848, the Genesee circuit court in Batavia ruled that an individual Indian had no legal standing and could not maintain the action of ejectment; and that Fellows and Kendle, although not having the right of possession of the parcel, were in two years entitled to possession notwithstanding the omission of the arbiters to award the plaintiff the improvement money. The New York Supreme Court at Buffalo, nevertheless, denied the motion for a new trial and insisted that the award of the improvement money and its acceptance by the Indians were a precondition to the Ogdens' right of possession.[22]

In December, 1848, one month after the national election, James S. Wadsworth, accompanied by appraiser Cook, a surveyor, and an armed force of fifty men invaded the reservation to commence the appraisal. A descendant of one of the white founding fathers of western New York, Wadsworth, a proprietor of the Ogden Land Company, promoted this action. The Indians did not yield, with the result that "many blows with fists and clubs were made by the company of whites upon the Indians."[23] Wadsworth, the scion of the famous family that had pioneered the Genesee Country, had enemies besides the Tonawandas. He had leased some of these lands to tenants who were given high rents with little or no hope of ownership. During this same time in the 1840s, tenant wars were erupting in the eastern part of the state against the Van Rensselaers and their vast domain. Taking advantage of this climate of class warfare, the savvy attorney Martindale clearly understood how public opinion could influence judicial thinking. He took advantage of these increasing divisions in white society and exploited them for his Tonawanda clients' benefit. Hence, some local whites saw the Indians' effort to resist the Ogdens as their way to get back at the Wadsworths. Conable has perceptively written: "Better to have Indian neighbors than to deal with men who had built large personal estates by exploiting the labor of poor farmers."[24]

Perhaps spurred by the Senate's rejection of the Tonawandas' efforts and by the national election of 1848, one in which Millard Fillmore, an ally of the Ogdens, was elected vice president, Fellows, Wadsworth, and other proprietors became more emboldened. They convinced the War Department to appoint a new appraiser, Horace Gay, to determine if the previous appraisal of $15,018.36 was accurate.[25] After the Ogden Land Company again attempted to have the improvement money deposited for the Indians in trust in the United States Treasury, the Tonawanda chiefs once again refused to accept the money. Consequently, Secretary of War Thomas Ewing Jr. did not allow the removal of the Indians to be carried out. Ewing could also not ignore the exposure of the "Stryker scandal," which revealed that the federal Indian subagent in New York pocketed Seneca annuity moneys for a three-year period (1837–1839), during the time that the Ogdens were "negotiating" the Treaty of Buffalo Creek of 1838.[26] Inaction became the policy of the federal government toward the Tonawanda situation until after 1853.

Martindale continued Blacksmith's strategy of delay. The attorney reiterated the same arguments he had made earlier, adding the point that the reservation was now worth more than what the appraisers had stated. He also claimed that there was no law allowing the secretary of war to appoint Gay as appraiser. The attorney suggested that the Indians did not need new obstacles put in their way by the federal government. To carry out Washington's trust responsibility to these Indians, he suggested that these officials should act as guardians and allow the Indians the benefit of judicial decisions.[27]

Martindale had previously forwarded a letter to the chiefs, outlining how to deal with this renewed threat. He informed them that they should reject another appraisal, that they never signed the deed (the treaty of 1842), and "by Indian customs and laws," the deed was worthless and had no validity. Martindale insisted that Gay's appointment was superfluous since the government had already appointed an initial arbiter (Love); that by doing so seven years after the treaty had been finalized made the appointment void, and that instead, the federal government need appoint a protector "to guard the rights of the Indians" since they viewed the Ogdens as the enemy.[28]

While Martindale was busy in the courtroom, the chiefs, with Blacksmith leading the way, were bombarding Washington with petitions and repeating Martindale's points one by one. On March 15, 1849, the council of chiefs once again insisted that all outstanding issues could be settled only in the "legal tribunals of the country." Any and all arguments were to be employed to save Tonawanda lands. In an interesting twist, the chiefs maintained that they were against removal to the West since they needed to be surrounded by "civilized" white people and would perish if they returned "to the habits" of their forefathers: "We cannot live by hunting—we are agriculturists" who depend "on the shops and stores of the white men." They also indicated that they were averse to going to Cattaraugus or Allegany. Using Schoolcraft's findings, they stressed that all of the most desirable lands on those two other reservations had already been apportioned.[29] In another petition dated June 23, 1849, they insisted that they were now forced with destruction: "On our controversy with the Ogden Company is a struggle for life or death."[30] Because the issue is now a judicial matter, the secretary of war and the newly created cabinet post—the secretary of the interior—that housed the Office of Indian Affairs, once again refused to intervene, leaving the matter to the courts to decide.

Often Martindale worked closely with Ely S. Parker, employing him as a conduit to carry news to and from the Tonawanda chiefs. Just as Blacksmith had mentored Parker in chiefly ways, Martindale did the same in educating the young Seneca about American law. Moreover, Parker's military experiences were shaped by the Whig attorney. Martindale, the West Pointer and later a prominent general in the Union Army during the Civil War, was clearly a role model to Parker, and the Seneca followed the career trajectory set by the attorney. Parker served in the New York State Militia in 1853–1854 and later received an officer's commission in the Union Army in 1863; subsequently, he rose to General Grant's staff in the Army of the Potomac and played an important role at Appomattox Courthouse on April 9, 1865. Hence, from 1846 onward, both men were on the same page using everything to fight removal and the efforts of the Ogden Land Company to take all of the Tonawanda Reservation and force the Indians to the West.

Both Parker and Martindale understood the desperate situation that the Tonawandas faced. Despite the long odds of achieving success, Parker remained optimistic and his faith in Martindale's abilities were unwavering. He wrote his father that once New York's highest court adjudicates the Blacksmith case favorably to the Tonawandas, the Indians would not have "a great deal of trouble removing the settlers."[31] He earnestly believed that his lobbying efforts and Martindale's courtroom skills would win the day.

Parker frequently wrote to Washington officials about the issues, maintaining that the Senecas were "civilized" Indians who had the right to choose their form of government. In July 1853, Parker wrote George Manypenny, the new commissioner of Indian affairs, insisting that the Senecas at Allegany and Cattaraugus had a right to change their form of government "that destroyed the national character they once enjoyed." To him, the Tonawandas also had the right to go in their own direction, one that had to be respected by federal authorities. Washington had to finally recognize the Tonawanda Senecas "as a distinct and separate Band of the Seneca Nation, living under the ancient government of chiefs which form of government they prefer to live under."[32] In a second letter to Commissioner Manypenny in September 1853, Parker described his community, one that had framed barns and "neatly furnished homes with white paint"; that farm cultivation had doubled since 1842, producing a large surplus of grains; that Tonawanda produce was netting high prices in the market; and that many of their children were learning the "arts of civilization" in the reservation school.[33]

Justices of the lower courts in western New York had found for Chief Blacksmith; now Blacksmith's widow as executor and Ely S. Parker as trustee of the chief's estate were to bring their action to the state's highest court in Albany. In March 1852, at the New York State Court of Appeals, Martindale argued that the Tonawanda Indian chiefs had never signed the deed, that is, the treaty of 1842; that no individual Seneca "by custom or usage" had the "power to grant away the lands" in question; that the New York State Legislature had never consented to the Ogden deed; that the Ogden Land Company had never secured the state of Massachusetts' approval required by the Hartford Convention of 1786; that Thomas Love's appointment as appraiser was illegal since he had no official papers from the commissioner of Indian affairs to serve in that capacity; that the Indians had objected to the appraisal by Love and Cook and therefore had "no authority" to carry out their work; and that the improvement money was never accepted by the Indians, nor a statement of its delivery filed with the Office of Indian Affairs as required under Article 5 of the treaty of 1842.[34]

By a vote of six to one, the Court of Appeals affirmed the lower courts' decisions. In the majority opinion of the New York State Court of Appeals, Justice Edmonds declared that the defendant, Joseph Fellows, was a trespasser and had no right of possession. Importantly, the justices insisted that the band—the Tonawandas—were not individual parties to the treaty of 1842 and that "it was not shown that the appraisement and award" could not have been made "without an actual entry upon the reservation." The case was also noteworthy in that John C. Spencer, the former secretary of war and son of Ambrose Spencer, the United States Indian commissioner at the 1842 treaty, was now the attorney for the Ogden Land Company.[35]

While Martindale was taking the lead in the courtroom, he was coordinating his efforts with Parker and the chiefs council. When the new Pierce administration came into office in 1853, both men attempted to educate the new officials on Tonawanda matters. George Manypenny was named commissioner of Indian affairs, now housed in the Interior Department. In one of the new commissioner's early decisions, Manypenny replaced Benjamin Pringle, Indian agent in New York and one detested by the Tonawandas, with the competent Marcus Johnson. Now, for the first time, an Indian agent accurately reported the Tonawanda situation back to Washington. Johnson detailed the history of the Indians' legal struggles with the Ogden Land Company, presented a generally favorable picture of the Tonawandas and their educational efforts, and transmitted complaints and memorials by the chiefs against accepting the "improvement money" or the removal of these Indians to another Seneca reservation.[36]

No longer in the shadow of Chief Blacksmith, Parker became more and more adamant in his letters to Washington. He feared that Philip Thomas, whom he judged to be a Quaker meddler and an enemy of the Tonawandas, would be appointed to mediate again as he had done in 1842. Parker suspected that Thomas was interested in getting hold of the "improvement money" to further his goal of building his orphan asylum/school at Cattaraugus. Parker also reminded officials of the Iroquois League's ancient greatness, the federal commitment made in the Treaty of 1794 to protect the Senecas, and the substantial military service that his people had made to the United

States' war effort in 1812. He insisted that his people would not concede to their destruction and lose their national character. He recognized that other Senecas at Allegany and Cattaraugus had the right to change their government to an elected system, although he and other Tonawandas disagreed with that choice.[37] Parker made it clear that what he and the chiefs council were seeking was that the United States "respect the Tonawanda of the Seneca Nation, living under the ancient government of chiefs which form of government they prefer to live under."[38] The Tonawanda sachem warned Washington officials about former Indian agent Stephen Osborn, who was lobbying for the carrying out of the 1842 treaty. Parker went on to challenge Joseph Fellows' arguments. He produced affidavits attested to by Senecas John Hill, Isaac Doxtator, and Tommy White indicating that they had never signed petitions asking for the "improvement money," and repeated the charges previously made against Indian subagent Stryker. Later, in a letter to President Pierce, Parker indicated that he had grown weary of repeating his points, since the crisis had gone on "fourteen years with a great cost of labor and money" fighting the "land company for our lands and homes, yes our lives."[39]

In 1856, the United States Supreme Court heard arguments made by Martindale for the Indians and Ransom Gillet for the Ogden Land Company. Gillet, a staunch Jacksonian Democrat, had been the United States commissioner in charge of the negotiations at the fraudulent Buffalo Creek Treaty of 1838.[40] Fellows had appealed the decisions in the courts of New York in a writ of error bringing his case to the nation's highest tribunal. He continued to claim that the Indians were trespassers on the Ogden Land Company's lands.

Chart 4. The United States Supreme Court in 1856

1. Roger Taney, Chief Justice (Maryland), appointed by Jackson
2. John Campbell, Associate Justice (Georgia), appointed by Fillmore
3. John Catron, Associate Justice (Tennessee), appointed by Jackson
4. Benjamin Curtis, Associate Justice (Massachusetts), appointed by Fillmore
5. Peter Daniel, Associate Justice (Virginia), appointed by Van Buren
6. Robert Grier, Associate Justice (Pennsylvania), appointed by Polk
7. John McLean, Associate Justice (Ohio), appointed by Jackson
8. Samuel Nelson, Associate Justice (New York), appointed by Polk
9. James Wayne, Associate Justice (Georgia), appointed by Jackson

The constitutional issue involved whether the Tonawanda Senecas and their lands fell under the provisions of the treaty of 1842, one that had been unanimously opposed by the Tonawanda chiefs. In the same United States Supreme Court that had heard the momentous Dred Scott case, one heavily laden with southern Democrats and Jacksonians, Martindale, now a staunch Republican, achieved a great victory for the Tonawandas in the decision rendered the next year.[41] Attorney Gillet unsuccessfully argued that Fellows and the Ogden Land Company had legal title to the reservation and that as land-holders could enter their lands; that the Indians were tenants living there at the sufferance of the landlords; that the distribution of the improvement fund was merely "an arrangement" between the government of the United States and the Seneca Nation with which Ogden and Fellows had no concern; and that the Ogden Land Company's obligation was "discharged by payment of the gross sum into the treasury."[42]

After recounting the background to the two treaties of 1838 and 1842 and the facts behind the 1846 trespass and battery incident on the Blacksmith property at Tonawanda, Justice Nelson declared that the treaty of 1842 was a legal instrument even though no Tonawanda chief assented to it. Since it became the "supreme law of the land" because it was "executed and ratified by the proper authorities of the Government," it could not be overturned. Yet Justice Nelson affirmed the New York courts' rulings that the appraisal and monetary award of improvements to the Indians was a precondition to their surrender of and removal from their lands. In this noteworthy decision by a much-maligned United States Supreme Court Justice, Nelson, a Polk Democrat born in Hebron and residing in Cooperstown, New York, concluded:

> We think, therefore, that the grantees [the Ogden Land Company] derived no power, under the treaty, to dispos-sess by force these Indians, or right of entry, so as to sus-tain an ejectment in a court of law; that no private remedy of this nature was contemplated by the treaty, and that a forcible removal must be made, if made at all, under the direction of the United States; that this interpretation is in accordance with the usages and practice of the Govern-ment in providing for the removal of Indian tribes from

their ancient possessions, with the fitness and propriety of the thing itself, and with the fair import of the language of the several articles bearing upon the subject.[43]

The Tonawandas had won; however, there was no mechanism in place to restore all or part of their land base. While they had staved off removal, they were still homeless peoples in the eyes of American officials. Once again, the brilliant Whig attorney would find a way to rectify the Tonawandas' precarious situation.

The Tonawanda Treaty

The Tonawanda Seneca victory in the Blacksmith case in the United States Supreme Court was one of the greatest legal achievements by any American Indian nation in the nineteenth century; however, the decision did not resolve major problems. While recognizing that the Tonawandas were a separate Indian nation and not a party to the Seneca Treaty of 1842, the decision did not remove the Ogden Land Company's preemption right to the Tonawanda Reservation. Indeed, a significant portion of the Indians' 12,800 acres had already been sold or auctioned off by the company's agents, and between sixty and seventy non-Indian families were residing within the pre-1838 boundaries of Tonawanda by 1856.[1] Questions arose about what to do with the Ogden Land Company's claim and whether the United States could or would aid the Indians by helping them buy back their lands. The Tonawandas were now in a twilight zone: They could not be forcibly removed, but they had no clear title to their lands!

The origins of the federal-Tonawanda Treaty of 1857 can only be understood by first examining what was transpiring in the boardroom of the proprietors of the Ogden Land Company in the 1840s and 1850s. Even before the death of Thomas Ludlow Ogden in 1844, the Ogden Land Company faced numerous problems as well as increased scrutiny by the general public as well as by federal officials. Quaker publications and United States congressional reports exposed its corrupt dealings.[2] Besides these challenges and Tonawanda resistance, the proprietors had to deal with other major problems. Some whites who had purchased reservation lands had failed to meet their mortgage payments, leading the proprietors to initiate ejectment suits.[3] The company's "ownership" of resources on the Tonawanda reservation also came under attack. Whites periodically came onto Ogden-claimed lands at Tonawanda and carried off valuable timber.[4] White squatters, with no loyalty to the Ogdens or the Tonawanda Senecas, occupied reservation lands.[5] Significantly, after Thomas Ludlow Ogden died in 1844, his estate, which included lands in Canada and the Midwest as well as Tonawanda lands, was tied up in litigation during much of the next decade.[6] In addition to losses in court in the Blacksmith case from 1846 to 1856, the Ogdens were to be dealt a major blow, namely, the collapse of the American economy in 1857.

Until the Blacksmith ruling by the United States Supreme Court, the majority of the Ogden Land Company proprietors still believed that they would triumph in their battle with the Tonawandas. In July 1853, proprietor R. L. Tillotson sent a circular letter to the proprietors about the lingering battle with the Tonawandas. He noted that the lands at Tonawanda "have greatly risen in price," approaching $25 an acre, and that Tonawanda Creek's water power would lead to higher land prices in the future. Tillotson proposed a "new" arrangement to deal with the "unsettled concerns of the Trust" since the Indians still had the "power to do us harm." Blaming the Tonawandas' noncompliance with the Treaty of 1842 on the influence of the Indians' outside advisers—presumably John H. Martindale—he maintained that further litigation should be avoided since this route would be more costly "to obtain a full and undisturbed possession." Despite the Tonawandas' firm resistance, Tillotson believed that the Indians could be easily bought out, showing a lack of understanding about the Tonawandas' will. Incredibly, he suggested that all the proprietors needed to do to secure Tonawanda lands was to offer the Indians an additional $1 per acre and they would subsequently leave their reservation behind![7] The proprietors were to slowly come to realize that what Tillotson, a hard-line proprietor, had proposed was unrealistic at best. It is clear that by that time other proprietors such as Alfred Ogden had concluded that a resolution to the controversy was in the best interests of the company.

After the New York Court of Appeals decision in the Blacksmith case in 1852, the Tonawanda Council of Chiefs, through the efforts of John H. Martindale and Ely S. Parker, began preparing other strategies. If the 1842 treaty could not be completely set aside by Congress, they would seek a new federal-Tonawanda treaty to win back their lands. The Tonawanda Council of Chiefs also continued to resist all efforts at data collection. In 1854 and 1855, despite efforts by New York State to employ a discredited Seneca, N. T. Strong, to gather statistical information, the effort once again faced resistance. The New York State Census of 1855 noted: "In this reservation the pagan party very reluctantly afforded any information, and in some instances refused to answer the inquiries."[8]

In December 1855, the chiefs petitioned federal authorities asking for a treaty council. Once again, they reiterated that they were united in rejecting the application of the Treaty of 1842 to their community, refusing to accept the required "improvement moneys," the so-called Gay-Cook assessment. Finding more sympathetic ears in federal Indian subagent Marcus Johnson and George Manypenny, the commissioner of Indian affairs, they were more optimistic than they had been in the past.[9] Johnson frequently insisted that the Tonawandas were united about resisting all efforts to carry out the Treaty of 1842 and that the Indian residents of the reservation had no intention of moving anywhere—to Cattaraugus or to Kansas.[10] Attempting to delay Tonawanda removal, Manypenny wrote Secretary of the Interior Robert M. McClelland that no formal decision on carrying out the Treaty of 1842 should be undertaken until the United States Supreme Court rendered its final decision in the Blacksmith case.[11]

Until his replacement as commissioner of Indian affairs in March of 1857, Manypenny expressed more sympathy for Indian rights, including those of the Tonawandas, than had previous office-holders. Appointed on March 28, 1853, he frequently battled with the newly-appointed governor of Kansas Territory, Andrew H. Reeder, who violated Indian treaty rights and "the territory's organic law which excluded Indian lands from the jurisdiction of the territorial government." In his annual report for 1856, the commissioner chastised the whites, caught up in the sectional conflict over slavery, who were violating the rights of these Indians. With the election of James Buchanan to the presidency, Manypenny resigned from office in March 1857.[12]

All this was occurring at a time when some of the Ogden Land Company's proprietors, realizing that their longtime efforts to have the Tonawandas removed were slipping away, increased their lobbying for enforcement of the provisions of the Seneca Treaty of 1842. H. J. Redfield, an agent of the Ogdens from Batavia, had urged the appointment of a special federal agent to pay over the improvement fund to the Seneca Indians of Tonawanda under this treaty. Redfield urged that the federal government insist that the Tonawandas should

go to Cattaraugus, that federal officials should accommodate the interests of "the white settlers and not the Indians" who "should command
our sympathies and protection," and that the 1842 treaty "be carried
into effect." Redfield, a close associate of proprietor James S. Wadsworth, blamed the situation on "designing white men," undoubtedly
referring once again to Martindale. The Ogden representative urged
that the commissioner of Indian affairs listen to the "most intelligent and temperate Indians," not the chiefs. He recommended that
Henry J. Glowacki, law partner of the chief counsel of the Ogden
Land Company, be appointed special federal agent to distribute the
improvement fund and carry out the 1842 treaty. After all, Redfield
pointed out, white families occupying Tonawanda lands were "nearly
equal to the whole number of Indians yet remaining," and these same
whites had already built school houses and churches there. They were
"among the most thrifty and intelligent inhabitants in the county."
Redfield went so far as to defend Asa Cutler, a local resident and
Ogden ally, and his seedy efforts to convince Washington officials of
the merits of Indian removal. A month later, Redfield maintained that
"the most intelligent and temperate Indians have, on several occasions,
expressed a desire to receive their share of the improvement fund to
go to Cattaraugus."[13] Importantly, Redfield was now aided in his
efforts by R. H. Gillet, who had argued the Ogdens' position in the
Blacksmith case.[14]

Importantly, at Manypenny's urging, McClelland sent George
Whiting, assistant secretary of the interior, to investigate the situation on the ground at Tonawanda. After a brief visit to the reservation, Whiting filed his report on May 28, 1855, indicating that some
whites working on behalf of the Ogden Land Company, specifically
Cutler and Henry Forward, had tried to bribe Tonawandas to accept
the improvement fund; that all the Indians he had met were opposed
to the appointment of a special agent to distribute these moneys; and
that they had forged Tonawanda names on petitions favoring distribution that were sent to Washington.[15] Manypenny also sent special
agent George Herrick to investigate the situation at Tonawanda in
the early fall of 1855. Herrick praised the Tonawandas, finding an
industrious community of Indians unanimously opposed to ceding
their land and leaving New York. It was becoming clear to policy
makers in the Office of Indian Affairs that the Ogdens had "pulled

the wool over their eyes" and that previous Indian agents had been in collusion with the company.[16]

In September 1856, Whiting had made a second visit to Tonawanda, this time as a special emissary of President Franklin Pierce. Many of the chiefs were away from the reservation at the Green Corn ceremonies at the Six Nations Reserve in Canada, but Whiting finally secured a public meeting at the council house. He asked the ninety or so Tonawandas to rise from their seats if they opposed taking the money for the improvement fund. Whiting repeated to Manypenny that all rose from their seats. "There was not a single exception."[17]

With the advent of a new administration in Washington in March 1857, each party—the Tonawandas, the Ogdens, and the whites who had settled on the reservation—continued to lobby. Initially, the new commissioner of Indian affairs, General James W. Denver, appeared to side with the Ogdens' and the white settlers' positions.[18] The Indians' fears were warranted. Denver, later governor of Kansas and Civil War general, was a speculator in western lands.[19] In the spring of 1857, Tillotson and Joseph Fellows, one of the company's proprietors, again requested that a special federal agent be appointed to distribute the improvement fund, carrying out the Treaty of 1842, and removing the Indians.[20] On April 20, 1857, white residents of the towns of Alabama and Pembroke petitioned the new president, James Buchanan, asserting that they had settled on Tonawanda lands for "upwards of eleven years" on acreage sold to them by Thomas Ludlow Ogden and Joseph Fellows; that they had cleared land, brought numerous acres into cultivation, built barns and homes "and made various other valuable improvements," such as repairing and constructing bridges and highways. Disturbed by the decision of the United States Supreme Court in the Blacksmith case, including the opinion that the Indians still had a right of occupancy to their lands, they asked the president for protection, fearing that local authorities would now evict them. To these white settlers, Washington officials should fully carry out the provisions of the treaties of 1838 and 1842.[21]

The new commissioner followed this up by preparing an inter-office memorandum, one that clearly showed that he was perplexed about the situation and generally ill-informed about Tonawanda. He admitted that the Tonawandas "forcibly resisted" the appraisal of their

reservation and that in the past Secretary of War Ewing suspected fraud and irregularities in obtaining the 1842 treaty and in the
Ogdens' push to have a special federal agent appointed to distribute
the improvement fund. Yet, he refused to set aside the 1838 and 1842
treaties or recognize the existence of a separate Tonawanda Seneca
Nation. Denver insisted, in 1838, 1842, or even after the Blacksmith
decision in 1856: "The Tonawandas have never been regarded as a
distinct band, but as constituting a part of the Seneca Nation." To
him, in both treaties, negotiations were "made with the chiefs and
head men of the tribe" before Allegany and Cattaraugus established
an elected system and a republican form of government.[22] Yet, the
commissioner was to change his opinions substantially by the summer of 1857.

The key to changing the direction of federal Indian policy relative to the Tonawandas was largely the result of Martindale's use of
his wide network of political and legal associates and their lobbying
efforts. While Parker, much of the time away working as a civil engineer, kept the Tonawanda issues alive by constantly detailing in letters
the nefarious actions of the Ogdens, the damage done by the treaties
of 1838 and 1842, and the federal government's trust responsibilities
to his people, Martindale was "pulling strings" and calling in favors to
help his Tonawanda clients, allowing them to be heard in the highest circles of the state and federal governments.[23] In New York State,
Martindale was aided by his Whig-Republican friends and his junior
law partner William Bryan, and by western New Yorkers—Frederick
Follett and Judge G. A. Verplanck—dedicated to helping the struggling Tonawandas.[24]

The shrewd Martindale even went so far as renewing friendship with Montgomery Blair, his classmate at West Point in the early
1830s. Blair, whose powerful family dominated the politics of two
states—Maryland and Missouri—had just unsuccessfully argued the
Dred Scott case before the United States Supreme Court. Although
his family had been Jacksonian Democrats, their political affiliation
shifted with the wind. Indeed, by 1861, President Lincoln appointed
Blair to his cabinet as his first Postmaster General.[25] Consequently,
Martindale sought support from Blair and his family, thus preparing
the way for formal treaty negotiations.

On April 15, 1857, Martindale had approached Blair, asking
him to help delay Commissioner Denver's decision relative to the

Tonawandas, since he feared that the commissioner would decide to have a knee-jerk response to the situation. Martindale informed Blair that under the Treaty of 1838, the Indians had to resettle in the West within five years and that he feared that the Tonawandas may have "forfeited their right to the western lands by failing to remove by a specific time."[26] Blair immediately wrote on Martindale's behalf to Commissioner Denver. Two months later, Martindale wrote to Blair about the situation, this time detailing the issues. He told Blair that the award for improvements and payment to individual Indians "are made conditions precedent to their own removal by the treaties." Appealing to his kindness and friendship, he emphasized that the Indians had "a right to be heard." Martindale outlined the history of the treaties of 1838 and 1842 as well as the Blacksmith case. He insisted that there was federal trust responsibility to the Tonawandas that had never been performed. Again recounting the troubles besetting the Indians, he asked Blair to help him "reach the ear of the Secretary of the Interior," thereby going over Commissioner Denver's head to a federal cabinet officer. Thus, Martindale used his longtime friend from West Point as a conduit to help secure a new treaty for the Tonawandas.[27]

By this time, a formula had been worked out that was to help resolve the Tonawanda situation. With the appointment of a new secretary of the interior, Jacob Thompson, the Office of Indian Affairs began to consider a swap. The federal government would sell off the Tonawandas' interest in Kansas lands, provided for in the Buffalo Creek Treaty of 1838, and use the money to extinguish the Ogden Land Company's preemptive right to Tonawanda. This was the exact solution needed to unlock the impasse.[28]

Several months earlier, to further the possibility of a new federal treaty, the Tonawanda Council of Chiefs had previously designated Ely and Nicholson Parker "lawful attorney agents and representatives" and ordered them once again to proceed to Washington to lobby for a new treaty.[29] Yet, because of Ely Parker's work schedule as a civil engineer, his contributions were as a persistent letter writer to various federal officials from late 1856 onward, explaining the position of the Tonawanda Council of Chiefs. Their position was eloquently presented in his correspondence right up to the formal negotiations of a treaty in late June 1857.[30]

The question arises about why the swap formula arose when it did? Sectionalism had contributed to a change of direction in federal

Indian policies. With the passage of the Kansas-Nebraska Act in 1854 out of lands that had formerly been designated the Indian Territory, two territories were created and a land rush began. The monetary value of these lands skyrocketed as plans to build railroads through the region multiplied. The commissioner of Indians' annual report clearly spelled out this frontier land rush occurring in Kansas. Under the Buffalo Creek Treaty of 1838, the Iroquois families were promised 320 acres in Kansas if they agreed to surrender their land rights in New York. The report suggested that those Iroquois who had already left should be settled on their 320-acre plots in Kansas; however, no additional Iroquois should be encouraged to migrate there. The report recommended that "the remainder of the lands be brought into market for the benefit of our citizens who are so rapidly filling up the Territory."[31]

By 1856, increasing tensions and resulting violence caused by the sectional crisis led to a reconsideration of further Indian removal to Kansas. The region was beset by a mini-civil war. The Indians already residing there or relocated there were now faced with violent pro-slavery and abolitionist elements as well as others seeking to take advantage of the situation to "acquire" Indian lands. Thus, "Bleeding Kansas" had an impact on what could be done with the Tonawandas.[32] On June 16, 1857, the Tonawanda Council of Chiefs once again gave over power of attorney to Martindale, to Judge Verplanck, and to Ely Parker. The document referred to Parker as a "respected chief" and to Martindale and Verplanck as "our brothers" whom the chiefs had "special confidence" in because of their "integrity." They were commanded to proceed to Washington to do business with the president and commissioner of Indian affairs to gain "the full and complete restoration and recognition of our ancient and vested rights in our homes and lands."[33]

Throughout the summer and fall of 1857, Martindale and Parker perceptively picked up on the importance of events in Kansas and used it as an excuse to plead the Tonawandas' case. Parker subtly pointed out to Commissioner Denver that the Kansas lands were more valuable than the Tonawanda Reservation, suggesting that an exchange could be made. On June 30, 1857, Martindale, Parker, Bryan, and Follett met in Washington with Commissioner Denver. They discussed swapping Kansas lands and the Indians' claim to them for Tonawanda land. In a preliminary agreement, the federal government once again refused to accept the Gay and Cook appraisal moneys for improvements on the reservation under the Treaty of 1842, acknowledged the frauds committed by the Ogden Land Company in the past, put a moratorium on future sales of the Tonawanda Reservation lands, and agreed that the Indians had suffered enough and would not be removed from their homes. While the commissioner insisted on strict obedience to the law, Martindale emphasized that public opinion had shifted away from removing the Indians in a Jacksonian-like manner.[34] Parker attached a letter to a transcript of this meeting which he sent to Commissioner Denver on the same day. Parker insisted that the Kansas lands were much more valuable than Tonawanda, but his community was determined to "cling to our homes for security and for our continued existence."[35] Quite importantly, Parker emphasized:

> The Tonawandas are a separate band of Senecas, easily identified as such, by their residence on a well known reservation, quite removed from the homes of other Senecas in New York and Canada and Ohio, also by their governmental organization under chiefs and headmen according to the ancient customs and ways of their race . . . separate from Allegany and Cattaraugus.[36]

When the delegates met with Secretary Thompson on July 2 and 3, they presented him with a memorial addressed to President Buchanan that stressed that the Indians had valuable lands in Kansas that were recognized as theirs by the federal government and that Washington officials had given their word that these western lands should "never be included in any state or territory of this union." They pointed out that the congressional passage of the Kansas-Nebraska Act of 1854 had violated this treaty commitment made to the Indians.[37]

After discussions with Secretary Thompson ended, the Interior Department signed off on the principles of this accord, a formal shift in Washington officials' views about the Tonawanda Senecas and their future. Tonawanda Seneca claimed-lands in Kansas would be sold off by the United States and deposited in the federal treasury to pay for the repurchase of a part of the Tonawanda Reservation as it existed before the Treaty of 1838. Important to note, not one representative of the Ogden Land Company or the white settlers on Tonawanda lands were a party to this preliminary accord worked out in a four-day period whose terms would later be formalized in a federal treaty.

Almost immediately after this preliminary agreement, Martindale sent his associate O. M. Benedict to a meeting of the proprietors of the Ogden Land Company in New York City. Benedict's assignment was to ascertain the "terms on which they [Ogden Land Company] would sell *all* [including Cattaraugus and Allegany] their Indian lands occupied by the Senecas." Martindale clearly understood that this proposal was a long shot and too complex to deal with, since he insisted that his priority was to his Tonawanda clients, not to other Seneca councils. He did not want to impede a solution for the Tonawandas "which I have so much at heart."[38]

The Whig attorney also approached the Hicksite Quakers for help in aiding the Tonawandas.[39] From March onward through July 1857, Martindale tried to convince Thomas of the Tonawandas' cause, even though Thomas had been one of the detested federal commissioners at the Seneca Treaty of 1842; however, in a letter on July 21, 1857, Thomas did not budge in his opinion that the 1842 treaty was a legal instrument and that the federal government had to find another home for the Tonawandas. Although he recognized that the Tonawandas "are unquestionably a grievously injured and oppressed people," he favored that these Indians join in with their kin at Cattaraugus, where he had recently founded the Thomas Asylum for Orphan and Destitute Indian Children.[40]

As late as July 1857, Ogden Land Company representatives continued to "play hardball." Faced with a nationwide depression in 1857 and stymied in their efforts to rid New York State of its Indian population, they, nevertheless, took the offense. On July 8, 1857, John Van Rensselaer, a company proprietor, reacting to the exclusion of the Ogdens from the negotiations of June 30–July 3, indicated his total dissatisfaction with the accord and insisted that the Treaty of 1842 be carried out at once.[41] While some Ogden representatives were insisting that the Treaty of 1842 had to be carried out forthwith, others in the company took a different tack. On August 14, 1857, James S. Wadsworth, Frederic Bronson, and W. D. Waddington wrote Commissioner Denver that the company would dispose of their preemptive interest to the United States "in exchange for Kansas lands or for money." They would "cheerfully" entertain a proposition for the preemption title of Allegany, Cattaraugus, Tuscarora "and for the sale of such portions of their Tonnewanta [*sic*] Reservation as have not been sold or contracted to be sold." Presenting themselves as defenders of the white settlers on the reservation, they foresaw complications if the Indians wanted all of their 12,800 acres back. To them, it would be "insurmountable and lead to endless trouble and inconvenience to the Government."[42] Hoping to finally make a significant profit out of this never-ending and costly controversy with the Tonawandas that sullied their names, the Ogden proprietors finally saw an opportunity in a new federal treaty.

In the late summer of 1857, Martindale met with Wadsworth, the chairman of the committee appointed by the Ogden Land Company to negotiate. On September 18, 1857, the attorney for the Tonawandas wrote to Secretary Thompson that he had personally met with Wadsworth and that the Ogdens would sell about half of the reservation "lying principally on the south side of the Tonawanda Creek where the largest portion and nearly all of the Indians reside."[43] On October 10, 1857, Martindale wrote Thompson that the company expected "speedy payment," but the repurchase of some lots were "extravagant" and "extortionate."[44] By October 16, Martindale indicated to the secretary that the Ogdens had jacked up the price, demanding $30–$100 per acre.[45] Finally, after three months of haggling, the Ogdens agreed to the price-fixed rate of $20 per acre for lands lying south of Tonawanda Creek. The Tonawandas would receive approximately $256,000 from the sale of their Kansas lands, now formally recognized by the United States, and would use that money to repurchase part of their reservation from the Ogdens.[46]

As early as July 1857, Parker and Martindale had already approached the new and timid President James Buchanan with the idea of an exchange. They accused the United States government of violating the Buffalo Creek Treaty of 1838, since the Iroquois were promised lands in the West that would "never be included in any state or territory of this union." They insisted that they would be in imminent danger if they left to settle in the West. The petitioners concluded by asking Buchanan to "buy their peace."[47] In September and October, Martindale continued to plead the Tonawandas' cause before Secretary Thompson, pointing out to him the substantial cost savings if Washington officials allowed this exchange.[48] On October 16, Martindale stated that the 614 Tonawandas would give up their claims to Kansas lands, totaling 196,480 acres, if they were allowed to use this money, along with the $400 thousand allocated by the federal government for the Indians' removal from New York, to purchase their reservation lands back. He suggested that the Indians would pay the Ogden Land Company $20 per acre as long as the Tonawandas received at least 5,673.4 acres of farm lands.[49] On October 18, the delegates and the commissioner came to a preliminary agreement on what later was the treaty accord. The Tonawanda delegates agreed that they would buy back lands "lying south of Tonawanda Creek, at a rate not to exceed twenty dollars per acre" but "yield up that portion lying north of the same."[50] Two weeks later, Secretary Thompson sent Charles Mix, later commissioner of Indian affairs, to Tonawanda to hold council with the chiefs and confirm this treaty. The treaty was confirmed by the chiefs in council on November 5, 1857; nevertheless, to be a lawful accord, it had to be ratified by the United States Senate.[51]

Both Parker and Martindale lobbied right down to the ratification of the treaty. Even after Parker's return to Galena, Illinois, he urged passage of the treaty without delay. On May 14, 1858, Parker wrote the new commissioner, Charles E. Mix, adding a new argument. By permanently recognizing the Tonawanda Indians and their reservation lands, the treaty "will settle the complicated case and relieve the [Interior] Department of much trouble."[52] Four days later, Martindale wrote Mix indicating that "the times are propitious." He said that he had met with Wadsworth and that the Ogden proprietors were anxious to sell. Perhaps naively, Martindale had "strong hope of buying the whole reservation or nearly all of it."[53]

Martindale had already called on his political connections to help him lobby for Senate ratification. Besides Montgomery Blair, Martindale's solid Whig-Republican credentials helped him secure the support of powerful Senator William Seward.[54] The unity of the New Republican Party and the increasing schism in the Democratic Party contributed to ratification. On June 4, 1858, the Senate voted by a 31 to 7 margin to ratify the treaty.[55] Four of the votes against ratification were cast by Southerners. Five of the six senators had been Jacksonian Democrats. Strangely, the famous Sam Houston, an adopted Cherokee for his earlier opposition to Jacksonian Indian policies, voted against the treaty. He had joined the Know-Nothing Party during the decade of the 1850s! On March 31, 1859, just before John Brown's raid at Harper's Ferry, President Buchanan formally proclaimed the treaty.[56] In the darkening clouds leading to the Civil War, the Tonawandas had "won." They were now formally recognized by the federal government as a separate entity, the Tonawanda Band

Chart 5. United States Senators in the 35th Congress Who Voted Against the Ratification of the Federal–Tonawanda Seneca Treaty (1857)*

Name	State	Years of Service in the Senate	Party Affiliation
1. Bayard, James Asheton, Jr. (1799–1880)	Delaware	1851–1864	Democrat
2. Clay, Clement Claiborne, Jr. (1816–1882)	Alabama	1853–1861	Democrat
3. Houston, Samuel (1793–1863)	Texas	1846–1855	Democrat; American (Know-Nothing)
4. Hunter, Robert Mercer Taliaferro (1798–1871)	Virginia	1847–1861	Democrat
5. Mason, James Murray (1798–1871)	Virginia	1847–1861	Democrat
6. Pugh, George Ellis (1822–1876)	Ohio	1855–1861	Democrat

*Information derived from: U.S. Congress, *Senate Executive Journal* (June 4, 1858), 438–439; and *Biographical Dictionary of the American Congress*. There were 41 Democrats, 20 Republicans, and 5 American (Know-Nothing) Party members in the 35th U.S. Senate, 1857–1859. The vote on the treaty was 31 in favor, 6 opposed.

of Senecas, apart from the Seneca Nation, and governed by a council of chiefs. The Tonawandas were not to be removed from their homes on the reservation. They were now allowed to use the money from the federal sale of their Kansas lands to pay the Ogdens for at least part of their tribal lands they had held in 1838; in this way, they would buy out the Ogden preemption on these reacquired lands.

Thus, the Tonawanda Senecas were awarded the "opportunity" to repurchase approximately 60 percent of the lands that they had held before the Treaty of 1838; however, for the first time since 1826, one of the chiefs dissented, undoubtedly on the grounds that the accord allowed only a partial restoration of Tonawanda lands.[57] Despite this break with consensus-styled governance, the accord was accepted as a "done deal" by the Tonawanda community. Now Martindale had to find a way to use the Kansas money to repurchase the lands back and once more make Tonawanda a contiguous reservation community.

Buying Back the Reservation

The Treaty of 1857 did not return reservation lands to the Tonawandas. It only provided a vague formula to allow the repurchase of some Tonawanda lands. The two parties to the accord, as well as the proprietors of the Ogden Land Company and individual non-Indian purchasers of lands from the company, had to work out the complex details to allow the Tonawandas to regain clear title to their reservation. Two weeks after Buchanan's proclamation, Martindale and Bryan met with the chiefs in the Tonawanda Council House "for the purpose of contracting for and making purchase" of Tonawanda lands on the terms and conditions of the 1857 treaty. Martindale was approved as attorney to buy back the southern portion of reservation lands, while Follett was appointed to "apportion the improvement fund" under provisions of the 1842 treaty.[1] Thus, while the country was heading for civil war, Martindale and Follett set their designs on "reacquiring lands" and removing the Ogden title and non-Indian occupants of Tonawanda.

On May 5, 1859, the Office of Indian Affairs formally approved Martindale's contract with the Tonawanda Council of Chiefs authorizing him to serve as its agent to repurchase the reservation.[2] For the next year and a half, the attorney set out to accomplish this difficult task. He had to clear title on contracts made with non-Indians that at times involved complicated legal negotiations. In the process, Martindale had to contend with three distinct realities: first, Tonawanda lands "owned" outright by the Ogden Land Company and its proprietors; secondly, lands sold at auction and purchased by whites from the Ogden Land Company, some of which had liens attached to them since some white settlers had taken out mortgages from the company and a few were in delinquency; and thirdly, white squatters who had taken up residence on reservation lands. Moreover, Martindale's repurchase of the reservation faced two other complicated hurdles.

A major complication arose from the beginning since the 1857 treaty did not define the procedures about the repurchase.[3] After a meeting with Martindale in Washington, A. B. Greenwood, the United States commissioner of Indian affairs, subsequently spelled out a set of instructions. Martindale was to contract with the landowners, be it the Ogden proprietors or white settlers at $20 per acre, then forward documents showing clear title. If the purchase contracts and abstracts of title were in order and satisfactory to both a federal judge and the Interior Department, the United States Treasury would then pay out moneys from the fund previously set aside for the Tonawandas to acquire lands in Kansas under the Buffalo Creek Treaty of 1838. Moreover, if contracts exceeded $20 per acre, only the president of the United States could approve the sale.[4] On the "class of contracts that had mortgage liens," Commissioner Greenwood described what had to be done: "You can take the assignments in your name, as suggested, to be held until the title can be perfected when the same shall be transferred to the Secretary of the Interior agreeably to the terms of the treaty."[5] Yet, the commissioner and Martindale also failed to see another impediment, namely, once the repurchase occurred, the lands acquired would be subject to taxation and foreclosure, which would torpedo efforts to aid the Tonawandas.

By June 1859, Martindale had devoted all his time and energy to his assignment and was making "most strenuous efforts" to "prepare abstracts of title."[6] Writing to Greenwood in mid-June, the attorney indicated that he had already made contracts for certain lots in his "desire to secure for the Indians a contiguous body of land."[7] Within ten days, he started forwarding purchase contracts and abstracts of titles to Washington.[8] Much of the early purchases were from the long-standing mainstays of the Ogden Land Company: the Fellows, Ogden, Rogers, Tillotson, Troup, and Wadsworth families. On June 24, 1859, Martindale forwarded six deeds contracted by him, totaling over 480 acres, at a cost of $10,745.62.[9] The process sped up so rapidly that as early as July 1, Commissioner Greenwood requisitioned $100,000 for purchases, allowing Martindale a credit line at the United States Treasury office in New York City.[10] It is important to note that among Martindale's contracting parties were some of the oldest families in New York State, including the Brinckerhoffs and the Van Rensselaers.[11] Prominent Whig-Republicans appeared on the list of lot owners. Besides James S. Wadsworth, the name of William Seward, the United States senator and former governor of New York State, appears as an owner of a lot on the old reservation, land that was repurchased by the Tonawandas in 1859.[12] By the end of that year, Martindale had expended approximately 60 percent of the Kansas moneys or $150,194.60 out of the $256,000 available.[13]

In order to reconfigure the reservation and make it one contiguous parcel again, Martindale had to take a flexible approach in his wheeling and dealing. In making a contract with James S. Wadsworth, he made a land exchange, one thousand acres for lands "required for the Indians."[14] Martindale was faced with obstacles that frequently delayed his efforts. In a revealing letter to the commissioner of Indian affairs in February 1860, the attorney indicated that the Ogdens had foreclosed on two lots for failure of white settlers to provide mortgage payments, and hence the company's efforts to contract with Martindale was delayed on 150 acres until the late spring.[15] The sale of three other lots contracted in November 1859 was also suspended "by reasons of the inability of the proprietor to make a clear title."[16] In the same letter, Martindale reported that the sheriff of Genesee County had also removed numerous "white intruders" who had refused to leave lands. The attorney hoped that by removing "the army of intruders" from Indian lands, by reestablishing the reservation, and by distributing the improvement fund to the Tonawandas as quickly as possible, these Senecas would be in a "most favorable position for prosecuting agricultural labor in the Spring" and thus overcome their "impoverished state."[17]

Martindale had to deal with other time-consuming matters besides buying back the reservation. He aided Frederick Follett in his efforts to distribute the moneys in the improvement fund to the Tonawandas. For a decade and a half, the desperately impoverished Indians had refused to accept $15,018.36 in compensation allotted to them in the Treaty of 1842 for the loss of their improvements—residences, barns, and orchards. In the spring of 1859, Follett, with the approval of the Tonawanda Council of Chiefs, was appointed as the special agent to dispense this "improvement" fund.[18] Thus, in order to get the right to repurchase some of their tribal lands back, the Tonawandas had to "hold their nose" and agree to finally recognize the Ogdens' purchase of their lands in the treaties of 1838 and 1842.

Follett, a defender of Tonawanda rights since the mid-1840s, was a key figure in restoring a viable economic base to the Tonawanda community. By December 1859, Follett had filed his report to the Office of Indian Affairs, making recommendations supported by the Tonawanda Council of Chiefs.[19] Part of the problem he faced was that nowhere in the Treaty of 1842 or Treaty of 1857 was the process of distributing the improvement fund spelled out. Moreover, there were delays in reimbursing Follett for his services. Both Martindale and Ely Parker complained that these delays were creating hardships, both to the Indians as well as to Follett. Martindale referred to Follett as "not rich," and Parker asked the commissioner of Indian affairs to immediately release the improvement fund to the Tonawandas since they needed money to plant and overcome their desperate economic situation.[20] These moneys were finally released in 1860, although there is no indication if it reached the reservation in time for planting.

Martindale faced two more challenges in 1860. One of these involved Daniel Willard of the town of Alabama who claimed that a covenant with the Ogden Land Company prevented his ejectment from Tonawanda lands. Willard and a group of white settlers appealed directly to the secretary of the interior. They insisted that Martindale had "suckered" the Indians, taking money out of their annuities to pay for his own sustenance, and that the government had abandoned them.[21] Martindale carefully sidestepped the slander to his reputation. He described Willard as an honest but poor man whose real desire was to go prospecting at Pike's Peak. Martindale deflected Willard's and other settlers' appeals to the commissioner by insisting that these white settlers had to litigate against the Ogden Land Company, not the Tonawandas. "I think the settlers have no claims against the Indians, or rights in the reservation, legal or equitable."[22] After a series of letters back and forth to Washington, Willard's appeal appears to have been filed away, never to be acted on by officials. Finally, on August 1, 1860, the Tonawanda Council of Chiefs formally ended the repurchase efforts, with the exception of two farm lots totaling 79.67 acres that were in foreclosure proceedings at that time. Martindale was ordered by the chiefs to end his contracting in the three-county area of Erie, Genesee, and Niagara.[23]

For much of 1859 onward into early 1860, Martindale and the Tonawanda Senecas were faced with a major dilemma. By repurchasing lands, the Tonawandas were formally recognizing that their reservation had been alienated out of their possession in 1842, thus recognizing the hated "compromised treaty." If their lands were no longer in their possession, these lands were now subject to taxation. The federal government in the Treaty of 1857 had not formally put these lands back into trust, thus making them subject to state taxation. This vexing problem stumped Martindale and required him to work out a compromise between the Tonawanda Senecas and New York State.

On January 20, 1860, Martindale sent New York State's Republican governor Edwin D. Morgan a report, who then transmitted it to the New York State Legislature. After briefly recounting the history of the Tonawanda struggle, Martindale indicated that these Indians had already secured nearly 7,000 acres and intended "to surrender up about five thousand acres"; that the Indians would "avail themselves of the provisions of the treaty, by which the money" would be used "to extinguish the pre-emption right to that portion of their lands." However, Martindale noted that these newly regained lands were now subject to New York State taxation.[24]

While Martindale was busy contracting for Tonawanda lands, the New York State Comptroller's Office was putting tax liens and planning to foreclose on the same property. Consequently, throughout the winter and early spring of 1860, Martindale attempted to secure tax relief by putting these newly repurchased lands into trust. With federal officials distracted by the growing sectional conflict, the attorney turned to his Republican ally in Albany, Governor Morgan, with hopes that this potentially disastrous development would not destroy Martindale's decade and a half of efforts to aid his Indian clients.

In the January 1860 report written by Martindale and subsequently forwarded by Governor Morgan to the New York State Legislature, the attorney had asked that a bill be passed designating some public officer of the state to receive these repurchased lands "in trust to be held for the exclusive use, occupation, and enjoyment of the Tonawanda Band of Indians, according to the provisions of said treaty [United States-Tonawanda Seneca Treaty of 1857]." Martindale went further, adding that the Tonawandas would "submit themselves to the protecting care and guardianship of the State of New York, to aid in their improvement, and given the peace in their ancient home, now happily confirmed to them."[25]

As a result of this appeal and the sizable political influence of Martindale with the Republican governor Morgan, the New York State Legislature passed two bills in April 1860, both directed at the Tonawanda Senecas. On April 16, 1860, the New York State Legislature passed a bill "authorizing the comptroller "to hold the Tonawanda Indian reservation in trust for the Tonawanda Band of Indians."[26] This act created a unique status for the Tonawanda Reservation, unlike any other Iroquois landholding in New York State. As part of Martindale's lobbying, the very next day the New York State Legislature passed a bill "to relieve the Tonawanda Band of Seneca Indians from certain taxes on the Tonawanda reservation, and to prevent intrusions thereon." Provision 5 of this second act provided that warrants for removal of trespassers or intruders could be issued by any justice of the peace in the state.[27] The Tonawanda Council of Chiefs had sent a memorial in favor of this second bill, while two disgruntled Ogden associates had unsuccessfully attempted to stymie the effort by forwarding a "remonstrance against passage" of the legislation. Both bills passed overwhelmingly.[28] Finally, on February 14, 1863, the secretary of the interior conveyed the 7,549 acres purchased by Martindale to Lucias Robinson, the state comptroller, to be held in trust for the Tonawandas by New York State.[29]

In 1862 and revised substantially in April 1863, the New York State Legislature passed bills that formally incorporated the Tonawandas into its purview. In the middle of the Civil War, the legislature enacted "An Act for the protection and improvement of the Tonawanda Band of Seneca Indians, residing on the Tonawanda reservation in this state." This comprehensive act "authorized and empowered" the Tonawandas to select a clerk, treasurer, and marshal as well as peacemaker judges who would be elected by all Tonawandas over the age of twenty-one. This New York State act defined the roles and responsibilities of each elected officer. The peacemaker court was recognized as having jurisdiction in controversies between Indians residing on the Tonawanda reservation. Unlike the past when clan mothers determined issues relating to Indian lands, the act recognized the Tonawanda Council of Chiefs as having the ultimate authority to make decisions about the tribal estate. Any controversy over eligibility to vote in tribal elections or to overturn decisions of the Peacemaker Court could be appealed to the Tonawanda Council of Chiefs. Non-Indians residing at Tonawanda had to obtain a permit from the Council of Chiefs. The bill also had restrictions on non-Indian employment on the reservation as well as on the cutting and sale of reservation timber. Other provisions granted the Indians the right to cut their own timber to manufacture shingles or staves or gave permission to clear land to allow for their agricultural endeavors.[30]

Thus, while achieving a great victory against all odds, the Tonawanda Senecas paid a price for regaining a small part of their reservation. To ward off the threat to their community's existence in their do-or-die struggle against the Ogden Land Company, they had to compromise with their old enemies in Albany who had done them in so many times in the past. They now, much like their kin within the Seneca Nation at Allegany and Cattaraugus, had to reluctantly accept the long arm of the state in certain aspects of their life, including the operation of a state-administered school on the reservation, state regulations on resource management, and even intrusions into their tribal governmental operations.

10

Conclusion

Tonawanda Seneca history from the American Revolution to the American Civil War is reminiscent of the Seneca story "The Race of the Turtle and the Beaver." In it, Beaver has invaded a stream and swamp where Turtle lives. No longer are there rushes, and the habitat has been transformed into a lake. By building his dam, Beaver has made the stream unlivable for Turtle. Turtle tells Beaver that he intends to break down the dam and restore his home. He challenges Beaver to a swimming race to determine ownership of the habitat. After repeatedly hanging on to Beaver's tail and biting it, Turtle outwits Beaver by projecting himself through the air like a flying squirrel, allowing him to land first on the shore. Thus, Turtle reclaims the right to his habitat, albeit a changed one from the time he lived before Beaver's invasion.[1] The changed habitat, one that exists to the present day, is the Tonawanda Indian Reservation, situated on 7,549 acres between Akron and Basom, New York.

Like the slow-moving, deliberate turtle, the Tonawanda Seneca leadership used guile more than violent confrontation. As conservative activists, the Tonawanda leadership was truly exceptional from the War of 1812 onward. The Tonawanda chiefs and less well-known clan mothers who bolstered their cause were peaceful but relentless in fighting for their lands; however, they adapted their strategies to meet changing circumstances. They pushed furiously and consciously attempted to foster the "Good Mind," the Iroquois ideal of what is best for the community, not the individual, and kept their council unified until 1857.

The evolution of a separate Tonawanda Seneca Nation and a distinct tribal identity occurred in several stages. Periodic migrations of Senecas from other communities occurred from the American

Revolution to at least 1830. In 1812, John Sky had clearly set forth that the Tonawandas were a distinct community apart from the chiefs at Buffalo Creek. Red Jacket, although hardly a Tonawanda, reinforced this separation of the Tonawandas from other Seneca communities by insisting that the 1826 treaty, one that reduced Tonawanda lands by 70 percent, was unacceptable and needed to be resisted. His impassioned oratory and stubbornness in the face of being deposed at Buffalo Creek won support for him among conservatives at Tonawanda. At Tonawanda, Jemmy Johnson's annual speech, combined with the recitation of the *Gaiwiio* and the revival of the Condolence ceremony, made this reservation a revered place for all Haudenosaunee followers of Handsome Lake.

More than any other single individual, the sachem John Blacksmith stood tall as the "founding father" of the Tonawanda Senecas. He helped set forth every strategy that Parker as well as Martindale used to accomplish that one objective: retaining a Tonawanda community in the homeland. By employing an old Indian strategy, namely, the use of delaying tactics, the Blacksmith-led Tonawanda Council of Chiefs pushed their cause long enough until events in the Trans-Mississippi West and circumstances on the ground in New York State forced a change in federal Indian policies.

As a Confederacy sachem, Chief Blacksmith was "the main man," representing the values of the ancient League of Peace and Power and attempting to build unity. As his Confederacy title suggests, he was the doorkeeper. He carefully allowed outsiders to enter his village but respected the women's right to screen them. Blacksmith selected one, the right one—the brilliant Martindale—to be his as well as the Tonawandas' mouthpiece in the courtroom, a setting that must have seemed quite alien to the chief. As was true of great sachems of days gone by, Blacksmith learned lessons from the past. As a student of history, he understood that his Seneca people had withstood previous times of troubles—the massive invasion by the French in 1687, the devastation of Seneca villages in the Sullivan-Clinton Campaign of 1779, and disastrous treaties—the Fort Stanwix (1784), the Big Tree (1797), and the Buffalo Creek treaties (1826, 1838, 1842)—to maintain their way of life. Blacksmith insisted that the federal government honor the Iroquois' most solemn accord with Washington—the Treaty of 1794—and recognize the time-honored Indian custom of consensus decision making. He drew strength from the support of Tonawanda clan mothers. Besides his deference to these powerful women, Blacksmith also had the sachem's responsibility of preparing leaders to meet future crises. Consequently, even after his death in April 1851, Blacksmith's legacy, in the person of Ely S. Parker, was felt.

Hence, Blacksmith, the chiefs, and the clan mothers could be labeled "conservative activists." They resisted in so many distinct ways: They brought up federal obligations and responsibilities under the Treaty of Canandaigua of 1794, insisting that Washington officials had promised them protection; they reminded whites of the Senecas' military sacrifices as American allies in the War of 1812; they attended and spoke at mass audiences to win support from their non-Indian neighbors; they took out advertisements in local newspapers; they used the distinguished Lewis Henry Morgan as their publicist and his Grand Order of the Iroquois as their petition gatherers; they convinced Henry Rowe Schoolcraft to provide them with valued information but restricted his access to statistical data that they thought could be harmful to their interests. At times, the Tonawandas' strategy turned more aggressive: endless litigation in state and federal courts, reaching the United States Supreme Court in 1856; forcibly removing surveyors and assessors from their lands; and even physically confronting Ogden Land Company henchmen who attempted to drive the Indians off their tribal lands.

In the process, these remarkable Native Americans preserved a parcel of what is today seen by most Haudenosaunee as a special place in their history, namely, the Tonawanda Seneca Territory between Akron and Basom, New York. There the *Gaiwiio* became a formal religion, where a few hundred Indians resisted the efforts of a powerful land company and state and national political forces intent on moving them out of the empire state. Indeed, the formation of the Tonawanda Seneca Band of Indians is a heroic epic, nearly comparable to their emergence story from Bare Hill, Canandaigua Lake. Once again, they met the insatiable appetite of a monster serpent and came away with their survival as a people.

Appendix I

Tonawanda Seneca Clan Mothers' Support of Chiefs' Efforts to Protest Treaty of Buffalo Creek of 1838, March 14, 1841, OIA, NYAR, M234, MR584, RG75, National Archives.

Tonawanda March 14th 1841*
His Excellency
    John Tyler
            President of the United States
Father: We write to you, and desire you to hear our words. His Excellency, we pray most earnestly to listen to us. We, the women of our race, feel troubled[.] We feel deep anxiety for our children. We feel as though we were bound up with our children in our arms—We pray our great father, the President, to loosen our bondage, for we are in great trouble. Our Great Father the President, the women of the Tonawanda Reservation, have exerted our influence, in trying to have our Chiefs united in their minds, in their councils, and they have been so, [since] not one of our chiefs have signed the Treaty [Buffalo Creek Treaty of 1838], and [yet] we are astonished to hear that we have to give up the Tonawanda Reservation. All our women of the other reservations [Allegany, Buffalo Creek, Cattaraugus] are of the same mind, and are all in trouble. We therefore pray you our great Friend to remove our troubles[.] We now take hold of your hand for protection. We ask the Great Spirit to grant our request and aid us.

Our great father: You may be surprised to hear from us, as we have never done the like before[.] We think much of our homes, and are strongly attached to the places which the great Spirit gave to his Red children of this country. We say as our Chiefs have often said, and which they repeated in the great council, which was opened at Cattaraugus, two years ago by J. R. Poinset[t] late secretary of war, that we are willing that the emigration party should have their share and proportion of the lands, and dispose of it as they pleased.

The former treaty [Treaty of Canandaigua in 1794] made with our nation, and the first President George Washington is good[,] the continuation of which is compared to the rising and setting sun, and to the waters which continue to flow. Washington trusted in the Great Spirit, and he was crowned with [success?][.] By his wisdom[,] this country is blessed with freedom, and it was his mind that this freedom should also be secured to us, and our children.

The number of women is two hundred and seven. Our Father the President this is all we have to say[.]

Signed on behalf of the whole by

Minerva Black Smith X
their marks   Widow Little Beard X
Susan Black Smith X
Lo-no-que-no X
Gar-near-no-wit X
O-no dy X
Dor-wa loes X
Gao-e war ha dus X

*Note: This petition is a verbatim transcript found in the National Archives that was probably drafted to be sent to President William Henry Harrison who died one month after his inaugural. Apparently, the eight Tonawanda Seneca clan mothers did not bother to change the date of the letter when John Tyler became President on April 6, 1841.

Appendix II

"TO THE PUBLIC"—Tonawanda Chiefs' Advertisement Asking the Non-Indians of Western New York Not to Purchase Reservation Lands from the Ogden Land Company. *Spirit of the Times* [Batavia, New York newspaper], June 19, 1844

TO THE PUBLIC

Whereas great injustice has been and is continued towards us by persons desirous of driving us from the lands where repose the ashes of our father,—lands conveyed to us by the great and good Washington, and which were to remain in our possession forever: Now therefore, we the undersigned Chiefs, delegated by the Council held at Tonnawanda [*sic*], on the 21st day of May, last, do protest against such innovations upon our rights, and would call upon all good men to aid us in the premises.

We do not deem it necessary to enter into a lengthy publication of the wrongs which we have suffered. We would not create any disturbance. We ask only Justice and look with confidence to the American people for it. We offer you a simple statement.

In the infancy of this Republic, when the now majestic and firmly planted Oak was but a sapling, our friendship was solicited, and was granted. One of the results of Treaties which have been made between us was, that our fathers and their posterity should remain in possession of the Lands we now occupy forever. Shall the Treaties which have been made be trampled in the dust? Shall we be thus driven from our homes! We raise our voices against the injustice.

Our Lands are advertised to be sold from us. We warn and entreat our white brothers not to purchase them. Copies of the treaties we have, and invite Americans to examine.

JOHN X BLACKSMITH,
JIMMY X JOHNSON,
BLUE X SKY,
JOHN X SKY,
BIG X FIRE,
JESSE X SPRING,
DAVID X SPRING,
SAMUEL X PARKER,
LEWIS X POODRY,
LEWIS X KENNEDY,
WING X WASHINGTON,
JESSE X TIFFANY,
ISAAC X SHANKS.

Notes

Preface

1. George H. J. Abrams, *The Seneca People* (Phoenix: Indian Tribal Series, 1976), 6–7.

2. Ibid., 6.

3. 7 *Stat.*, 601 (Sept. 15, 1797); 7 *Stat.*, 550 (Jan. 15, 1838); 7 *Stat.*, 586 (May 20, 1842); *Whipple Report*, 23–24 (August 31, 1826).

4. 11 *Stat.*, 735; 12 *Stat.*, 991 (November 5, 1857).

5. Arthur C. Parker, *The History of the Seneca Indians* (Port Washington, New York: Ira J. Friedman, Inc., 1967), 151–152 (originally published as "An Analytical History of the Seneca Indians" (Rochester, New York: Researches and Transactions of the New York State Archaeological Association, Lewis Henry Morgan Chap., 6 (1926): 1–162.

6. William H. Armstrong, *Warrior in Two Camps: Ely S. Parker, Union General and Seneca Chief* (Syracuse: Syracuse University Press, 1978), 19–43, 51–68. Arthur C. Parker virtually ignores this important chapter in his granduncle's life: *The Life of General Ely S. Parker: Last Grand Sachem of the Iroquois and General Grant's Military Secretary* (Buffalo: Buffalo Historical Society, 1919; reprint, Lynchburg, Virginia: Schroeder Publications, 2005).

7. Mary H. Conable, "A Steady Enemy: The Ogden Land Company and the Seneca Indians" (PhD diss., Rochester: University of Rochester, 1994); see also Laurence M. Hauptman, *Conspiracy of Interests: Iroquois Dispossession and the Rise of New York State* (Syracuse: Syracuse University Press, 1999).

8. Most notable are the writings by Elisabeth Tooker: "On the Development of the Handsome Lake Religion," *Proceedings of the American Philosophical Society* 133 (1989): 35–50; "The Structure of the Iroquois League: Lewis Henry Morgan's Research and Observations," *Ethnohistory* 30 (1983): 141–154; "Lewis Henry Morgan and His Contemporaries," *American Anthropologist* 94 (1992): 357–375; *Lewis H. Morgan on Iroquois*

Material Culture (Tucson: University of Arizona Press, 1994). For Morgan's classic study, see Lewis Henry Morgan, *The League of the Ho-dé-no-sau-nee, or Iroquois* (Rochester: Sage, 1851; reprint with introduction by William N. Fenton, New York: Corinth Books, 1962).

9. Deborah Doxtator, "What Happened to the Iroquois Clans? A Study of Clans in Three Nineteenth-Century Rotinonhsyoni Communities" (PhD diss., London, Ontario: University of Western Ontario, 1996).

10. Ibid., 294.

11. Ibid., 2.

12. Ibid., 277.

13. For the case, see *Fellows v. Blacksmith*, 19 *Howard* 366 (December 1856).

14. Benjamin S. Cohn, "History and Anthropology: The State of Play," *Comparative Studies in Society and History* 22 (April 1980): 198–221.

15. Laurence M. Hauptman, *The Iroquois and the New Deal* (Syracuse: Syracuse University Press, 1981).

Chapter 1. The Tonawanda Community: Early History

1. For the Seneca conquest of the Neutrals and Eries, see *JR*, XXVI: 117–119 (Neutrals); *JR*, XVII: 25–29; *JR*, LXII: 71 (Eries). See also Marian White, "Neutral and Wenro," in: *Handbook of North American Indians.* XVI: *The Northeast* (Washington, D.C.: Smithsonian Institution, 1978), 407–415; and "Erie," in: *Handbook of North American Indians*, XV: 412–417. On his visit in 1788 Samuel Kirkland described in his journal that he was told of a battle waged by the Senecas against "Western Indians" at the exact location of Tonawanda about 250 years before (100 years before the Wenro war). Samuel Kirkland, *The Journals of Reverend Samuel Kirkland*, Walter Pilkington, ed. (Clinton, New York: Hamilton College, 1980), 141.

2. Kirkland, *Journals*, 141.

3. Parker, *The Life of General Ely S. Parker*, 42, 313–314.

4. Kurt A. Jordan, *The Seneca Restoration, 1715–1754* (Gainesville, Florida: University Press of Florida, 2008), 187. William Engelbrecht, p.c., September 8, 2008; Engelbrecht is a leading authority on Iroquoian archaeology in western New York.

5. Frederick Houghton, "The Migrations of the Seneca Nation," *American Anthropologist* 29 (April 1927): 242.

6. 7 *Stat.*, 70 (June 30, 1802); *Whipple Report*, 144–150. See also chap. 3.

7. Parker, *The Life of General Ely S. Parker*, 18–20.

8. Justus Ingersoll [federal Indian agent] Census Report for the Six Nations Agency, October 1, 1830, SNAR, 1824–1832. M234. MR832, RG75, NA.

9. Arthur C. Parker, "The White Man Takes Possession, 1783–1842," in: *History of the Genesee County*, Lockwood R. Doty, ed. (Chicago: S. J. Clarke Publishing Co., 1925), I: 278.

10. Timothy Alden, *Account of Sunday Missions Performed Among the Senecas and Munsees* (New York: J. Seymour, 1827), 104–105.

11. Wallace L. Chafe, *Handbook of the Seneca Language* (Albany: New York State Museum and Science Center, Bulletin No. 388, 1963), 56.

12. Parker, *The Life of General Ely S. Parker*, 16–17, 30.

13. Kirkland, *Journals*, 141. Morgan, *The League of the Ho-dé-no-sau-nee, or Iroquois*, 426–433; Orasmus Turner, *Pioneer History of the Holland Purchase of Western New York* (Buffalo: George H. Derby, 1850), 62–63.

14. Parker, *The Life of General Ely S. Parker*, 16–17, 30. See also Stanley Vanderlaan, "Tonawanda Village" [New York State], *Museum Service* 37 (February 1964): 24–26.

15. Kirkland, *Journals*, 141.

16. Dorcas R. Brown, "The Reservation Log House" (MA thesis, Cooperstown: Cooperstown Graduate Program and SUNY Oneonta, 2000), 29–32.

17. Ibid., 29.

18. Ibid.

19. Ibid.

20. Anonymous [Duncan Ingraham?], "Extract from a Letter from a Gentleman Upon His Return from Niagara, 1792," in: *Studies of the Niagara Frontier*, Frank Severance, ed. (Buffalo: Buffalo Historical Society Publications, No. 15, 1911), 390–391.

21. News report on Iroquois "Sachems and Head Warriors" meeting with "Colonel Pickering," in Philadelphia, *General Advertiser*, March 28, 1792, 2.

22. 7 *Stat.*, 44 (November 11, 1794).

23. "Jacob Lindley's Journal," in: *Buffalo Historical Society Publications*, Frank Severance, ed. (Buffalo: Buffalo Historical Society, 1903), VI: 177–178.

24. Doxtator, "What Happened to the Iroquois Clans," 280. For the "clearing-forest world" dichotomy, see Elisabeth Tooker, "Women in Iroquois Society," in: *Extending the Rafters*, Jack Campisi, Michael Foster, and Marianne Mithun, eds. (Albany: State University of New York Press, 1984), 109–123.

25. Doxtator, "What Happened to the Iroquois Clans," 285. For women and the Great Law, see William N. Fenton, *The Great Law and the Longhouse* (Norman, Oklahoma: University of Oklahoma Press, 1998).

26. Doxtator, "What Happened to the Iroquois Clans," 337–338. See also Ibid., 288.

27. Anthony F. C. Wallace and Deborah Holler, "Reviving the Peace Queen: Revelations from Lewis Henry Morgan's Field Notes on the Tonawanda Senecas," *Histories of Anthropology Annual* 5 (2009): 90–109. Caroline Parker was graduated from Albany Normal School. Kendall A. Birr, *A Tradition of Excellence: The Sesquicentennial History of the University at Albany, State University of New York, 1844–1994* (Virginia Beach, Virginia: Donning Company Publishers, 1994), 34. A teacher, she was bestowed the title Jigonsasee (Peace Queen), the legendary Neutral Indian woman who was the first to accept the message of Deganawidah, the Peacemaker. Parker later married Tuscarora chief John Mountpleasant, a prominent musician, and moved to the Tuscarora Reservation. Deborah Holler is currently writing an autobiography of this extraordinary woman's life. Unfortunately, most of Caroline Parker's early correspondence, which is housed at the American Philosophical Society, deals with educational and family concerns, not the political fight to regain lands lost from 1838 to 1842.

28. Thomas Morris, "Account of the Treaty of Big Tree," Henry O'Reilly MSS., NYHS. See also "Rough notes of speech of Thomas Morris to the Seneca Indians, 1797. Miscellaneous MSS., M., NYHS. Robert Morris to Thomas Morris and Charles Williamson, August 1, 1797, Skivington Collection, Box 26, Folder 1, UR.

29. 7 *Stat.*, 601 (September 15, 1797). For more on the "treaty-making" at Big Tree, see Wallace, *The Death and Rebirth of the Seneca*, 179–183; Norman B. Wilkinson, "Robert Morris and the Treaty of Big Tree," *Mississippi Valley Historical Review* 40 (September 1951): 257–278; Barbara A. Chernow, "Robert Morris: Genesee Land Speculator," *New York History* 58 (April 1977): 195–220.

30. Robert W. Bingham, ed., *Holland Land Company Papers: Reports of Joseph Ellicott* (Buffalo: Buffalo Historical Society Publications, 1941), II: 352–354.

31. Arthur C. Parker, *Red Jacket: Seneca Chief* (1952) (Reprint edition, Lincoln, Nebraska: University of Nebraska Press, 1998), 166.

32. *Laws of New York*, chap. XLVII (March 19, 1802): 73–75.

33. Julian Ursyn Niemcewicz, "Journey to Niagara, 1805," Metchie J. E. Budka, ed., *New-York Historical Society Quarterly* 74 (January 1960): 102–104.

34. Carl Benn, *The Iroquois in the War of 1812* (Toronto: University of Toronto Press, 1998), 65. Charles M. Snyder, ed., *Red and White on the*

New York Frontier; A Struggle for Survival: Insights from the Papers of Erastus Granger, Indian Agent (Harrison, New York: Harbor Hill Books, 1978), 44, 56, 57. Wallace, *The Death and Rebirth of the Seneca*, 294–296.

35. "John Sky's Speech," *National Aegis* (April 8, 1812): 4.

36. Ibid.

37. Ibid.

38. Ibid.

39. Ibid.

40. For the death of the elder and more well-known Chief Little Beard in 1806, see Orasmus Turner, *History of the Pioneer Settlement of Phelps and Gorham's Purchase and Morris Reserve* (Rochester: William Alling, 1851), 328.

41. "List of Indian Volunteers Who Served in the War of 1812 and Who Volunteered at Tonawanda Reservation"; and "Minutes of Old Soldier Meeting," November 3, 4, 5, 1873, Ely S. Parker MSS., APS; Arthur C. Parker, "The Senecas in the War of 1812," *Proceedings of the New York State Historical Association* XV (1916): 78–90; New York State Adjutant General's Office, *Index of Awards: Soldiers of the War of 1812* (Baltimore, Maryland: Genealogical Publishing Co., 1969), 569–570.

42. John Sky I, #10,078 Award Application, War of 1812 Claims, Series A3352, Box 39, Folder 16, NYSA. John Sky died in 1819 and his son John Sky I, who lived into the 1850s, should not be confused with his father.

43. Lockwood R. Doty, ed., *History of Livingston County, New York* (Jackson, Michigan: W. J. Van Deusen, 1905), 43.

44. Benn, *The Iroquois in the War of 1812*, 65.

45. Minutes of a council at Buffalo Creek, July 25, 1813, DHI, MR45.

46. Parker, "The Senecas in the War of 1812," 78–90.

47. Snyder, ed., *Red and White on the New York Frontier*, 71, 81–85.

48. *Whipple Report*, 211–213. For more on this "sale," see Hauptman, "Who Owns Grand Island (Erie County, New York)?" *Oklahoma City University Law Review* 23 (Spring/Summer 1998): 151–174. In 2002, the federal courts dismissed the Seneca claim based on a misreading of history and making a distinction between Indian ownership and "aboriginal title." *Seneca Nation of Indians and Tonawanda Band of Seneca Indians* vs. *The State of New York, the New York State Thruway Authority, et al.* 206 F. Su 2d 448 (Western District of N.Y., 2002).

49. For canal building's impact on the Senecas, see Laurence M. Hauptman, "Ditches, Defense, and Dispossession: The Iroquois and the Rise of the Empire State," *New York History* 79 (October 1998): 325–358.

50. For a British Quaker woman's account of the troupe and their many travails, see Elizabeth Fothergill's memoir, "Account of Seven American Indians of the Senecas Who Visited York, England in the Month of May, 1818," BV-Seneca MSS., NYHS.

51. Quoted in Carolyn Foreman, *Indians Abroad* (Norman, Oklahoma: University of Oklahoma Press, 1943), 121–122.

52. Quoted in Ibid., 124.

53. Ibid., 121–124.

54. Estwick Evans, *A Pedestrious Tour of Four Thousand Miles, Through the Western States and Territories During the Winter and Spring of 1818* (Concord, New Hampshire: 1819), 52, 57. Reprinted in: Clayton Mau, ed., *The Development of Central and Western New York: From the Arrival of the White Man to the Eve of the Civil War* (Rochester, New York: DuBois Press, 1944), 223–224.

55. Alden, *An Account of Sunday Missions*, 83, 98–105. Sky died soon after. See his obituary in *New York Daily Advertiser*, February 24, 1819, 2.

56. New York State Legislature. Assembly. *Doc. No. 90: Report Relative to Indian Affairs*, March 4, 1819, DHI, MR46.

Chapter 2. The Awakener

1. For the best works on Red Jacket, see Christopher Densmore, *Red Jacket: Iroquois Diplomat and Orator* (Syracuse, New York: Syracuse University Press, 1999); and Granville Ganter, ed., *The Collected Speeches of Sagoyewatha, or Red Jacket* (Syracuse, New York: Syracuse University Press, 2006). See also Ganter's recent article "Red Jacket and the Decolonization of Republican Virtue," *American Indian Quarterly* 31 (Fall 2007): 559–581. For earlier studies, see Parker, *Red Jacket*; and Henry S. Manley, "Red Jacket's Last Campaign," *New York History* 31 (April 1950): 149–168.

2. Densmore, *Red Jacket*, xv; Arthur C. Parker, *Parker on the Iroquois*, William N. Fenton, ed. (Syracuse: Syracuse University Press, 1968), 68n2; Laurence M. Hauptman, Tonawanda and Seneca field notes, February–May 2009.

3. Parker, *Parker on the Iroquois*, 68n2; Parker, *The Life of General Ely S. Parker*, 202.

4. Wallace, *The Death and Rebirth of the Seneca*, 182–183.

5. Densmore, *Red Jacket*, xv. For his speeches, see Ganter, ed., *The Collected Speeches of Sagoyewatha*.

6. Parker, *The Life of General Ely S. Parker*, 51, 214–218, 264–268. See chapter 5n55.

7. *Whipple Report*, 134–141.

8. Conable, "A Steady Enemy, 1–5, 49–55.

9. Ibid.; *Whipple Report*, 172–189.

10. Robert Troup to Jasper Parrish, August 24, 1810, DHI, MR45.

11. David A. Ogden to Bishop J. H. Hobart, December 14, 1814, DHI, MR45.

12. For the relationship of transportation development to rising land speculation and sales, see Nathan Miller, *Enterprise of a Free People: Aspects of Economic Development in New York State During the Canal Era, 1792–1838* (Ithaca, New York: Cornell University Press, 1962).

13. I have developed this point in my *Conspiracy of Interests*. For a summary, see my "Ditches, Defense and Dispossession," 325–358. In his classic on the canal system, Noble E. Whitford lists the names of the original state commissioners who oversaw the building of the canal system, almost all of whom were involved in land speculation. See *History of the Canal System of the State of New York* (Albany: Brandow Printing, 1906), II: 1130–1131.

14. David A. Ogden to the sachems, chiefs, and warriors of the Seneca Nation, May 26, 1817, DHI, MR45.

15. David A. Ogden to John C. Calhoun, March 16, 1819; Calhoun to Ogden, March 24, 1819; Calhoun to Morris S. Miller, March 27, 1819; in: John C. Calhoun, *The Papers of John C. Calhoun*, W. Edwin Hemphill, ed. (Columbia, South Carolina: University of South Carolina Press, 1969), III: 667–670, 688, 698; IV: 175–176, 216.

16. David A. Ogden Memorial to President of the United States [Monroe], ? 1819, DHI, MR46.

17. Joseph Delafield, *The Unfortified Boundary*. Robert McElroy and Thomas Riggs, eds. (New York: privately printed, 1943), 229–243; *The Collected Speeches of Sagoyewatha*, 198–219; Snyder, ed., *Red and White on the New York Frontier*, 93–95; Densmore, *Red Jacket*, 90–91.

18. For the Ogden-allied conspirators aiming to work together to defraud the Iroquois, see *Conspiracy of Interests*, 121–161.

19. Red Jacket Reply to David Ogden at Buffalo Creek, July 7–9, 1819, in: *The Collected Speeches of Sagoyewatha*, 198–219.

20. Ibid., 213–214.

21. Ibid., 215.

22. Peter B. Porter to John C. Calhoun, September 22, 1822, in: *The Papers of John C. Calhoun*, VII: 276–277.

23. Densmore, *Red Jacket*, 97.

24. Ibid., 95–98. See also Alyssa Mt. Pleasant, "After the Whirlwind: Maintaining a Haudenosaunee Place at Buffalo Creek, 1780–1825" (PhD diss., Ithaca, New York: Cornell University, 2007), 103–132. For Spencer's

later role as U.S. Secretary of War and its impact on Seneca history, see
Laurence M. Hauptman, "State's Men, Salvation Seekers and the Senecas:
The Supplemental Treaty of Buffalo Creek, 1842," *New York History* 78
(January 1997): 51–82.

25. *Laws of the State of New York* (April 22, 1822): 222.

26. The murder and trial coverage can be found in the *New York
Gazette*, August 1, 1821, 2; *Ithaca Republican Chronicle*, August 1, 1821,
3.

27. "An Indian Tried for Murder," *Eastern Argus*, April 15, 1833, 2.
In this murder by Steep Rock of his wife, the case was adjudicated off the
Tonawanda Reservation in a state court at Batavia, New York.

28. Mt. Pleasant, "After the Whirlwind," 133–175.

29. *Laws of the State of New York*, 44th sess. (March 31, 1821), chap.
CCIV, 183–185.

30. Densmore, *Red Jacket*, 92–95.

31. Jabez B. Hyde, "A Teacher Among the Senecas: Narrative of Jabez
Hyde," in: *Buffalo Historical Society Publication* VI, Frank H. Severance, ed.
(Buffalo: Buffalo Historical Society, 1903): 261n.

32. John Cumming, ed., "A Missionary Among the Senecas: The
Journal of Abel Bingham, 1822–1828," *New York History* 60 (April 1979):
157–193. For Reverend Ely Stone's influence on Tonawanda, see Armstrong,
Warrior in Two Camps, 1, 17.

33. Ibid.

34. Ibid.

35. Red Jacket to Jasper Parrish, January 18, 1821, DHI, MR46.

36. Young King and Other Deputies of the Christian Party of the
Six Nations, September 2, 1822, *Papers of John C. Calhoun*, VII: 264–265;
Porter to Calhoun, September 23, 1822; Col. Pollard, Silver Smith, Big
John, and 21 Chiefs to John C. Calhoun, ? 1820, Ibid., V: 198–199. Both
Parrish and Jones helped defraud the Senecas in 1826. For undeserved praise
of these two men, see *Buffalo Historical Society Publications* VI: 493–546.
For Jones' earlier involvement in the 1797–1802 doings and his reward,
see Ibid., 501–504; and 7 *Stat.*, 72 (June 30, 1802). For Parrish's payment
(Squaw Island) for the 1815 state "treaty," see *Laws of New York*, chap. 63
(April 5, 1816): 65–66. See also Daniel D. Tompkins to New York State
Senate, February 21, 1816, DHI, MR45.

37. Red Jacket, Jemmy Johnson, Blue Sky, Cornplanter, Blackchief,
John Sky (the Younger) to New York State Legislature, March 22, 1821,
DHI, MR46.

38. Densmore, *Red Jacket*, 104.

39. See note 36.

40. Tonawanda Council Petition to Remove Parrish and Jones and Refusal to Move to Green Bay, May 3, 1823, in: *Collected Speeches of Sagoyewatha*, 233–236.

41. Well before receiving Porter's report, Calhoun labeled the charges against Parrish as being "without foundation." Porter insisted that Chief Pollard was "entirely satisfied with the official integrity and good conduct of the Agent [Parrish]. *Papers of John C. Calhoun*, VII: 276–277, 283, 407.

42. For a fuller treatment of the "Gardeau purchase," see Hauptman, *Conspiracy of Interests*, 149–152; James M. Seaver, Comp., *A Narrative of the Life of Mrs. Mary Jemison* (1824), George H. J. Abrams, ed. (Syracuse: Syracuse University Press. Paperback reprint, 1990); Lockwood L. Doty, *History of Livingston County, New York*, 1st ed. (Geneseo, New York: Edward L. Doty, 1876), 56–103; Lockwood L. Doty, *History of Livingston County, New York*, 2nd ed. (Jackson, Michigan: W. J. Van Deusen, 1905), 2: appendixes 4 and 6; Lockwood R. Doty, *History of the Genesee County* (Chicago: S. J. Clarke, 1925), 597–598.

43. U.S. Congress. House of Representatives. *Report No. 209*, May 13, 1825, DHI, MR46.

44. Conable, "Steady Enemy," chap. 2; see also Hauptman, *Conspiracy of Interests*, 148–162.

45. *Whipple Report*, 144–150.

46. For Dr. Jacob Jemison, see William N. Fenton, ed., "Answers to Governor Cass's Questions by Jacob Jameson, a Seneca (ca. 1821–1825)," *Ethnohistory* 16 (Spring 1969): 113–119.

47. *Whipple Report*, 21, 147–150; Manley, "Red Jacket's Last Campaign," 149–162.

48. Buffalo Creek Treaty of August 30, 1826, Unratified Treaties, OIA, T494, MR8, RG75, NA.

49. Samuel Parsons and Willet Hicks to Philip Thomas, July 1, 1827, OIA, SNAR, M234, MR832, RG75, NA.

50. Manley, "Red Jacket's Last Campaign," 149–162.

51. Richard Montgomery Livingston Report to Secretary of War Peter B. Porter, December 25, 1828, OIA, SAR, M234, MR808, RG75, NA.

52. Quoted in Manley, "Red Jacket's Last Campaign," 151.

53. Quoted in Ibid., 153.

54. Oliver Forward to the President of the United States, January 30, 1827, OIA, SNAR, M234, MR832, RG75, NA.

55. Manley, "Red Jacket's Last Campaign," 155.

56. Memorial of Red Jacket and Seneca Chiefs and Principal Men to President of the United States, May 19, 1827, Oliver Forward MSS.,

BECHS; Charles Francis Adams, ed., *Memoirs of John Quincy Adams* (Philadelphia: J. B. Lippincott, 1875), 7: 484–485.

57. Seneca Petition to Governor DeWitt Clinton asking for inquiry into the 1826 Land Sale [Red Jacket et al., including Tonawandas Jemmy Johnson, Big Fire, Squire Brooks, John Sky I], March 15, 1827, OIA, SAR, M234, MR808, RG75, NA. The vote against the 1826 treaty is confirmed in Willett Hicks to Philip Thomas and Thomas Ellicott, July 1, 1827, OIA, SNAR, M234, MR832, RG75, NA.

58. Memorial of Red Jacket and Seneca Chiefs and Principal Men to President of the United States, May 19, 1827, Oliver Forward MSS., BECHS.

59. U.S. Congress. Senate. *Journal of the Executive Proceedings* (February 29, 1828), 3: 601.

60. Ibid. (April 4, 1828), 3: 603.

61. Adams, ed., *Memoirs of John Quincy Adams*, 7: 484–485.

62. Richard Montgomery Livingston Report.

Chapter 3. He Carries a Heavy Weight on His Shoulders

1. "Grand Indian Council," *Watchtower* (Cooperstown, New York), September 20, 1830, 1.

2. Tooker, *Lewis Henry Morgan on Iroquois Material Culture*, 297n12.

3. Conversation [of Lewis Henry Morgan] with Chiefs Blacksmith and Johnson, June 1, 1849, Rochester, N.Y. LHM MSS., A.M. 85, Journal Vol. 1, UR.

4. Parker, *The Life of General Ely S. Parker*, 18–20.

5. Wallace, *The Death and Rebirth of the Seneca*, 149–236.

6. Ibid.

7. Armstrong, *Warrior in Two Camps*, 8.

8. Quoted in Ibid.

9. Parker, *The Life of General Ely S. Parker*, 55, 87.

10. I have written extensively about this family before, especially Ely and Isaac Newton Parker. See Laurence M. Hauptman, *Between Two Fires: American Indians in the Civil War* (New York: Basic Books/Simon & Schuster, 1995), 161–184.

11. Lewis Henry Morgan dedicated his classic to Hasanoanda, Ely S. Parker. See *League of the Ho-de-no-sau-nee, or Iroquois*, frontispiece.

12. Wallace, *The Death and Rebirth of the Seneca*, 335–336.

13. Elisabeth Tooker, "The Iroquois since 1820," in: *Handbook of North American Indians*, 15: 452–453.

14. Elisabeth Tooker, "On the Development of the Handsome Lake Religion," 37–38.

15. Ibid., 40–41.

16. Robert E. Bieder, "The Grand Order of the Iroquois: Influences on Lewis Henry Morgan's Ethnology," *Ethnohistory* 27 (Autumn 1980): 349–361; Elisabeth Tooker, "Isaac N. Hurd's Ethnographic Studies of the Iroquois, Their Significance and Ethnographic Value," *Ethnohistory* 27 (Autumn 1980): 363–369; and Tooker, "The Structure of the Iroquois League: 141–154. See chapter 5n55.

17. *Rochester Daily American*, September 27, 1845.

18. William N. Fenton, *The Great Law and the Longhouse* (Norman, Oklahoma: University of Oklahoma Press, 1998), 8. For its importance in Iroquoian diplomacy, see William N. Fenton, "Structure, Continuity and Change in the Process of Iroquois Treaty-Making," in: *The History and Culture of Iroquois Diplomacy: An Interdisciplinary Guide to the Treaties of the Six Nations and Their League*, Francis Jennings et al., eds. (Syracuse, New York: Syracuse University Press, 1985), 3–36.

19. Fenton, *The Great Law and the Longhouse*, 6.

20. Ibid., 99, 209; Fenton, "Structure, Continuity and Change," 16–18.

21. Fenton, "Structure, Continuity and Change," 21–27.

22. Fenton, *The Great Law and the Longhouse*, 6.

23. Ibid., 27, 130, 618.

24. Tooker, "The Structure of the Iroquois League," 146–148.

25. Ibid., 150. See also Lewis Henry Morgan to Ely S. Parker, August 2, 1850, ESP MSS., BOX 3, APS.

26. Tooker, "On the Development of the Handsome Lake Religion," 41–45.

27. Bieder, "The Grand Order of the Iroquois," 347–361. The hobbyist quality of the Grand Order of the Iroquois can easily be seen. George Brush to Lewis Henry Morgan, "Moon of Gr-hon-gut, 12th day," and May 9, 1846, LHM, UR.

28. Jemmy Johnson and John Blacksmith to Lewis Henry Morgan, April 12, 1846, LHM MSS., AM85, Journal, Vol. I, UR.

29. Charles T. Porter to Henry Rowe Schoolcraft, January 10, 1846, LHM MSS., AM85, Correspondence, Box 1, Folder 7, UR.

30. Ibid.; Conable, "A Steady Enemy," 300–304.

31. Charles T. Porter to Henry Rowe Schoolcraft, January 10, 1846, HRS MSS., MR35, LC. Porter was a member of Morgan's Grand Order of the Iroquois.

32. Lewis Henry Morgan to William Medill, July 24, 1847, HRS MSS., MR36, LC.

33. Morgan, *The League of the Ho-dé-no-sau-nee*, 107.

34. See, for example, Lewis Henry Morgan to Caroline Parker, May 28, 1846, Box 2; Caroline Parker to Nicholson Parker, February 28, 1847, Box 2; Morgan to [Isaac] Newton Parker, December 19, 1849, Box 3, ESP MSS., APS. Both were attending or planning to return to the Albany Normal School. See Birr, *A Tradition of Excellence: The Sesquicentennial History of the University at Albany, State University of New York*, 34. Nicholson Parker also attended. Later, Morgan wrote recommendations for Ely Parker's efforts to become an assistant engineer on the Genesee Canal, as a commissioned officer in the American Civil War, and to be named United States Commissioner of Indian Affairs.

35. Henry Rowe Schoolcraft, *Notes on the Iroquois or Contributions to American History, Antiquities and General Ethnology* (Albany: Erastus Pease, 1847), 461.

36. Chief Blacksmith was condoled and given the league title Deonihogáhwa, replacing the deposed Little Johnson. Thomas Abler, "Seneca Moieties and Hereditary Chieftainships: The Early Nineteenth-Century Political Organization of an Iroquois Nation," *Ethnohistory* 51 (Summer 2004): 459–487, at table 2.

37. Chiefs of the Six Nations of N.Y. Indians to President Andrew Jackson, December 25, 1831, OIA, M234, SNAR, 1824–1832, MR832, RG75, NA. Jemmy Johnson was the first signatory; all the signatories appear to be Tonawandas.

38. Seneca Council Resolutions at the Onondaga Council House at Buffalo Creek, July 29, October 15, 1833. The deposed chiefs were Young King, Captain Strong, Captain Billy, Destroy Town, Seneca White, Job Pierce, John Snow, and James Stephens. OIA, M234, SNAR, MR832, RG75, NA.

39. John H. Eaton to James W. Stryker, November 30, 1830, OIA, M234, NYAR: Emigration, 1829–1851, MR597, RG75, NA.

40. James W. Stryker to Elbert Herring, November 12, 1833, OIA, M234, SNAR, MR832, RG75, NA.

41. Indian Petition (Chiefs Big Kettle, Johnson, etc.) to Remove James Stryker, February 5, 1834, OIA, M234, SNAR, MR832, RG75, NA.

42. Articles of Agreement between T. L. Ogden and Joseph Fellows and Henan Potter, Orlando Allen, and James Stryker, February 23, 1837, Indian Treaties, A00-723, BECHS. See also Conable, "A Steady Enemy," 129–138.

43. See note 40.

44. For a fuller treatment of Schermerhorn, see James W. Van Hoeven, "Salvation and Indian Removal: The Career Biography of Rev. John Freeman Schermerhorn, Indian Commissioner" (PhD diss., Nashville,

Tennessee: Vanderbilt University, 1972.). For a summary of his work on Indian removal in the Jacksonian era, see Laurence M. Hauptman, *Tribes and Tribulations: Misconceptions About American Indians and Their Histories* (Albuquerque, New Mexico: University of New Mexico Press, 1995), 39–48.

45. John F. Schermerhorn to Commissioner of Indian Affairs, May 5, 1836; Schermerhorn to Indian Office, July 12, 1836, OIA, M234, NYAR, 1824–1880, MR583, RG75, NA.

46. John F. Schermerhorn to Andrew Jackson, October 29, 1836, OIA, M234, NYAR, 1824–1880, MR583, RG75, NA.

47. John F. Schermerhorn to C. A. Harris, October 27, 1836, OIA, M234, NYAR, 1824–1880, MR583, RG75, NA.

48. 7 *Stat.*, 550 (January 15, 1838); Van Hoeven, "Salvation and Indian Removal," 264–265.

49. Silas Wright et al. (R. H. Gillet, C. C. Cambreleng, William Seymour) to Indian Office, May 10, 1836, OIA, M234, NYAR, 1824–1880, MR583, RG75, NA. Later Wright was governor of New York State and secretary of war.

50. For more on Gillet, see Laurence M. Hauptman, "Four Eastern New Yorkers and Seneca Lands: A Study in Treaty Making," *Hudson Valley Regional Review* 13 (March 1996): 11–15.

51. "[Stryker] Talks of Seneca Chiefs at a Special Meeting Held at Buffalo Creek, October 29, 1834, OIA, M234, SNAR, M832, RG75, NA.

52. Memorial of Seneca "Chiefs" at a Council at Buffalo Creek to Secretary of War Lewis Cass, January 10, 1836, OIA, M234, NYAR, 1824–1880, MR583, RG75, NA.

53. [Six Nations] Memorial to President of the United States, October 7, 1837, OIA, M234, NYAR, 1824–1880, MR583, RG75, NA.

54. 7 *Stat.*, 550 (January 15, 1838).

Chapter 4. The Compromised Treaty

1. 7 *Stat.*, 586 (May 20, 1842). After its quick approval in the United States Senate, the treaty was proclaimed by President John Tyler on August 26, 1842. The other treaties that allowed for the return or repurchase of Iroquois lands are the Pickering (Canandaigua) Treaty of 1794 and the Tonawanda Treaty of 1857.

2. Ibid.

3. This observation is based on forty years of fieldwork among the Senecas in western New York—the Seneca Nation of Indians as well as the Tonawanda Band of Senecas. I was the featured speaker at the Seneca cer-

emony commemorating this 1842 treaty on May 20, 2008, at West Seneca, New York.

4. See chap. 3; see also Manley, "Buying Buffalo from the Indians," 313–329; and Hauptman, *Conspiracy of Interests*, 175–212.

5. Ambrose Spencer to General John Armstrong, May 25, 1842, Rokeby Collection, NYHS.

6. Society of Friends (Hicksite), Executive Committee of the Yearly Meetings, *Proceedings of an Indian Council Held at the Buffalo Creek Reservation, State of New York, Fourth Month, 1842* (Baltimore: William Wooddy for the Executive Committee of the Yearly Meetings, 1842), 72–74. Despite its title, it should be noted that the council included proceedings through May 20, 1842.

7. Tonawanda protest (Jemmy Johnson, John Blacksmith, et al.) to Governor William H. Seward, June 4, 1842, William H. Seward MSS., Box 18, Folder: "Seneca," UR. Tonawanda protest (Jemmy Johnson, John Blacksmith, et al.) to Secretary of War, June 17, 1842, DHI, MR 49.

8. "From the President [Polk] of the United States Communicating a Petition of the Tonawanda Band of Seneca Indians, praying that steps may be taken to abrogate the treaties of 1838 and 1842." United States Congress. *Senate Doc. 273*. Series Set 474 (1846).

9. Society of Friends (Hicksite), *Proceedings of an Indian Council* 1842), 72.

10. Tonawanda protest to Seward, June 4, 1842; Tonawanda protest to Secretary of War, June 17, 1842.

11. Maris B. Pierce to John Canfield Spencer, April, 9, 1842, Haviland Record Room, Records of the New York Yearly Meeting. New York City. These Society of Friends Records have been transferred to the Quaker Collection at Haverford College.

12. The literature on the Society of Friends interaction with the Senecas is too extensive to cite in its entirety. For a start, see Hugh Barbour, *Quaker Crosscurrents: Three Hundred Years of Friends in the New York Yearly Meetings* (Syracuse: Syracuse University Press, 1995), 97–99, 316; Lois Barton, *A Quaker Promise Kept: Philadelphia Friends' Work with the Allegany Seneca, 1795–1960* (Eugene, Oregon: Spencer Butte Press, 1990). Rayner W. Kelsey, *Friends and the Indians, 1655–1917* (Philadelphia: Associated Committee of Friends on Indian Affairs, 1917), chap. 5 and 6. For more critical studies of the Friends, see Diane Rothenberg, "The Mothers of the Nation: Seneca Resistance to Quaker Intervention," in: *Women and Colonization: Anthropological Perspectives*, Mona Etienne and Eleanor Leacock, eds. (New York: Praeger, 1980), 63–87; Thomas S. Abler, "Friends, Factions and the Seneca Nation Revolution of 1848," *Niagara Frontier* 21 (Winter 1974):

74–79; and Robert F. Berkhofer Jr., *Salvation and the Savage: An Analysis of Protestant Missions and American Indian Response, 1787–1862* (Lexington, Kentucky: University of Kentucky Press, 1965; paperback reprint, New York: Atheneum, 1976), 56, 72–84, 104, 135–137.

13. For more on Thomas, see Albro Martin, *Railroads Triumphant: The Growth, Rejection, and Rebirth of a Vital American Force* (New York: Oxford University Press, 1992), 250; William N. Fenton, "Toward the Gradual Civilization of the Indian Natives: The Missionary and Linguistic Work of Asher Wright (1803–1875) Among the Seneca of Western New York," *Proceedings of the American Philosophical Society* 100 (December 1956): 567–581.

14. See the subagents' reports for the New York Indians, S. Osborn to T. Hartley Crawford, February 21 and March 1, 1842, OIA, NYAR, M 234, MR 584, RG 75, NA.

15. Society of Friends (Hicksite), *Proceedings of an Indian Council . . . 1842*, 59.

16. For Clay's racism toward Indians, see Adams, *The Memoirs of John Quincy Adams*, 7: 89–90. Ironically, because of his opposition to Cherokee removal, he was praised by Indians. See Robert V. Remini, *Henry Clay: Statesman for the Union* (New York: W. W. Norton and Company, 1991), 315.

17. Webster's role was noted later in the *Whipple Report*, 28–29.

18. For the Second Seminole War, see John K. Mahon, *History of the Second Seminole War, 1835–1842* (Gainesville, Florida: University of Florida Press, 1967); James W. Covington, *The Seminoles of Florida* (Gainesville, Florida: University of Florida Press, 1993), chap. 4 and 5. For the Indian issue in the political campaign of 1840, see Robert G. Gundersen, *The Log-Cabin Campaign* (Lexington, Kentucky: University of Kentucky Press, 1957), 94.

19. John Canfield Spencer was later secretary of the treasury and a failed Whig nominee to the United States Supreme Court in 1844. On the Spencer family's dealings with the Holland Land Company, see John Canfield Spencer to Gentlemen [John Townsend, Benjamin Hale, et al.], July 10, 1822, DC13209, NYSL, MD; and Paul D. Evans, *The Holland Land Company* (Buffalo: Buffalo Historical Society, Publication XXVIII, 1924), 344–345, 374–378, 384–385. For Spencer's anti-Masonry, see Elizabeth B. Haigh, "New York Antimasons, 1826–1833" (PhD diss., Rochester, New York: University of Rochester, 1980), 239–326.

20. Haigh, "New York Antimasons," 237–244. More information of Spencer can be found in Robert A. Trennert Jr., *Indian Traders on the Middle Border: The House of Ewing, 1827–1854* (Lincoln, Nebraska: University of Nebraska Press, 1981), 103, 106–109, 122; and Ronald M. Satz,

American Indian Policy in the Jacksonian Era (Lincoln, Nebraska: University of Nebraska Press, 1975), 265–278.

21. Quoted in Satz, *American Indian Policy in the Jacksonian Era*, 265–268.

22. Ibid., 211–236, and Satz' "Thomas Hartley Crawford," in: *The Commissioners of Indian Affairs, 1824–1977*, Robert M. Kvasnicka and Herman Viola, eds. (Lincoln, Nebraska: University of Nebraska Press, 1979), 24–25.

23. Society of Friends (Hicksite), *Proceedings of an Indian Council . . . 1842*, 30.

24. There is no full-scale biography on Ambrose Spencer. Some biographical materials were found in the *DAB*, the *Biographical Directory of Congress, 1789–1949*, in Haigh's study of anti-Masonry, and in the writings of Jabez Hammond.

25. 20 *Johns* 188 (1822).

26. Ibid. Chancellor James Kent reversed the decision on appeal. In this case, and in an earlier one (*Jackson v. Wood*), and in his *Commentaries*, Kent helped predict Marshall's decisions in the later Cherokee cases. The Chancellor argued that because of their state of "dependence," the Indian tribes within the territorial jurisdiction of the government of the United States must have the right to protection, that the United States had the "exclusive right of extinguishing the Indian title by possession," and that the "Indian possession is not to be taken from them, or disturbed without their free consent, by fair purchase, except it be by force of arms in the event of a just and necessary war." James Kent, *Commentaries on American Law* (New York: O. Halsted, 1826; New York: Da Capo Press, 1971), 3: 311–312.

27. Joseph C. Burke, "The Cherokee Cases: A Study in Law, Politics, and Morality," *Stanford Law Review* 21 (February 1969): 506–508, 511, 506n31. Jeremiah Evarts, *Cherokee Removal: The "William Penn" Essays and Other Writings*, Francis Paul Prucha, ed. (Knoxville, Tennessee: University of Tennessee Press, 1981), 16 (introduction by Prucha).

28. Satz, *American Indian Policy in the Jacksonian Era*, 159–160, 259, 283n28.

29. T. Hartley Crawford to Ambrose Spencer, February 17, 1842, DHI, MR 49.

30. Ambrose Spencer to T. Hartley Crawford, March 1, 1842, DHI, MR 49.

31. See, for example, the reprint of several of these Hicksite pamphlets from 1840–1842: *The Case of The Seneca Indians* (Stanfordville, New York: Earl Coleman, 1979).

32. For Pierce, see Howard A. Vernon, "Maris Bryant Pierce," in: *Indian Lives: Essays on Nineteenth- and Twentieth-Century Native American Leaders*, L. G. Moses and Raymond Wilson, eds. (Albuquerque: University of New Mexico Press, 1985). For Pierce's opposition during the deliberations of the Treaty of Buffalo Creek (1838), see Frank Severance, ed., *Journals of Henry A. S. Dearborn* (Buffalo: Buffalo Historical Society Publications, 1904), 7: 92, 136. For one of Pierce's speeches against the Treaty of Buffalo Creek of 1838, see M. B. Pierce, *Address on the Present Condition and Prospects of the Aboriginal Inhabitants of North America with Particular Reference to the Seneca Nation* [speech at the Baptist Church in Buffalo, August 28, 1838] (Buffalo: Steele's Press, 1838).

33. Maris B. Pierce to Abraham Bell, January 29, December 10, December 18, December 28, 1841; Pierce to Jacob Harvey, February 19, June 18, 1841, April 19, 1842; Pierce to John Canfield Spencer, April 9, 1842. Records of the New York Yearly Meeting, Haviland Record Room, New York City. Pierce to T. Hartley Crawford, January 15, 1842; Pierce and Henry Two Guns to William Henry Harrison, early March, March 6, 1841; Pierce to John Bell, April 14, 1841; Pierce et al. to Daniel Kurtz, October 1, October 11, 1841, OIA, NYAR, M234, MR 584, RG75, NA.

34. Tonawanda protest to Secretary of War, June 17, 1842; Tonawanda protest to Governor William H. Seward, June 4, 1842, William Seward MSS. Box 18, Folder: "Seneca," UR.

35. Dixon was there because on January 29 and February 24, 1841, both houses of the New York State Legislature petitioned the Congress to investigate the circumstances involving the Treaty of Buffalo Creek of 1838 and determine whether it had been voluntarily assented to by the Seneca. New York State Legislature, *Assembly Journal*. 64th Session, 1841 (Albany: Thurlow Weed State Printer, 1841), 222, 408.

36. Society of Friends (Hicksite), *Proceedings of an Indian Council . . . 1842*, 42.

37. Ibid., 50.

38. Ibid., 6.

39. Tonawanda protest to Secretary of War, June 17, 1842; Society of Friends (Hicksite), *Proceedings of an Indian Council . . . 1842*, 27–28.

40. Maris Pierce to John Canfield Spencer, April 9, 1842.

39. Society of Friends (Hicksite), *Proceedings of an Indian Council . . . 1842*, 60–61.

41. Ibid., 5–6, 11–12.

42. Ibid., 61. See also 40, 44, 51, 60, 72.

43. Ibid., 37–55, 61–62, 68–69, 72.

44. Ibid., 62.
45. Ibid., 73–74.

Chapter 5. The Activist Sachem

1. "Death of John Blacksmith," *Rochester American* (reprinted in *The Farmers' Cabinet* [New Hampshire], May 8, 1851), 2.

2. For a thorough discussion of this term, see William N. Fenton, "Northern Iroquoian Culture Patterns," in: *Handbook of North American Indians*, 15: 319–321. Fenton was aided by Ives Goddard, Floyd Lounsbury, Hanni Woodbury, and Michael Foster in this endeavor.

3. Fenton, *The Great Law and the Longhouse*, 6, 8, 12, 135–140, 191–202. Elisabeth Tooker, "The League of the Iroquois: Its History, Politics, and Ritual," in: *Handbook of North America Indians*, 15: 418–448.

4. See note 3.

5. Ibid.

6. Asher Wright, Minutes of the Six Nations Council at Onondaga, July 17, 1839, ESP MSS., Box 1, APS.

7. Thomas Abler, "Seneca Moieties and Hereditary Chieftainships: The Early Nineteenth-Century Political Organization of an Iroquois Nation," *Ethnohistory* 51 (Summer, 1004): 472; Fenton, *The Great Law and the Longhouse*, 193–194, 712; Armstrong, *Warrior in Two Camps*, 49.

8. For the Iroquois skill in "real politique" diplomacy, see Wallace, *The Death and Rebirth of the Seneca*, 111–114. See also Francis Jennings, *The Ambiguous Iroquois Empire* (New York: W. W. Norton, 1984); Daniel Richter, *The Ordeal of the Longhouse: The Peoples of the Iroquois League in the Era of European Colonization* (Chapel Hill, North Carolina: University of North Carolina Press, 1992).

9. Treaty of Fort Stanwix 7 *Stat.*, 15 (October 22, 1784).

10. John Blacksmith's Pension Application No. 10,043 and 13,983, New York State Division of Military and Naval Affairs, Adjutant General's Office, Claims, Applications and Awards for Service in the War of 1812, NYSA, Albany. Please note that these pension applications were filed by his widow Susan in the late 1850s. For Tonawanda Seneca involvement in the War of 1812, see chap. 1. See also Report of Indian Subagent Marcus Johnson to the Commissioner of Indian Affairs, September 22, 1853, OIA, NYAR, M234, MR588, RG75, NA.

11. 7 *Stat.*, 586 (May 20, 1842).

12. Nicholson Parker Address, 1842, ESP MSS., Box 1, APS. Ely S. Parker referred to Thomas as "a d--n rascal" and, in 1853, he warned the

commissioner of Indian affairs that Thomas was the Tonawandas' enemy and not a spokesman for his community. Ely S. Parker to Nicholson H. Parker, July 15, 1846, ESP MSS., Box 2, APS; Ely S. Parker to George Manypenny, July 18, 1853, NYAR, M234, MR588, RG75, NA.

13. Orasmus H. Marshall, "Narrative of the Expedition of Marquis De Denonville, Against the Senecas in 1687," *Collections of the New-York Historical Society* 2, 2d. ser. (1848): 161–162. Ely S. Parker to Charles Mix, OIA, NYAR, M234, MR588, RG75, NA; Robert E. Bieder and Christopher Plant, "Annuity Censuses as a Source for Historical Research: The 1858 and 1869 Tonawanda Annuity Censuses," *American Indian Culture and Research Journal* 5 (1981): 33–46.

14. Horace Gay and Ira Cook, Appraisal Report to the Secretary of War, March 31, 1849, OIA, NYAR, M234, MR587, RG75, NA.

15. Henry R. Schoolcraft, *Notes on the Iroquois or Contributions to American History, Antiquities and General Ethnology* (Albany: Erastus H. Pease and Co., 1847; paperback reprint, Kila, Montana: Kessinger, 2006), 461–468 (Jemmy Johnson) and 451–452, 461 (John Blacksmith). Tooker, *Lewis H. Morgan on Iroquois Material Culture*, 4. For Jemmy Johnson, see Lewis Henry Morgan, *The League of the Ho-de-no-sau-nee, or Iroquois*, 230–231.

16. Schoolcraft, *Notes on the Iroquois*, 461. See the cover illustration of this book.

17. Ibid., 451–452.

18. Cf. Conable, "A Steady Enemy," 296–305.

19. N. L. Benton [New York State Secretary of State] to Henry Rowe Schoolcraft, June 25, 1845, HRS MSS., MR35, LC.

20. Quoted in: Henry Rowe Schoolcraft, *Notes on the Iroquois or Contributions to American History, Antiquities and General Ethnology* (Albany: Erastus H. Pease, 1847), 8.

21. Schoolcraft's statement in New York State, *Indian Census of 1845*, Part VIII: Tonawanda, NYSA. Blacksmith feared that the census—collection of data by outsiders—was somehow related to the carrying out of the Treaty of 1842. *ARCIA*, 1846, 97–98.

22. I examined over fifty petitions presented to United States and New York State governmental officials in the period of 1838 to 1851, the latter the year of Chief Blacksmith's death. On most of the petitions/memorials from 1843 onward, Blacksmith's name is placed above that of Chief Jemmy Johnson. See, for example, Tonawanda Chiefs to President John Tyler, February 1, July 12, 1843, January 26, April 16, 1844, OIA, NYAR, M234, MR585, RG75, NA. Tonawanda Chiefs to President James Polk, May 7, 1846; Tonawanda Chiefs to Commissioner of Indian Affairs, April 1, 1846, OIA, NYAR, M234, MR586, RG75, NA; Tonawanda Chiefs to

President Zachary Taylor, March 15, June 23, 1849, Tonawanda Chiefs to Secretary of the Interior Thomas Ewing, March 8, September 28, 1849, OIA, NYAR, M234, MR587, RG75, NA. In a petition sent to Washington on August 27, 1844, Blacksmith is listed as "Head Chief." Tonawanda Chiefs to the Secretary of War, August 27, 1844, OIA, NYAR, M234, MR585, RG75, NA.

23. The Society of Friends (Hicksite), *The Case of the Seneca Indians in the State of New York Illustrated by Facts*, 116.

24. For their united stand, see Ibid., 120.

25. Ibid., 137–139.

26. Ibid., 124–125.

27. Henry A. S. Dearborn, *Journals of Henry A. S. Dearborn*, Frank Severance, ed., in: *Publications of the Buffalo Historical Society* 7 (1904): 204–205.

28. John Blacksmith and Lewis Poodry [Tonawanda Chiefs] to President William Henry Harrison, January 25, 1841; see also T. L. Ogden and Joseph Fellows to John Bell [Secretary of War], June 8, 1841, OIA, NYAR, M234, MR584, RG75, NA.

29. Petition of Tonawanda Seneca Women to President John Tyler, March 14, 1841, OIA, NYAR, M234, MR584, RG75, NA. For more information about this petition, see note in Appendix I.

30. Thomas Ludlow Ogden and Joseph Fellows to John Bell, June 8, 1841, Joseph Fellows MSS., Box 2, Folder: Indian Reservation Papers Letters Relating to Reservations, CU.

31. Nicholson Parker Address, 1842, ESP MSS., Box 1, APS; Tonawanda Chiefs Protest to President John Tyler, June 1, 1842, February 1, 1843, OIA, NYAR, M234, MR584, RG75, NA. In this letter of June 1, 1842, they refer to the 1842 treaty as the "compromised treaty."

32. 7 *Stat.*, 586 (May 20, 1842).

33. *ARCIA*, 1843: 4.

34. Tonawanda Council of Chiefs to President Tyler, January 9, July 12, 1843, March 30, April 21, 1844; Tonawanda Council of Chiefs to Secretary of War, December 30, 1843, OIA, NYAR, M234, MR585, RG75, NA.

35. Tonawanda Council of Chiefs to President Tyler, January 9, 1843, OIA, M34, MR585, RG75, NA.

36. Osborn gave the false impression to the commissioner of Indian affairs that the Tonawandas would eventually agree to leave their homes and "remove quietly" to join their Seneca kin at Allegany and Cattaraugus. *ARCIA*, 1843: 184.

37. The incident of June 19 was reported in Tonawanda Council of Chiefs to President Tyler, July 12, 1843, OIA, NYAR, M234, MR585, RG75, NA.

38. Ibid.

39.Ira Cook and Thomas Love to T. Hartley Crawford [Commissioner of Indian Affairs]. December 28, 1843, OIA, NYAR, M234, MR585, RG75, NA.

40. Tonawanda Council of Chiefs to President Tyler, March 30, April 21, 1844, OIA, NYAR, M234, MR585, RG75, NA.

41. Thomas Ludlow Ogden to Secretary of War John Spencer, May 8, June 5, 1843, OIA, NYAR, M234, MR584, RG75, NA; Ogden to Spencer, May 8, 1844, Ogden to Commissioner of Indian Affairs T. Hartley Crawford, April 16, 1844, Ogden to Secretary of War James Porter, January 13, 1844, OIA, NYAR, M234, MR584, RG75, NA. When Ogden died in 1844, Joseph Fellows became the Ogden Land Company's chief lobbyist. See Joseph Fellows to Commissioner of Indian Affairs, May 14, 1846, OIA, NYAR, M234, MR586, RG75, NA.

42. Tonawanda Chiefs to the Secretary of War, August 27, 1844.

43. Tonawanda Chiefs to President Tyler, April 16, 1844.

44. "To the Public"—advertisement by John Blacksmith, Jemmy Johnson, and eleven other Tonawanda chiefs, *Spirit of the Times*, June 19, 1844. See Appendix II.

45. Chiefs John Blacksmith and Jemmy Johnson, August 20, 1844, 1844, OIA, NYAR, M234, MR585, RG75, NA.

46. See, for example, *Spirit of the Times*, March 31, 1846.

47. "Council of the Seneca Nation," *Buffalo Commercial Advertiser*, August 27, 1845, 3, found in OIA, NYAR, M234, MR586, RG75, NA.

49. See chap. 7.

50. Previously Governor Wright had said that he had no power to intervene in the controversy. William C. Bouck to chiefs Blacksmith and Jemmy Johnson, June 17, 1844, ESP MSS., APS. Wright later repeated this point to the Tonawanda chiefs. Wright to Tonawanda Chiefs, March 4, 1845, DHI, MR 49. The chiefs also approached the New York State Legislature but without success from 1846 to 1851. See chiefs Jesse Spring and William Parker to Ely S. Parker, with petition of Tonawanda chiefs, headmen and warriors, May 8, 1846, DHI, MR 49.

51. Tonawanda Council of Chiefs to Governor Silas Wright, February 22, 1845, ESP MSS., Box 1, APS. See also Tonawanda Council of Chiefs to Governor Silas Wright, November 9, 1846; Nicholson Parker Memorandum, June 12(?), 1846, ESP MSS., Box 2, APS.

52. R. B. Warren, a friend of Ely S. Parker, earlier warned the Tonawandas about Wright and his previous involvement in pushing the Buffalo Creek Treaty of 1838, labeling the governor as a two-faced "snake in the grass." R. B. Warren to Ely S. Parker, July 22, 1846, ESP MSS., Box 2, APS.

53. Tonawanda Council of Chiefs to President James Polk, May 7, 1846, OIA, NYAR, M234, MR586, RG75, NA.

54. Armstrong, *Warrior in Two Camps*, 49–50.

55. The late Elisabeth Tooker identifies Ely S. Parker's mother Elizabeth as the niece of Jemmy Johnson. Hence, he was a grand-uncle to Parker. Tooker, *Lewis Henry Morgan on Iroquois Material Culture*, 62. Jaré Cardinal, the director of the Seneca-Iroquois National Museum, who has spent a quarter of a century collecting Tonawanda genealogy, confirms this relationship. Jaré Cardinal to Laurence Hauptman, p.c., August 2, 2010. Arthur C. Parker states that his relative Jemmy Johnson (Sos-he-o-wa) was Caroline Parker's and Ely S. Parker's grandfather. Arthur C. Parker, *The Life of General Ely S. Parker*, 31. I do not think that Parker made a mistake. I believe that the distinguished Arthur C. Parker, who as of Seneca ancestry, was honoring his ancestor with this designation since "grandfather" is often applied as a fictive term by the Senecas to honor revered elders. I think Deborah Holler for pointing out Jemmy Johnson's relationship to Caroline and Ely S. Parker.

Chapter 6. The Runner

1. Tonawanda Council of Chiefs, List of Expenditures "in defense of national rights" from 1838 to 1847, October 30, 1847, ESP MSS., Box 2, APS.

2. *ARCIA*, 1847/1848: 171.

3. For the role of "runners," see Morgan, *The League of the Ho-dé-no-sau-nee, or Iroquois*, 109–110; and Laurence M. Hauptman, "Samuel George (1795–1873): A Study of Onondaga Indian Conservatism," *New York History* 70 (January 1989): 9–10.

4. Armstrong, *Warrior in Two Camps*, 1–24; Parker, *The Life of General Ely S. Parker*, 50–70.

5. Morgan, *The League of the Ho-de-no-sau-nee, or Iroquois*, 109–110.

6. For the life of one modern-day runner, see "Joyondawde Lee A. Lyons, Wolf Clan, Seneca Nation," *Akwesasne Notes* 18 (Midwinter 1986): 3. In July 1984, I attended ceremonies at the Cattaraugus Indian Reservation, at which time Iroquois runners were sent cross-country to the site of the Olympic Games in Los Angeles. For wampum's use in diplomacy, see Mary Druke, "Iroquois Treaties: Common Forms, Varying Interpretations," in: *The History and Culture of Iroquois Diplomacy: An Interdisciplinary Guide to the Treaties of the Six Nations and Their League*, Francis Jennings, William N. Fenton, et al., eds. (Syracuse: Syracuse University Press, 1985), 88–98; Michael K. Foster, "Another Look at the Function of Wampum in Iroquois-White Councils," in: *The History and Culture of Iroquois Diplomacy*, Jennings, Fenton, et al., eds., 99–114.

7. Armstrong, *Warrior in Two Camps*, 31, 50–51.

8. Ibid., 1–24.

9. Ibid., 16. Fenton, *The Great Law and the Longhouse*, 28–29.

10. Parker, *The Life of General Ely S. Parker*, 189–190. Parker refers to Spencer Cone's "blunder" but does not identify the nature of the blunder. Despite this family split, Ely continued to correspond with his brother, and Spencer Cone was later reconciled with his family. See Ely S. Parker to S. H. Cone, June 8, 1846, ESP MSS., Box 2, APS.

11. Ely S. Parker Diary (excerpt), May 18–21, 1846; Parker Diary, January 1–13, 1847, ESP MSS., Box 2, APS. He had complete support of the Tonawanda chiefs and he and his brother Nicholson were reporting their every move. See Nicholson H. Parker Memorandum, June 12 (?), 1846, ESP MSS., Box 2, APS; Tonawanda Chiefs to Ely S. Parker, July 15, 1846, ESP MSS.

12. Ely S. Parker to Reuben B. Warren, January 14, 1846, RBW MSS., WHS.

13. Ely S. Parker to Reuben B. Warren, January 27, 1846, RBW MSS., WHS.

14. Ely S. Parker to Reuben B. Warren, March 22, 1846, RBW MSS., WHS.

15. Ibid.

16. Ely S. Parker to Reuben B. Warren, May 9, 1846, RBW MSS., WHS.

17. Ely S. Parker to President James Polk, May 18, 1846; Nicholson Parker to Ely S. Parker, May 7, 1846; Tonawanda Council of Chiefs to President James Polk, May 7, 1846, OIA, M234, MR585, RG75, NA; Ely S. Parker Diary Entry, May 18 and 21, 1846, ESP MSS., Box 2, APS; Ely S. Parker to Reuben B. Warren, May 19, 1846, RBW MSS., WHS.

18. Ely S. Parker to Reuben B. Warren, June 10, 1846, RBW MSS., WHS.

19. Ely S. Parker to Reuben B. Warren, June 25, 1846, RBW MSS., WHS.

20. Ely S. Parker to Reuben B. Warren, July 10, 1846, RBW MSS., WHS.

21. Ely S. Parker to Reuben B. Warren, July 17, 1846, RBW MSS., WHS.

22. For their continued support of Parker, see Tonawanda Council of Chiefs letter of support to Ely S. Parker, July 15, 1846, ESP MSS., Box 2, APS.

23. See note 11.

24. John Blacksmith and Jemmy Johnson to Ely S. Parker, January 25, 1847, ESP MSS., Box 2, APS.

25. Ely S. Parker to Reuben B. Warren, January 8, 1847, RBW MSS., WHS.

26. Ibid.

27. Ely S. Parker to Reuben B. Warren, January 29, 1847, RBW MSS., WHS.

28. United States Congress, Senate Committee on Indian Affairs, *Report* on whether "Tonawanda band of the Seneca tribe of Indians may be exempted from the operation of the treaty of the 20th May, 1842," U.S. Senate Document No. 156, 29th Cong., 2d sess. (February 19, 1847), 1–2.

29. Ely S. Parker to Reuben B. Warren, July 11, 1847, RBW MSS., WHS.

30. See chap. 5.

31. For Schoolcraft and the Grand Order of the Iroquois, see Lewis Henry Morgan to Henry Rowe Schoolcraft, February 25, 1845; Schoolcraft to My Brothers, May 10, 1845; Morgan to Schoolcraft, May 21, 1845; Morgan to Schoolcraft, July 24, 1847, HRS MSS., MR26, LC; Schoolcraft to Morgan, May 7, 1846, LHM MSS., AM85, UR. For Schoolcraft's efforts to secure a new federal position based on his work on the Iroquois, including the Census of 1845, see Schoolcraft to Senator Folsom, George Folsom MSS., Box: 1844–1845, NYHS; Schoolcraft to John Romeyn Brodhead, May 22, 1847, Misc. MSS.; Schoolcraft, Henry Rowe, Folder 1, Re: Indian tribes, nd, 1835–1862, NYHS.

32. Ely S. Parker to Henry Rowe Schoolcraft, May 2, 1846, LHM MSS., Correspondence Series, Box 1, Folder 8, UR.

33. Henry Rowe Schoolcraft to Ely S. Parker, May 7, 1846, ESP MSS., Box 2, APS.

34. Ely S. Parker to Henry Rowe Schoolcraft, May 31, 1847, HRS MSS., MR36, LC.

35. Ely S. Parker to Henry Rowe Schoolcraft, April 10, 1848, ESP MSS., Box 2, APS.

36. Henry Rowe Schoolcraft to Ely S. Parker, March 11, 1849, ESP MSS., Box 3, APS.

37. Armstrong, *Warrior in Two Camps*, 36.

38. Ely S. Parker, "Notes on the Road," January 18, 1848, ESP MSS., Box 2, APS.

39. Ely S. Parker to Reuben B. Warren, November 11, 1847, RBW MSS., WHS.

40. Ibid.

41. Lewis Henry Morgan to Ely S. Parker, December 14, 1848, ESP MSS., Box 2, APS.

42. For Parker's outstanding military career, see Hauptman, *Between Two Fires*, 161–184. Parker received praise for his brief service in the militia.

See H. S. Fairchild to Ely S. Parker, August 29, 1854, ESP MSS., Box 4, APS.

43. "Death of John Blacksmith," 2.

44. Armstrong, *Warrior in Two Camps*, 44–60.

Chapter 7. The Whig Mouthpiece

1. For Brown's brief on behalf of the Tonawandas, see U.S. Senate Document No. 156 (February 19, 1847), 15–193. William Linn Brown to Tonawanda Indians, April 22, 1846, ESP MSS., Box 2, APS; Brown to Senator A. H. Sevier, June 2, 1846; Tonawanda Chiefs to Silas Wright, November 9, 1846, ESP MSS., Box 2, APS.

2. John Vance, "Martindale, John Henry," in: *Dictionary of American Biography* (New York: Charles Scribner's Sons, 1933), 12: 349–350. For Henry F. Martindale, see *Biographical Directory of Congress, 1774–1949* (Washington, D.C.: U.S. Government Printing Office, 1949).

3. George W. Cullum, *Biographical Register of the Officers and Graduates of the United States Military Academy at West Point, New York, from Its Establishment, March 16, 1802 to the Army Re-organization of 1866–1867* (New York: D. Van Nostrand, 1868): Class of 1835, 588. These statistics are gleaned from Ibid. For the resignations, see United States Congress, House of Representatives, *Report* by R. Jones, Adjutant General, to Benjamin F. Butler, Secretary of War: *Statement of the Number of Company Officers of the Army in Service Against the Creek and Seminole Indians in Florida in 1836; the Number and Rank of Those Who Resigned*, 24th Cong., 2d sess. (1837).

4. See Martindale's arguments in favor of taxing the Indians while serving as New York State attorney general. *The New York Indians*, 72 US 761 (May 16, 1867).

5. F. W. Beers, ed., *Gazetteer and Biographical Record of Genesee County, N.Y., 1788–1890* (Syracuse: J. W. Vose, 1890), 58–60.

6. "Mass Meeting for the Indians," *Spirit of the Times*, March 31, 1846.

7. Ibid.

8. Ibid.

9. Nicholson H. Parker Memorandum, June 12 (?), 1846, ESP MSS., Box 2, APS.

10. *Blacksmith v. Fellows*, 4 N.Y. 401, New York Court of Appeals, 1852, traces the history of the case from 1846.

11. *John Blacksmith v. Joseph Fellows and Robert Kendle*, October 13, 1847, Circuit Court Records, 1834–1854, Genesee County Court Records, Genesee County Clerk's Office, Batavia, New York.

12. For examples of how the Tonawanda chiefs used the case as a delaying tactic, see Tonawanda Council of Chiefs to President of the United States, March 15, 1849; Tonawanda Council of Chiefs to Commissioner of Indian Affairs, June 23, 1849; [Martindale] "Brief and Protest on Behalf of the Indians," March 26, 1849, OIA, NYAR, M234, MR587, RG75, NA; *ARCIA*, 1851: 267. See also Conable, "A Steady Enemy," 296.

13. For example, Joseph Fellows to Commissioner of Indian Affairs Medill, April 14, May 14, 1846, OIA, NYAR, M234, MR586, RG75, NA. For the countersuits, see note 14 See also, for example, *Joseph Fellows and Robert Kendle v. John Blacksmith*, February 28, 1849, Genesee County Court Records, Miscellaneous Filings, F 1846–1873, Genesee County Clerk's Office, Batavia, New York.

14. *ARCIA*, 1847/1848: 171.

15. Ibid.

16. Armstrong, *Warrior in Two Camps*, 42–43. For example, *Isaac Doctor v. Philander Filkens*; *Tommy Hill v. Asa Cutler*; *David Printup v. Philander Filkens*, October 17, 1846, Genesee County Court Records, Genesee County Court of Pleas, Civil Filings A–F (1847), Genesee County Clerk's Office, Batavia, New York.

17. Ely S. Parker to [Isaac] Newton Parker, June 22, 1852, ESP MSS., Box 3, APS.

18. New York State *Statutes*. Chap. XCII (April 10, 1813): 155 ["An Act Relative to the Different Tribes and Nations of Indians Within This State"]; Tonawanda Chiefs to Governor Silas Wright, November 9, 1846, ESP MSS., Box 2, APS (relative to 1821 state law).

19. Tonawanda Chiefs to Ely S. and Nicholson H. Parker, July 15, 1846; Nicholson H. Parker to Ely S. Parker, May 19, June 11, 1846, June 14, 1848, ESP MSS., Box 2, APS. Armstrong, *Warrior in Two Camps*, 38.

20. Nicholson H. Parker to Ely S. Parker, May 19, June 11, 1846; Ely S. Parker to Spencer Cone, June 8, 1846; Spencer Cone to Ely S. Parker, November 26, 1848, ESP MSS., Box 2; R. B. Warren to Ely S. Parker, January 16, February 21, 1849, ESP MSS., Box 3, APS.

21. Ely S. Parker to Spencer Cone, June 8, 1846.

22. John H. Martindale, "In the Matter of the Tonawanda Indians: Brief and Protest on Behalf of the Indians," March 26, 1849, OIA, M234, NYAR, MR588, RG75, NA.

23. Spencer Cone to Ely S. Parker, November 26, 1848, ESP MSS., Box 2, APS; R. B. Warren to Ely S. Parker, January 16, 1849, ESP MSS., Box 3, APS; Ely S. Parker affidavit to R. H. Shankland, December 30, 1848, OIA, NYAR, M234, MR587, RG75, NA. Ely S. Parker even suggested that he feared that Wadsworth and the other company directors were determined

to go further with forcing the Indians to accept the appraisers' reports, "even if they resort to killing."

24. Conable, "A Steady Enemy," 302–303. The white tenants who challenged the Van Rensselaers dubbed themselves as "Indians." For the Van Rensselaer tenant wars, see the Court of Appeals case *Rensselaer v. Hays*, 19 N.Y. 68 (March 1859). See also Charles W. McCurdy, *The Anti-War Era in New York Law and Politics, 1839–1865* (Chapel Hill, North Carolina: University of North Carolina Press, 2000). It should be noted that a Van Rensselaer was heavily involved in the operations of the Ogden Land Company. [John?] Van Rensselaer to Commissioner of Indian Affairs James Denver, July 8, 1857, OIA, NYAR, M234, MR588, RG75, NA.

25. Horace Gay to Tonawanda Chiefs, March 1, 1849; Tonawanda Chiefs' Petitions to President of the United States, March 15, June 23, 1849, OIA, NYAR, M234, MR587, RG75, NA.

26. For the Stryker frauds, see Thomas B. Goddard Report to Commissioner William Medill, December 11, 1847, Ely S. Parker to William Medill with attached statement by the chiefs, January 20, 1847, OIA, NYAR, M234, MR586, RG75, NA. For Ewing's refusal for the United States Treasury to accept "improvement money" from the Ogden Land Company, see Tonawanda Delegates to Commissioner James Denver, June 30, 1857, ESP MSS., Box 4, APS.

27. [Martindale] "Brief and Protest," March 26, 1849; John H. Martindale to Commissioner of Indian Affairs Luke Lea, May 9, 1851; Martindale to Secretary of War William Marcy, March 14, 1849, OIA, NYAR, M234, MR587, RG75, NA.

28. John H. Martindale to Tonawanda Council of Chiefs, February 16, 1849, OIA, NYAR, M234, MR587, RG75, NA.

29. Tonawanda Council of Chiefs to President of the United States [Zachary Taylor], March 15, 1849.

30. Tonawanda Council of Chiefs to Secretary of War Thomas Ewing, September 28, 1849; Tonawanda Council of Chiefs to Office of Indian Affairs, June 23, 1849, OIA, NYAR, M234, MR587, RG75, NA. Chief Blacksmith's name appears first on all of these petitions.

31. Ely S. Parker to William Parker, April 14, 1852, ESP MSS., Box 3, APS.

32. Ely S. Parker to George Manypenny, July 18, 1853, OIA, M234, NYAR, MR588, RG75, NA.

33. Ely S. Parker to George Manypenny, September 18, 1853, OIL, M234, NYAR, MR588, NA.

34. 4 N.Y. 401 (1852).

35. Ibid.

36. Johnson's reports exposed the lie spread that the Tonawandas wanted to take the improvement moneys, as well as the nefarious actions to pressure the Indians off their reservation. See, for example, Marcus Johnson to Secretary of the Interior Robert McClelland, December 1, 1854; Marcus Johnson Agency Report to Office of Indian Affairs, September 30, 1853; Johnson to Commissioner of Indian Affairs George Manypenny, June 30, 1853, September 23, 1856, OIA, NYAR, M234, MR588, RG75, NA.

37. Parker to President Franklin Pierce, October 17, 1856; Parker to George Manypenny, July 18, September 18, 1853, September 25, 1856; Parker to Commissioner of Indian Affairs James Denver, May 3, 1857, OIA, NYAR, M234, MR588, RG75, NA.

38. Ely S. Parker to George Manypenny, September 18, 1853.

39. Ely S. Parker to President Franklin Pierce, October 17, 1856.

40. For Gillet, see Hauptman, *Conspiracy of Interests*, 178, 185–189.

41. *Joseph Fellows, Survivor of Robert Kendle, Plaintiff in Error v. Susan Blacksmith and Ely S. Parker, Administrators of John Blacksmith, Deceased*, 60 U.S. 366 (March 5, 1857).

42. Ibid.

43. Ibid. For Nelson's controversial twenty-seven–year judicial career on the United States Supreme Court, one that involved writing 347 opinions, see Jenni Parrish, "Samuel Nelson," in: *Biographical Encyclopedia of the Supreme Court: The Lives and Legal Philosophies of the Justices*, Melvin L. Urofsky, ed. (Washington, D.C.: Congressional Quarterly Press, 206), 378–380. Because of his opinion in the *Dred Scott* case, Peter Irons has dubbed the New York jurist "a Southerner in sheep's clothing," because of his states' rights position and his refusal "to acknowledge any federal power to ban slavery in the nation's territories." Peter Irons, *A People's History of the Supreme Court: The Men and Women Whose Cases Have Shaped Our Constitution*, rev. ed. (New York: Viking Penguin, 2006), 164. For further information about Nelson, see Richard Lerch, "The Rediscovery of Samuel Nelson," *New York History* 34 (1953): 64–71.

Chapter 8. The Tonawanda Treaty

1. Herman Redfield to Commissioner of Indian Affairs, February 27, 1856, OIA, M234, NYAR, MR588, RG75, NA.

2. For the Stryker frauds, see U.S. Congress, Senate *Report* No. 192. 31st Cong., 1st sess. (September 9, 1850); Manley, "Buying Buffalo from the Indians," 315; Hauptman, *Conspiracy of Interests*, 178–188. For bribes given in 1838 by the Ogden Land Company to the Indians, see Society of Friends (Hicksites), *The Case of the Seneca Indians in the State of New York*

(1840), 25 passim. For the continued "payments" to certain Senecas after the Buffalo Creek Treaty of 1838, see Joseph Fellows, "Reservation Accounts, 1845," Joseph Fellows MSS., Box 12, CorU.

3. Joseph Fellows to Alfred Ogden, November 7, 1847, Ogden Family MSS., Series I, Box 1: Letters to Alfred Ogden, NYHS.

4. Harry Forward to Alfred Ogden, February 9, 1852, Ogden Family MSS., Series I, Box 1, Letters to Alfred Ogden, NYHS.

5. Before the federal-Tonawanda Treaty of 1857 was ratified by the United States Senate in 1859, company agents were complaining about these white squatters, calling them "devils from the lower region." Harry Forward to Alfred Ogden, April 15, 1859, Ogden Family MSS., Series I, Box 1: Letters to Alfred Ogden, NYHS.

6. Estate problems continued well beyond the federal-Tonawanda Treaty of 1857. Richard Ogden to Proprietor, January 26, 1854; J. D. Ogden to Alfred Ogden, October 1, 8, 1861; C. Leroux Ogden, October 22, 1859, Ogden Family MSS., Series I, Box 1: Letters to Alfred Ogden, NYHS.

7. R. L. Tillotson, "Tonnewanda [sic] and Tuscarora Reservation Circular. Re: Lands, July 25, 1853." Miscellaneous MSS., NYHS.

8. Franklin B. Hough, Comp., *Census of the State of New York for 1855* (Albany: Charles Van Benthuysen, 1857), 500–530. N. T. Strong was accused of taking bribes to secure his approval of the Buffalo Creek Treaty of 1842. See Society of Friends, *The Case of the Seneca Indians in the State of New York*, 32–51.

9. Petition of the Tonawanda Council of Chiefs, December, 1855, OIA, M234, NYAR, MR588, RG75, NA.

10. Marcus Johnson to Commissioner of Indian Affairs George Manypenny, June 30, 1853; Johnson to Secretary of the Interior R. M. McClelland, December 1, 1854; Johnson to Manypenny, September 23, 1856, Johnson to President Franklin Pierce, October 17, 1856, OIA, M234, NYAR, MR 588, RG 75, NA.

11. George Manypenny to R. M. McClelland, January 30, 1855. See also Manypenny to McClelland, December 24, 1854; Manypenny Report, September 17, 1856, OIA, M234, NYAR, MR588, RG75, NA.

12. Robert M. Kvasnicka, "George W. Manypenny, 1853–1857," in: *The Commissioners of Indian Affairs, 1824–1977*, Robert M. Kvasnicka and Herman J. Viola, eds. (Lincoln, Nebraska: University of Nebraska Press, 1979), 57–67. Manypenny continued his efforts to promote better treatment of the Indians well after he left office. See George Manypenny, *Our Indian Wards* (Cincinnati: Robert Clarke & Co., 1880).

13. Redfield to Commissioner of Indian Affairs, March 27, 1856, OIA, M234, NYAR, MR588, RG75, NA.

14. Ransom H. Gillet to President Franklin Pierce, May 9, 1855, OIA, M234, NYAR, MR588, RG75, NA.

15. George C. Whiting to R. M. McClelland, May 28, 1855; Whiting Report, May 28, 1855, OIA, M234, NYAR, MR588, RG75, NA. Harry Forward and Asa Cutler, working for the Ogden Land Company, had written earlier that a "large portion" of the Tonawandas would accept the moneys from the improvement fund, thus putting into effect the Seneca Treaty of 1842. Affidavit by Harry Forward and Asa Cutler (witnessed by Herman Redfield), March 31, 1855, OIA, M234, NYAR, MR588, RG75, NA. For these fraudulent efforts, see also Johnson to Manypenny, September 23, 1856; George Manypenny Report, September 17, 1856; Ely S. Parker to President Franklin Pierce, October 17, 1856, OIA, M234, NYAR, MR588, RG75, NA.

16. George Herrick Report to Office of Indian Affairs, September 21, 1855, OIA, NYAR, M234, MR588, RG75, NA. This investigation was spurred on by Ely S. Parker's letter to Manypenny on September 18, 1853.

17. George Manypenny Report, September 17, 1856.

18. James Denver to Secretary of the Interior Jacob Thompson, May 1, 1857; Commissioner James Denver Memorandum Respecting Tonawanda Indians, 1857, OIA, M234, NYAR, MR588, RG75, NA.

19. Donald Chaput, "James W. Denver, 1857, 1858–1859," in: *Commissioners of Indian Affairs, 1824–1977*, 69–79.

20. For the lobbying of Tillotson and Fellows, see James Denver to Jacob Thompson, May 1, 1857, OIA, M234, NYAR, MR588, NA.

21. Petition of Towns of Alabama and Pembroke [New York] to the President of the United States, April 20, 1857, OIA, M234, NYAR, MR588, RG75, NA.

22. Commissioner James Denver Memorandum Respecting Tonawanda Indians, 1857.

23. For Ely Parker's lobbying efforts, see Parker to George Manypenny, September 25, 1856; Parker (with Nicholson Parker) to Franklin Pierce, October 7, 17, 1856, OIA, M234, NYAR, MR588, RG75, NA.

24. See, for example, G. H. Verplanck to William L. Marcy, October 10, 1856; Frederick Follett to R. M. McClelland, October 7, 1856, OIA, M234, NYAR, MR588, RG75, NA. Bryan was an attorney from Batavia associated with Martindale who had moved his law office to Rochester in 1851. Verplanck was a judge in Buffalo who had served as a co-counsel for the Tonawandas with Martindale in the late 1840s.

25. Jean H. Baker, "Blair, Montgomery," in: *American National Biography.* Mark C. Carnes and John A. Garraty, eds. (New York: Oxford University Press, 1999), II: 916–917; Elbert B. Smith, "Blair, Montgomery (1813–1883): U.S. Postmaster General," in: *Encyclopedia of the American*

Civil War, David S. & Jeanne T. Heidler, eds. (New York: W. W. Norton, 2000), 239–240. See also William Ernest Smith, *The Francis Preston Blair Family in Politics* (New York: Macmillan Co., 1933); and *Elbert S. Smith*, *Francis Preston Blair* (New York: The Free Press, 1980), 240–241.

26. John Martindale to Montgomery Blair, April 15, 1857. Blair almost immediately wrote to Commissioner Denver on behalf of his friend and the Tonawandas. Martindale to Blair, June 13, 1857, OIA, M234, NYAR, MR588, RG75, NA.

27. Martindale to Blair, June 13, 1857.

28. For discussions of this formula, see H. R. Selden and Nicholas Hill to Jacob Thompson, June 20, 1857, OIA, M234, NYAR, MR588, RG75 NA.

29. Tonawanda Council of Chiefs Resolution, October 4, 1856, OIA, M234, NYAR, MR588, RG 75 NA.

30. See notes 22 and 23.

31. *ARCIA*, 1857: 8. According to the federal Indian subagent, about two hundred Iroquois left for Kansas (the Indian Territory). Of these, seventy-four died of disease and other causes, eighty-nine returned to New York, and twenty-five remained in the West. W. H. Angel's List of Indians, June 25, 1848, OIA, M 234, NYAR, MR 597, RG75, NA.

32. See H. Craig Miner and William E. Unrau, *The End of Indian Kansas: A Study of Cultural Revolution, 1854–1871* (Lawrence, Kansas: Regents Press of Kansas, 1978).

33. Tonawanda Council of Chiefs Power of Attorney to John H. Martindale, G. H. Verplanck, and Ely S. Parker, June 16, 1857, ESP MSS., Box 4, APS.

34. Conference Transcript of Meeting with Commissioner of Indian Affairs, June 30, 1857, OIA, M234, NYAR, MR588, RG75, NA.

35. Ely S. Parker to James Denver, June 30, 1857, OIA, M234, NYAR, MR588, NA.

36. Ibid.

37. Ely S. Parker, John H. Martindale, Frederick Follett, and William Bryan memorial to President of the United States, July 2, 1857, OIA, M234, NYAR, MR588, RG75 NA.

38. John H. Martindale to James Denver, August 10, 1857, OIA, M234, NYAR, MR588, RG75 NA.

39. John H. Martindale to Philip Thomas, March 25, 1857; Thomas to George Manypenny, March 3, 1857; Thomas to Martindale, May 5, 1857; Thomas to Denver, July 21, 1857, OIA, M234, NYAR, MR588, NA.

40. Thomas to Denver, July 21, 1857.

41. John Van Rensselaer to James Denver, July 8, 1857, OIA, M234, NYAR, MR588, RG75 NA.

42. J. P. Wadsworth, Frederic Bronson, and W. D. Waddington to James Denver, August 14, 1857, OIA, M234, NYAR, MR588, RG75 NA.

43. John H. Martindale to Jacob Thompson, September 18, 1857, OIA, M234, NYAR, MR588, RG75, NA.

44. John H. Martindale to Jacob Thompson, October 10, 1857, OIA, M234, NYAR, MR588, RG75 NA.

45. John H. Martindale to Jacob Thompson, October 16, 1857, OIA, M234, NYAR, MR588, RG75, NA.

46. John H. Martindale to James Denver with attachment agreement signed by Ely S. Parker, Frederick Follett, William Bryan, and John H. Martindale, October 17, 1857, OIA, M234, NYAR, MR588, RG75, NA.

47. John H. Martindale to Jacob Thompson, September 18, 1857.

48. See notes 42, 43, and 44.

49. John H. Martindale to Jacob Thompson, October 16, 1857.

50. John H. Martindale to James Denver, October 17, 1859.

51. 11 *Stat.* 735; 12 *Stat.* 991 (November 5, 1857).

52. Ely S. Parker to [Commissioner of Indian Affairs] Charles E. Mix, May 14, 1858, OIA, M234, NYAR, MR589, RG75, NA.

53. John H. Martindale to Charles E. Mix, May 18, 1858, OIA, M234, NYAR, MR589, RG75 NA.

54. Blair had become a hero in the North for his defense of Dred Scott. For Seward's support of the Tonawandas' cause, see "The Six Nations," *New York Times*, March 5, 1859, 4.

55. United States, *Senate Executive Journal* (June 4, 1858), 439; see chart.

56. See note 50.

57. Tonawanda Council of Chiefs Resolution, April 14, 1859; John H. Martindale to Charles E. Mix, April 16, 1859, OIA, M234, NYAR, MR589, RG75, NA.

Chapter 9. Buying Back the Reservation

1. Tonawanda Council of Chiefs Resolution, April 14, 1859, OIA, MR234, NYAR, MR589, RG75, NA.

2. Commissioner of Indian Affairs [A. B. Greenwood] to John H. Martindale and William Bryan [Martindale's junior law partner], May 5, 1859, OIA, M234, NYAR, MR589, RG75, NA.

3. John H. Martindale to A. B. Greenwood, May 17, 1859, OIA, M234, NYAR, MR589, RG75, NA.

4. John H. Martindale to Charles Mix [Acting Commissioner], May 18, 1859; A. B. Greenwood to Martindale, May 18, 1859, OIA, M234, NYAR, MR589, RG75, NA.

5. A. B. Greenwood to Martindale, May 18, 1859.

6. John H. Martindale to A. B. Greenwood, June 8, 1859, OIA, M234, NYAR, MR589, RG75, NA.

7. John H. Martindale to A. B. Greenwood, June 15, 1859, OIA, M234, NYAR, MR589, RG75, NA.

8. John H. Martindale to A. B. Greenwood, June 23, 24, 1859, OIA, M234, NYAR, MR589, RG75, NA.

9. See note 8.

10. A. B. Greenwood to John H. Martindale, July 1, 1859, OIA, M234, NYAR, MR589, RG75, NA.

11. John H. Martindale to A. B. Greenwood, June 28, July 7, 1859, February 29, 1860, OIA, M234, NYAR, MR589, RG75, NA. See also note 10.

12. A. B. Greenwood to John H. Martindale, December 2, 1859, February 29, 1860, OIA, M234, NYAR, MR589, RG75, NA.

13. John H. Martindale to A. B. Greenwood, December 17, 1859, OIA, M234, NYAR, MR589, RG75, NA.

14. John H. Martindale to A. B. Greenwood, September 5, 1859, OIA, M234, NYAR, MR589, RG75, NA.

15. John H. Martindale to A. B. Greenwood, February 29, 1860, OIA, M234, NYAR, MR589, RG75, NA.

16. John H. Martindale to A. B. Greenwood, December 17, 1859, OIA, M234, NYAR, MR589, RG75, NA.

17. Ibid.

18. Frederick Follett to Office of Indian Affairs, September 10, 28, 1859, OIA, M234, NYAR, MR589, RG75, NA.

19. Frederick Follett, Report, December 14, 1859, OIA, M234, NYAR, MR589, RG75, NA. See also note 17.

20. For Parker, see Ely S. Parker to A. B. Greenwood, March 8, 1860, OIA, M234, NYAR, MR589, RG75, NA.

21. Daniel Willard to Secretary of the Interior [Jacob Thompson], March 23, 1860, OIA, M234, NYAR, MR589, RG75, NA.

22. John H. Martindale to G. W. Brown, March 12, 1860; Martindale to A. B. Greenwood, April 28, 1860, OIA, M234, NYAR, MR589, RG75, NA.

23. Proceedings of the Tonawanda Council of Chiefs, August 1, 1860, OIA, M234, NYAR, MR589, RG75, NA.

24. New York State Legislature. Assembly. Document No. 28 (January 21, 1860).

25. Ibid.

26. "An Act authorizing the comptroller of this state to hold the Tonawanda Indian reservation in trust for the Tonawanda Band of Indians." *Laws of New York*, 83rd sess., chap. 439 (April 16, 1860): 762–763. The act

passed the New York State Assembly by 81 to 1 and the New York State Senate 20 to 0. New York State Assembly, *Journal* (1860), 607, 1156, 1220, 1247, 1321–1322, 1401; New York State Senate, *Journal* (1860), 109, 185, 327, 329, 334, 926, 973.

27. "An Act to relieve the Tonawanda Band of Seneca Indians from certain taxes on the Tonawanda reservation, and to prevent intrusions thereon." *Laws of New York*, 83rd sess., chap. 491 (April 17, 1860): 980–981. The act passed the New York State Assembly by 88 to 3 and the New York State Senate 20 to 0. New York State Assembly, *Journal* (1860), 553, 607, 1156, 1220, 1252, 1361–1362, 1406; New York State Senate, *Journal* (1860), 107, 109, 176, 264, 270, 319, 323, 348, 964.

28. New York State Senate, *Journal* (1860), 107, 264.

29. *Centennial Pamphlet Commemorating the Hundredth Anniversary of the United States-Tonawanda Treaty of November 5, 1857* (Tonawanda Indian Reservation, 1957), 1.

30. "An Act for the protection and improvement of the Tonawanda Band of Seneca Indians, residing on the Tonawanda reservation in this state." *Laws of New York*, 86th sess., chap. 90 (April 7, 1863): 135–149. The act passed 79 to 1 in the New York State Assembly and unanimously in the New York State Senate. New York State Assembly, *Journal* (1863), 192, 226, 512; New York State Senate, *Journal* (1863), 154, 404. See Ely S. Parker's petition, February 10, 1863, in: New York State Assembly, *Journal* (1863), 192.

Chapter 10. Conclusion

1. Parker, *Seneca Myths and Folk Tales*, 309–311.

Bibliography

I. Archival Records and Manuscript Collections

American Philosophical Society
    Fenton, William N. MSS.
    Parker, Ely S. MSS.
    Speck, Frank G. MSS.
    Tooker, Elisabeth, MSS.
    Wallace, Anthony F. C. MSS.
Buffalo and Erie County Historical Society
    Forward, Oliver MSS.
    Granger, Erastus MSS.
    Holland Land Company MSS.
    Indian Collection [Indian Treaties]
    Parker, Arthur C. MSS.
    Parker, Ely S. MSS.
    Parker, Isaac Newton MSS.
    Parrish, Jasper MSS.
    Pierce, Maris B. MSS.
    Porter, Peter B. MSS.
    Potter, Henan MSS.
Columbia University, Butler Library
    Clinton, DeWitt MSS.
    Jay, John MSS.
    Morris, Gouverneur MSS.
Cornell University, Carl Kroch Library
    Fellows, Joseph MSS.
Genesee County Clerk's Office, Batavia
    County Court Records
        1. Circuit Court Records, 1834–1854
        2. County Court of Pleas, 1846–1849
        3. Miscellaneous Filings, 1846–1873

Hamilton College
    Kirkland, Samuel MSS.
Haverford College, Magill Library
    a. Elkinton, Joseph MSS. and Journals
    b. Friends, Society of. Indian Committee of the Society of Friends,
        1757–1896. Records of the Philadelphia Yearly Meeting.
    c. Records of the Tunesassa Boarding School
Haviland Record Room, New York Yearly Meeting of Friends, New York,
    New York (recently transferred to Swarthmore)
    Records of the New York Yearly Meeting of Friends
    Records of the Genesee Yearly Meeting of Friends
Library of Congress
    Grant, Ulysses S. MSS.
    Jackson, Andrew MSS.
    Morris, Robert MSS.
    Schoolcraft, Henry Rowe MSS.
    Troup, Robert MSS.
    Van Buren, Martin MSS.
    Wadsworth Family MSS.
Massachusetts Historical Society, Boston
    Pickering, Timothy MSS.
Miscellaneous Manuscript Collections
    Holland Land Company Archives (Frederica Safran, Comp.),
        microfilm publications.
    Indian Claims Commission, Expert Testimony on Dockets No. 342
        A, B, C, E, F, 368, 368 A (microfiche).
    Jennings, Francis, et al., Ed., *Iroquois Indians: A Documentary
        History of the Six Nations and Their League.* 50 microfilm reels.
        Woodbridge, Conn.: Research Publications, 1985.
National Archives, Washington, D.C.
    Cartographic Records—Archives II.
    Correspondence of the Office of Indian Affairs. Letters Received,
        1824–1881. M234, RG75.
        1. Records of the New York Agency, 1829–1880
        2. Records of the New York Agency Emigration, 1829–1851
        3. Seneca Agency in New York, 1824–1832
        4. Six Nations Agency, 1824–1834
        5. Office of the Secretary of War. Letters Received by the
            Secretary of War Relating to Indian Affairs, 1800–1823.
            M.271.
    Records of the Indian Claims Commission. RG 279.
    Records Relating to Indian Treaties
        1. Ratified Indian Treaties, 1722–1869. M668.

2. Documents Relating to the Negotiation of Ratified and Unratified Treaties, 1801–1869. T494.

3. Special Case File 29 (Re: Treaty of Buffalo Creek of 1838 and Kansas Claims)

New-York Historical Society

American Indian Collection

Folsom, George MSS.

Miscellaneous MSS.

1. Elizabeth Fothergill's "Account of Seven American Indians of the Senecas Who Visited York, England in the Month of May, 1818"

2. Rough Notes of Speech of Thomas Morris to the Seneca Indians [at Treaty of Big Tree, 1797]

Ogden Family (Alfred Ogden letters) MSS.

O'Reilly, Henry MSS.

Rokeby Collection

Schoolcraft, Henry Rowe MSS.

Troup, Robert MSS.

New York Public Library

Morse, Jedidiah MSS.

Schuyler, Philip MSS.

Troup, Robert MSS.

New York State Archives, Albany, New York

Office of the New York State Surveyor-General, Land Office Records, Series I and II.

Records of the New York State Court of Appeals—

Blacksmith v. Fellows (1852)

Rensselaer v. Hays (1859)

Records of Indian Deeds and Treaties, 1748–1847.

Records of the New York State Legislature. Assembly Papers. Indian Affairs.

Records of State Comptroller's Indian Annuity Claims, Receipts and Related Documents, 1796–1925.

Records of the Thomas Indian School.

Records of the War of 1812—Certificates of Claims by War of 1812 Veterans.

New York State Bureau of Land Management, Albany, New York

Minutes of the New York State Board of Land Commissioners— nineteenth-century minute books.

New York State Library, Manuscript Division

Beauchamp, William MSS.

Clinton, De Witt MSS.

Gillet, Ransom MSS.

Hough, Franklin Benjamin MSS.
Holland Land Company MSS.
Morgan, Edwin MSS.
Ogden Land Company Record Book, 1811–1882.
Parker, Arthur C. MSS.
Phelps and Gorham MSS.
Schoolcraft Population Census of Indian Reservations, 1845.
Schuyler Family MSS.
Seymour, Horatio MSS.
Stillman, Lulu MSS.
Troup, Robert MSS.
Van Buren, Martin MSS.
Van Rensselaer Family MSS.
Wadsworth Family MSS.
Watson, Elkanah MSS.
Onondaga Historical Association
Beauchamp, William MSS.
Vertical Files
Rochester Public Library
Fellows, Joseph MSS.
Pulteney Land Company MSS.
St. John Fisher College
Decker, George P. MSS.
State University of New York at Albany
Manley, Henry S. MSS.
State University of New York, College at Buffalo
Reilly, Paul G. MSS.—Indian Claims Commission
Swarthmore College—Friends Historical Society
Records of the Baltimore Yearly Meeting of Friends.
Records of the Indian Committee (Hicksite) of the Philadelphia
Yearly Meeting of Friends.
Minutes: Miscellaneous Records; Indian Concerns Subcommittee
MSS.
University of Rochester, Rush Rhees Library
Morgan, Lewis Henry MSS.
Parker, Arthur C. MSS.
Parker, Ely S. MSS.
Seward, William MSS.
Skivington, George J. Collection.
Wadsworth Family MSS. (Jeremiah and James S. Wadsworth) MSS.
Vassar College, Poughkeepsie, New York
Parrish, Jasper MSS.

Wisconsin Historical Society, Madison
  Draper, Lyman C. MSS.
  Warren, Reuben D. MSS.

II. Government Publications

American State Papers: Documents, Legislative and Executive of the Congress of the United States. 38 vols. [Class 2: Indian Affairs. 2 vols. 1832–1834] Washington, D.C.: Gales & Seaton, 1832–1861.

Donaldson, Thomas, Comp. *The Six Nations of New York.* Extra Census Bulletin of the 11th Census [1890] of the United States. Washington, D.C.: U.S. Census Printing Office, 1892.

Hastings, Hugh, ed. *The Public Papers of George Clinton.* 8 vols. Albany: Oliver Quayle, 1904.

Hastings, Hugh, ed. *Public Papers of Daniel D. Tompkins, Governor of New York, 1807–1817.* 3 vols. New York: Wynkoop, Hallenbeck & Crawford, 1898.

Kappler, Charles J., Comp. *Indian Affairs: Laws and Treaties.* 5 vols. Washington, D.C.: U.S. Government Printing Office, 1903–1941.

Lincoln, Charles Z., ed. *Messages from the [NYS] Governors.* Vols. I–III. Albany: J. B. Lyon Co., 1909.

Morse, Jedidiah. *A Report to the Secretary of War of the United States on Indian Affairs, Comprising a Narrative of a Tour Performed in the Summer of 1820 . . .* New Haven, Connecticut: S. Converse, 1822.

New York State Adjutant General's Office. *Index of Awards: Soldiers of the War of 1812.* Baltimore: Genealogical Publishing Co., 1969.

New York State Board of Canal Commissioners. *Annual Report* [1811–1878].

New York State. *Census of the State of New York for 1855.* Franklin B. Hough, Comp. Albany: Charles Van Benthuysen & Sons, 1857.

New York State Constitutional Convention. *Reprints of the Proceeds and Debates of the New York State Constitutional Convention, 1821.* New York: Da Capo Press, 1970.

New York State Legislature, Assembly, Document No. 51: *Report of the Special Committee to Investigate the Indian Problem of the State of New York.* Appointed by the Assembly of 1888. 2 vols. Albany: Troy Press, 1889. [Popularly known as the *Whipple Report.*]

New York State Legislature. *Assembly Journal.*

New York State Legislature. *Senate Journal.*

New York State Legislature. *Laws (Statutes) of the State of New York.*

New York State Secretary of State. *Census of the State of New York, 1825.* Albany, 1826.

New York State Secretary of State. *Census of the State of New York for 1835.* Albany: Croswell, Van Benthuysen & Burt, 1836.

New York State Secretary of State. *Census of the State of New York for 1845.* Albany: Carrol & Cook, 1846.

Richardson, James D., Comp. *A Compilation of the Messages & Papers of the Presidents, 1789–1897.* 10 vols. Washington, D.C.: U.S. Government Printing Office, 1896–1899.

Royce, Charles C., Comp. *Indian Land Cessions in the United States. 18th Annual Report of the Bureau of American Ethnology, 1896–1897.* Part 2. Washington, D.C.: U.S. Government Printing Office, 1899.

U.S. Bureau of the Census. 1st (1790)–9th (1860) Censuses.

U.S. Congress. *Annals of Congress,* 1789–1824.

U.S. Congress. *Congressional Globe.*

U.S. Congress. *Register of Debates in Congress,* 1825–1837.

U.S. Congress, House of Representatives. *Journal of the House of Representatives* [1789–1815]. Washington, D.C.: Gales & Seaton, 1826.

U.S. Congress, Senate. *Journal of the Senate* [1789–1815]. 5 vols. Washington, D.C.: Gales & Seaton, 1820–1821.

U.S. Congress, Senate. *Journal of the Executive Proceedings of the Senate* [1789–1828]. 3 vols. Washington, D.C.: Duff Green, 1828.

U.S. Congress, Senate Committee on Indian Affairs. Document No. 156, 29th Cong., 2d sess. (February 19, 1847).

U.S. Indian Claims Commission. *Decisions of the Indian Claims Commission* [microfiche edition]. New York: Clearwater Publishing Co., 1973–1978.

U.S. Interior Department, Secretary of the Interior. *Annual Report* [1849–1861].

U.S. Interior Department, Commissioner of Indian Affairs. *Annual Report* [1849–1861].

U.S. War Department, Commissioner of Indian Affairs, *Annual Report* [1824–1863].

U.S. War Department, Secretary of War. *Annual Report* [1789–1848].

Whitford, Noble E. *History of the Canal System of the State of New York.* . . . 2 vols. Albany: Brandon Printing [Supplement to the Annual Report of the State Engineer and Surveyor of the State of New York], 1906.

III. Books, Booklets, and Pamphlets

Abler, Thomas S. *Cornplanter: Chief Warrior of the Allegany Senecas.* Syracuse: Syracuse University Press, 2007.

Abler, Thomas S., ed. *Chainbreakers: The Revolutionary War Memoirs of Governor Blacksnake as Told to Benjamin Williams*. Lincoln: University of Nebraska Press, 1989.

Abrams, George H. J. *The Seneca People*. Phoenix: Indian Tribal Series, 1976.

Adams, Charles Francis, ed. *Memoirs of John Quincy Adams*. Vol. 7. Philadelphia: J. B. Lippincott & Co., 1875.

Alden, Timothy. *An Account of Sundry Missions Performed Among the Senecas and Munsees . . .* New York: J. Seymour, 1827.

Armstrong, William H. *Warrior in Two Camps: Ely S. Parker: Union General and Seneca Chief*. Syracuse: Syracuse University Press, 1978.

Austin, Alberta, Comp. *Ne Ho Ni Yo De: No—That's What It Was Like*. 2 vols. New York: Rebco Enterprises, 1986–1989.

Barbour, Hugh, et al., eds. *Quaker Crosscurrents: Three Hundred Years of Friends in the New York Yearly Meetings*. Syracuse: Syracuse University Press, 1995.

Barton, Lois. *A Quaker Promise Kept: Philadelphia Friends' Work with the Allegany Seneca, 1795–1960*. Eugene, Oregon: Spencer Butte Press, 1990.

Beauchamp, William M. *A History of the New York Iroquois*. New York State Museum *Bulletin* 78. Albany, 1905.

Benn, Carl. *The Iroquois in the War of 1812*. Toronto: University of Toronto Press, 1998.

Berkhofer, Robert F., Jr. *Salvation and the Savage: An Analysis of Protestant Missions and American Indian Response, 1787–1862*. Lexington, Kentucky.: University of Kentucky Press, 1965; reprint, New York: Atheneum, 1976.

Bieder, Robert E. *Science Encounters the Indian, 1820–1880: The Early Years of American Ethnology*. Norman: University of Oklahoma Press, 1986.

Bingham, Robert W., ed. *Holland Land Company Papers: Reports of Joseph Ellicott*. 2 vols. Buffalo: Buffalo Historical Society Publications, 1941.

Bragdon, George C. *Notable Men of Rochester and Vicinity*. Rochester, New York: D. J. Stoddard, 1902.

Bremer, Richard G. *Indian Agent and Wilderness Scholar: The Life of Henry Rowe Schoolcraft*. Mount Pleasant, Michigan: Clarke Historical Library Central Michigan University, 1987.

Brown, Thomas. *Politics and Statesmanship: Essays on the American Whig Party*. New York: Columbia University Press, 1985.

Calloway, Colin G. *Crowns and Calumet: British-Indian Relations, 1783–1815*. Norman: University of Oklahoma Press, 1987.

Campbell, William W., ed. *The Life and Writings of DeWitt Clinton*. New York: Baker & Scribner, 1949.

Campisi, Jack, Michael Foster, and Marianne Mithun, eds. *Extending the Rafters: Interdisciplinary Approaches to Iroquoian Studies*. Albany: State University of New York Press, 1984.

Caswell, Harriet S. *Our Life Among the Iroquois Indians*. (1892) paperback reprint. Lincoln: University of Nebraska Press, 2007. [Introduction by Joy Bilharz.]

Catlin, George. *Letters and Notes on the Manners, Customs and Conditions of North American Indians*. 2 vols.(1844); paperback reprint, New York: Dover, 1973. [Introduction by Marjorie Halpin.]

Chafe, Wallace L. *Handbook of the Seneca Language*. Albany: New York State Museum and Science Service, 1963.

Chazanoff, William. *Joseph Ellicott and the Holland Land Company: The Opening of Western New York*. Syracuse: Syracuse University Press, 1970.

Congdon, Charles E. *Allegany Oxbow: A History of Allegany State Park and the Allegany Reserve of the Seneca Nation*. Little Valley, New York: Straight Publishing Co., 1967.

Cornplanter, Jesse. *Legends of the Longhouse*. New York: Lippincott, 1938.

Cullum, Charles W. *Biographical Register of the Officers and Graduates of the United States Military Academy at West Point, N.Y. from Its Establishment, to the Army Re-organization of 1866–1867*. New York: D. Van Nostrand, 1868.

Curtin, Jeremiah. *Seneca Indian Myths* (1922). Paperback reprint edition. New York: Dover, 2001.

Cusick, David. *Sketches of Ancient History of the Six Nations . . . 1827*. 2d ed. Lockport, New York: Cooley & Lothrop, 1828.

Dearborn, Henry A. S. *Journals of Henry A. S. Dearborn*. Frank H. Severance, ed. Buffalo Historical Society *Publications* 7, Buffalo: Buffalo Historical Society, 1904. 35–235.

Delafield, Joseph. *The Unfortified Boundary*. Robert MacElroy and Thomas Riggs, eds. New York: privately printed, 1943.

Densmore, Christopher. *Red Jacket: Iroquois Diplomat and Orator*. Syracuse: Syracuse University Press, 1999.

Disturnell, John. *A Gazetteer of the State of New-York . . .* Albany: 1842.

Doty, Lockwood L. *History of Livingston County, New York*. 1st ed. Geneseo, New York: Edward E. Doty, 1876. [Second edition edited by Lockwood R. Doty, published in Jackson, Michigan by W. J. Deusen in 1905].

Doty, Lockwood R. *History of the Genesee Country*. Chicago: S. J. Clarke, 1925.

Downes, Randolph C. *Council Fires on the Upper Ohio . . .* Pittsburgh: University of Pittsburgh, 1940.

Ellicott, Joseph. *Holland Land Company Papers: Reports of Joseph Ellicott*. 2 vols. Robert W. Bingham, ed. Buffalo: Buffalo Historical Society, 1941.

Engelbrecht, William. *Iroquoia: The Development of a Native World*. Syracuse: Syracuse University Press, 2004.

Evans, Paul D. *The Holland Land Company*. Buffalo: Buffalo Historical Society, 1924.

Fenton, William N. *The Iroquois Eagle Dance: An Offshoot of the Calumet Dance*. 1953; paperback reprint, Syracuse: Syracuse University Press, 1991.

Fenton, William N. *The Little Water Society of the Senecas*. Norman: University of Oklahoma Press, 2002.

Fenton, William N., ed. *Symposium on Local Diversity*. Bureau of American Ethnology *Bulletin* 149. Washington, D.C., 1951.

Fenton, William N. *The Great Law and the Longhouse: A Political History of the Iroquois Confederacy*. Norman: University of Oklahoma Press, 1998.

Fenton, William N., and John Gullick, eds. *Symposium on Cherokee and Iroquois Culture*. Bureau of American Ethnology *Bulletin* 180 (1961).

Ferguson, E. James, ed. *The Papers of Robert Morris*. 7 vols. Pittsburgh: University of Pittsburgh Press, 1973.

Fitzpatrick, John C., ed. *The Autobiography of Martin Van Buren*. Reprint of 1920 edition, New York: Da Capo Press, 1973.

Foreman, Carolyn. *Indians Abroad*. Norman: University of Oklahoma Press, 1943.

Foreman, Grant. *The Last Trek of the Indians*. 1946; reprint, New York: Russell & Russell, 1972.

Fox, Dixon Ryan. *The Decline of Aristocracy in the Politics of New York, 1801–1840*. 1919; paperback reprint ed. by Robert V. Remini, New York: Harper Torchbook edition, 1965.

French, J. H., Comp. *Gazetteer of the State of New York*. Syracuse: R. Pearsall Smith, 1860.

Ganter, Granville, ed. *The Collected Speeches of Sagoyewatha, or Red Jacket*. Syracuse: Syracuse University Press, 2006.

Garraty, John. *Silas Wright*. New York: Columbia University Press, 1949.

Gerber, David A. *The Making of an American Pluralism: Buffalo, New York, 1825–1860*. Urbana: University of Illinois Press, 1989.

Glatthaar, Joseph, and James Kirby Martin. *Forgotten Allies: The Oneida Indians and the American Revolution*. New York: Hill and Wang, 2006.

Graymont, Barbara. *The Iroquois in the American Revolution*. Syracuse: Syracuse University Press, 1972.

Gunn, L. Ray. *The Decline of Authority: Public Economic Policy and Political Development in New York, 1800–1860*. Ithaca, New York: Cornell University Press, 1988.

Hale, Horatio E. *The Iroquois Book of Rites*. 2 vols. Philadelphia: D. G. Brinton, 1883.

Hammond, Jabez D. *The History of Political Parties in the State of New York*. 2 vols. Albany: Charles Van Benthuysen, 1842.

Hauptman, Laurence M. *Between Two Fires: American Indians in the Civil War*. New York: The Free Press, 1995.

Hauptman, Laurence M. *Conspiracy of Interests: Iroquois Dispossession and the Rise of New York State*. Syracuse: Syracuse University Press, 1999.

Hauptman, Laurence M. *The Iroquois in the Civil War*. Syracuse: Syracuse University Press, 1993.

Hauptman, Laurence M. *Seven Generations of Iroquois Leadership: The Six Nations Since 1800*. Syracuse: Syracuse University Press, 2008.

Hauptman, Laurence M. *Tribes and Tribulations: Misconceptions of American of Indians and Their Histories*. Albuquerque: University of New Mexico Press, 1995.

Hauptman, Laurence M., ed. *A Seneca Indian in the Union Army: The Civil War Letters of Sergeant Isaac Newton Parker, 1861–1865*. Shippensburg, Pennsylvania: Burd Street Press/White Mane Publishing Co., 1995.

Hauptman, Laurence M., and L. Gordon McLester III. *Chief Daniel Bread and the Oneida Nation of Indians of Wisconsin*. Norman: University of Oklahoma Press, 2002.

Haydon, Roger, ed. *Upstate Travels: British Views of Nineteenth-Century New York*. Syracuse: Syracuse University Press, 1982.

Hemphill, W. Edwin, et al., eds. *The Papers of John C. Calhoun*. 16 vols. Columbia, South Carolina: University of South Carolina Press, 1959–1984.

Hewitt, J. N. B. *Iroquois Cosmology*. Part I. Bureau of American Ethnology, *21st Annual Report*. Washington, D.C.: U.S. Government Printing Office, 1899–1900, 127–339.

Hewitt, J. N. B. *Iroquoian Cosmology*. Part II. Bureau of American Ethnology, *Annual Report*. Washington, D.C.: Bureau of American Ethnology, 1928.

Horsman, Reginald. *Expansion and American Indian Policy, 1783–1812*. East Lansing: Michigan State University Press, 1967.

Horsman, Reginald. *The Frontier in the Formative Years, 1783–1815*. New York: Holt, Rinehart & Winston, 1970.

Hough, Franklin Benjamin, comp. *Proceedings of the Commissioners of Indian Affairs Appointed by Law for the Extinguishment of Indian Titles in the State of New York*. 2 vols. Albany: Munsell, 1861.

Houghton, Frederick. *The History of the Buffalo Creek Reservation.* Buffalo Historical Society *Publication* 24. Buffalo: Buffalo Historical Society, 1920.

Howe, Daniel Walker. *The Political Culture of the American Whigs.* Chicago: University of Chicago Press, 1979.

Howe, Daniel Walker. *What Hath God Wrought: The Transformation of America, 1815–1848.* New York: Oxford University Press, 2007.

Irons, Peter. *A People's History of the Supreme Court.* Rev. Ed. New York: Viking Penguin, 2006.

Jennings, Francis, William N. Fenton, et al., eds. *The History and Culture of Iroquois Diplomacy: An Interdisciplinary Guide to the Treaties of the Six Nations and Their League.* Syracuse: Syracuse University Press, 1985.

Johnson, E. Roy. *The Tuscaroras: History—Traditions—Culture.* 2 vols. Murfreesboro, North Carolina: Johnson Publishing Co., 1968.

Johnson, Elias. *Legends, Traditions and Laws of the Iroquois, or, Six Nations, and History of the Tuscarora Indians.* Lockport, New York: Union Printing and Publishing, 1981.

Johnson, Marlene, comp. *Iroquois Cookbook,* 2d ed. Tonawanda Indian Reservation: Peter Doctor Memorial Fellowship Foundation, 1989.

Johnston, Charles M., ed. *The Valley of the Six Nation . . .* Toronto, Ontario: University of Toronto, 1964.

Jordan, Kurt. *The Seneca Restoration: A Local Political Economy.* Gainesville: University Press of Florida, 2008.

Kelsey, Isabel Thompson. *Joseph Brant, 1743–1807: Man of Two Worlds.* Syracuse: Syracuse University Press, 1984.

Kent, James. *Commentaries on American Law.* 3 vols. 1826; reprint, New York: Da Capo Press, 1971.

Ketchum, William. *An Authentic Comprehensive History of Buffalo.* 2 vols. Buffalo: Rockwell, Baker & Hill, 1864–1865.

Klinch, Carl F., and James J. Talman, eds. *The Journal of Major John Norton, 1816.* Toronto, Ontario: Champlain Society, 1970.

Kvasnicka, Robert, and Herman Viola, eds. *The Commissioners of Indian Affairs, 1824–1977.* Lincoln: University of Nebraska Press, 1979.

Lafitau, Joseph François. *Customs of the American Indians* (1724). 2 vols. William N. Fenton, ed.; Elizabeth Moore, trans. Toronto, Ontario: Champlain Society, 1974.

Larned, Josephus N. *A History of Buffalo, Delineating the Evolution of the City.* 2 vols. New York: Progress of the Empire State Co., 1911.

Livermore, Shaw. *Early American Land Companies: Their Influence on Corporate Development.* Cambridge: Harvard University Press, 1939.

Manypenny, George. *Our Indian Wards.* Cincinnati: Robert Clarke & Co., 1880.

Mau, Clayton, ed. *The Development of Central and Western New York.* New York: DuBois Press, 1944.

McCurdy, Charles W. *The Anti-Rent Era in New York Law and Politics, 1839–1865.* Chapel Hill, North Carolina: University of North Carolina Press, 2000.

McKelvey, Blake. *Rochester on the Genesee: The Growth of a City.* Syracuse: Syracuse University Press, 1973.

McKelvey, Blake. *Rochester: The Water-Power City, 1812–1854.* Cambridge: Harvard University Press, 1952.

McNall, Neil Adams. *An Agricultural History of the Genesee Valley, 1790–1860.* Philadelphia: University of Pennsylvania Press, 1952.

Meinig, D. W. *The Shaping of America: A Geographical Perspective on 500 Years of History.* 2 vols. New Haven: Yale University Press, 1986 and 1993.

Middleton, Richard. *Pontiac's War: Its Causes and Consequences.* New York: Routledge, 2007.

Miller, Nathan. *The Enterprise of a Free People: Aspects of Economic Development in New York State During the Canal Era, 1792–1838.* Ithaca: Cornell University Press, 1962.

Miner, H. Craig, and William E. Unrau. *The End of Indian Kansas: A Study of Cultural Revolution, 1854–1871.* Lawrence: Regents Press of Kansas, 1978.

Morgan, Lewis Henry. *League of the Ho-dé-no-sau-nee, or Iroquois.* Rochester: Sage & Bros., 1851; paperback reprint ed. by William N. Fenton, New York: Corinth Books, 1962.

Namias, June. *White Captives: Gender and Ethnicity on the American Frontier.* Chapel Hill: University of North Carolina Press, 1993.

Parker, Arthur C. *Parker on the Iroquois.* William N. Fenton, ed. Syracuse: Syracuse University Press, 1968.

Parker, Arthur C. *Red Jacket.* (1952). Paperback reprint, Lincoln: University of Nebraska Press, 1998. [Introduction by Thomas S. Abler.]

Parker, Arthur C. *Seneca Myths and Folk Tales* (1923). Paperback reprint, Lincoln: University of Nebraska Press 1989. [Introduction by William N. Fenton.]

Parker, Arthur C. *The Life of General Ely S. Parker, Last Grand Sachem of the Iroquois and General Grant's Military Secretary.* Buffalo Historical Society *Publication* 23. Buffalo: Buffalo Historical Society, 1919.

Pierce, Maris B. *Address on the Present Condition and Prospects of the Aboriginal Inhabitants of North America with Particular Reference to the Seneca Nation.* Speech at the Baptist Church in Buffalo, August 28, 1838. Buffalo: Steele's Press, 1838.

Pilkington, Walter, ed. *The Journals of Samuel Kirkland.* Clinton, New York: Hamilton College, 1980.

Prisch, Betty C. *Aspects of Change in Seneca Iroquois Ladles, A.D. 1600–1900*. Rochester: Rochester Museum and Science Center, 1982.

Prucha, Francis Paul. *American Indian Policy in the Formative Years: The Indian Trade and Intercourse Acts, 1790–1834*. Cambridge: Harvard University Press, 1962.

Prucha, Francis Paul. *The Great Father: The United States Government and the American Indians*. 2 vols. Lincoln: University of Nebraska Press, 1984.

Resek, Carl. *Lewis Henry Morgan: American Scholar*. Chicago: University of Chicago Press, 1960.

Richter, Daniel K. *Peoples of the Iroquois League in the Era of European Colonization*. Chapel Hill, North Carolina: University of North Carolina Press, 1992.

Richter, Daniel K., and James H. Merrell, eds. *Beyond the Covenant Chain: The Iroquois and Their Neighbors in Indian North America, 1600–1800*. Syracuse: Syracuse University Press, 1987.

Royce, C.C., comp. *Indian Land Cessions in the United States*. Bureau of American Ethnology. *13th Annual Report, 1896–1897*. Washington, D.C.: U.S. Government Printing Office, 1899.

Savery, William. *A Journal of the Life, Travels, and Religious Labours of William Savery, Late of Philadelphia, A Minister of the Gospel of Christ, in the Society of Friends*. London: Charles Gilpin, 1844.

Satz, Ronald. *American Indian Policy in the Jacksonian Era*. Lincoln: University of Nebraska Press, 1975.

Schoolcraft, Henry R. *Notes on the Iroquois, or Contributions to American History, Antiquities and General Ethnology*. Albany: Erastus H. Pense, 1847.

Seaver, James E., comp. *A Narrative of the Life of Mrs. Mary Jemison*. George H. J. Abrams, ed. 1824; reprint, Syracuse: Syracuse University Press, 1990.

Seaver, James E., comp. *A Narrative of the Life of Mrs. Mary Jemison*. June Namias, ed. 1824; paperback reprint, Norman: University of Oklahoma Press, 1995.

Severance, Frank H., ed. *Correspondence on the Holland Land Company and Canal Construction in Western New York*. Buffalo Historical Society *Publication* 14. Buffalo: Buffalo Historical Society, 1910.

Seward, William H. *The Works of William H. Seward*. 4 vols. George E. Baker, ed. Boston: Houghton, Mifflin & Co., 1884.

Shannon, Timothy. *Indians and Colonists at the Crossroads of Empire: The Albany Congress of 1754*. Ithaca: Cornell University Press, 2000.

Shaw, Ronald E. *Canals for a Nation: The Canal Era in the United States, 1790–1860*. Lexington, Kentucky: University Press of Kentucky, 1990.

Shaw, Ronald E. *Erie Water West: A History of the Erie Canal, 1792–1854*. Lexington, Kentucky: University Press of Kentucky, 1966.

Sheriff, Carol. *The Artificial River: The Erie Canal and the Paradox of Progress, 1817–1862.* New York: Hill & Wang, 1996.

Shirreff, Patrick. *A Tour Through North America* . . . Edinburgh, U.K.: Oliver & Boyd, 1835.

Smith, Elbert S. *Francis Preston Blair.* New York: The Free Press, 1980.

Smith, William Ernest. *The Francis Preston Blair Family in Politics.* New York: Macmillan Co., 1933.

Snyder, Charles M., ed. *Red and White on the New York Frontier . . . from the Papers of Erastus Granger, 1807–1819.* Harrison, New York: Harbor Hill Books, 1978.

Society of Friends (Hicksite). *The Case of the Seneca Indians.* [Three Quaker pamphlets dated 1840, 1841, and 1872.] Reprint, Stanfordville, New York: Earl M. Coleman, 1979.

Society of Friends (Hicksite), Executive Committee of the Yearly Meetings. *Proceedings of an Indian Council Held at the Buffalo Creek Reservation, State of New York, Fourth Month, 1842.* Baltimore: William Wooddy for the Executive Committee of the Yearly Meetings, 1842.

Society of Friends (Hicksite), Executive Committee. *Report of the Proceedings of an Indian Council at Cattaraugus in the State of New York . . . 1843.* Baltimore: William Wooddy, 1843.

Spafford, Horatio Gates. *A Gazetteer of the State of New-York* . . . Albany: B. D. Packard, 1824.

Stone, William L. *The Life and Times of Red Jacket or Sa-go-ye-wat-ha; Being the Sequel to the History of the Six Nations.* New York: Wiley & Putnam, 1841.

Syrett, Harold C., ed. *The Papers of Alexander Hamilton.* 26 vols. New York: Columbia University Press, 1961–1979.

Tanner, Helen Hornbeck et al., eds. *Atlas of Great Lakes Indian History.* Norman: University of Oklahoma Press, 1987.

Taylor, Alan. *The Divided Ground: Indians, Settlers, and the Northern Borderland of the American Revolution.* New York: Alfred A. Knopf, 2006.

Taylor, George Rogers. *The Transportation Revolution, 1815–1860.* New York: Rinehart & Co., 1951.

Thwaites, Reuben G., ed. *The Jesuit Relations and Allied Documents.* 73 vols. Cleveland: Burrows Bros., 1896–1901.

Tocqueville, Alexis de. *Democracy in America.* 2d ed. Henry Reeve, trans., preface and notes by John C. Spencer. New York: Adlard, 1838.

Tocqueville, Alexis de. *Journey to America.* George Lawrence, trans., J. P. Mayer and A. P. Kerr, eds. Garden City, New York: Anchor; paperback reprint, Doubleday & Co., 1971.

Tonawanda Band of Seneca Indians. *Centennial Pamphlet Commemorating the Hundredth Anniversary of the United States-Tonawanda Treaty of November 5, 1857.* Tonawanda Reservation: 1957.

Tooker, Elisabeth. *Lewis Henry Morgan on Iroquois Material Culture.* Tucson: University of Arizona Press, 1994.

Tooker, Elisabeth. *The Iroquois Ceremonial of Midwinter.* Syracuse: Syracuse University Press, 1970.

Trennert, Robert A. *Indian Traders on the Middle Border: The House of Ewing, 1827–1854.* Lincoln: University of Nebraska Press, 1981.

Trigger, Bruce G., ed. *Handbook of North American Indians.* Vol. XV: *The Northeast.* Washington, D.C.: Smithsonian Institution, 1978.

Truettner, William H. *The Natural Man Observed: A Study of Catlin's Indian Gallery.* Washington, D.C.: Smithsonian Press, 1979.

Turner, Orasmus. *History of the Phelps' and Gorham's Purchase.* Rochester: William Alling, 1851.

Turner, Orasmus. *Turner's Pioneer History of the Holland Purchase of Western New York.* Buffalo: George H. Derby, 1850.

Tuttle, Sarah. *Letters and Conversations on the Indian Missions at Seneca, Tuscarora, Cattaraugus, in the State of New York, and Maumee in Ohio.* Boston: Massachusetts Sabbath School Union, 1831.

Upton, Helen M. *The Everett Report in Historical Perspective: The Indians of New York.* Albany: New York State American Revolution Bicentennial Commission, 1980.

Vecsey, Christopher, and William A. Starna, eds. *Iroquois Land Claims.* Syracuse: Syracuse University Press, 1988.

Viola, Herman. *Thomas L. McKenney: Architect of America's Early Indian Policy, 1816–1830.* Chicago: Swallow Press, 1974.

Viola, Herman J. *Diplomats in Buckskin: A History of Indian Delegations in Washington City.* Washington, D.C.: Smithsonian Institution Press, 1981.

Wallace, Anthony F. C. *The Death and Rebirth of the Seneca.* New York: Alfred A. Knopf, 1969.

Washington, George. *The Writings of George Washington . . . , 1745–1799.* John C. Fitzpatrick, ed. 39 vols. Washington, D.C.: U.S. Government Printing Office, 1931–1944.

Waugh, Frederick W. *Iroquois Foods and Food Preparation.* Anthropological Series 12, Memoirs of the Canadian Geological Survey 86. Ottawa, Ontario, 1916.

White, Richard. *The Middle Ground: Indians, Empires, and Republics in the Great Lakes Region, 1650–1815.* New York: Cambridge University Press, 1991.

Wilson, Peter. Speech of Wa-o-wa-na-onk (Peter Wilson), an Indian chief addressed to the Committee of the Baltimore Yearly Meeting of Friends on Indian Concerns, October 29, 1848. Baltimore, 1848.

Wyckoff, William. The Developers' Frontier: The Making of the Western New York Landscape. New Haven: Yale University Press, 1988.

IV. Articles

Abler, Thomas S. "Friends, Factions and the Seneca Nation Revolution of 1848." *Niagara Frontier* 21 (Winter 1974): 74–79.

Abler, Thomas S., "Protestant Missionaries and Native Cultures: Parallel Careers of Asher Wright and Silas T. Rand." *American Indian Quarterly* 26 (Winter 1992): 25–37.

Abler, Thomas S. "Seneca Moieties and Hereditary Chieftainships: The Early Nineteenth-Century Political Organization of an Iroquois Nation." *Ethnohistory* 51 (Summer 2004): 459–488.

Abler, Thomas S., and Elisabeth Tooker. "Seneca." In: *North American Indians*. Vol. 15: *The Northeast*. Bruce G. Trigger and William C. Sturtevant, eds. Washington, D.C.: Smithsonian Institution, 1978. 505–517.

Allen, Orlando. "Personal Recollections of Captain Jones and Parrish, and the Payment of Indian Annuities in Buffalo." Buffalo Historical Society *Publications* 6. Buffalo: Buffalo Historical Society, 1903. 539–546.

Avery, Joseph. "Visit of Rev. Joseph Avery." In: Buffalo Historical Society *Publications* 6. Buffalo: Buffalo Historical Society, 1903. 223–230.

Bacon, David. "Rev. David Bacon's Visits to Buffalo in 1800." Buffalo Historical Society *Publications* 6. Buffalo: Buffalo Historical Society, 1903. 183–186.

Berkhofer, Robert F., Jr. "Faith and Factionalism Among the Senecas: Theory and Ethnohistory." *Ethnohistory* 12 (1965): 99–112.

Bieder, Robert E. "The Grand Order of the Iroquois: Influences on Lewis Henry Morgan's Ethnology." *Ethnohistory* 27 (Fall 1980): 349–361.

Bieder, Robert E., and Christopher Plant. "Annuity Censuses as a Source for Historical Research: The 1858 and 1869 Tonawanda Annuity Censuses." *American Indian Culture and Research Journal* 5 (1981): 33–46.

Bingham, Robert W. "The History of Grand Island." In: *Niagara Frontier Miscellany*. Robert W. Bingham, ed. Buffalo Historical Society *Publications* 34. Buffalo: Buffalo Historical Society, 1947. 59–78.

Bird, William A. "Reminiscences of the Boundary Survey Between the United States and the British Provinces." Buffalo Historical Society *Publications* 4. Buffalo: Buffalo Historical Society, 1896. 1–14.

Burrows, Roswell. "Visit of Rev. Roswell Burrows, 1806." Buffalo Historical Society *Publications* 6. Buffalo: Buffalo Historical Society, 1903. 231–238.

Chernow, Barbara A. "Robert Morris: Genesee Land Speculator." *New York History* 58 (April 1977): 195–220.

Coates, Isaac. "Journal of Journeys to the Indian Country." *The Friends' Intelligencer and Journal* 44 (1887), sec. II: 468–470; III: 482–484; VIII: 562–564; IX: 557–580; X: 593–595; XI: 610–612.

Cohn, Benjamin. "History and Anthropology: The State of Play." *Comparative Studies in Society and History* 22 (April 1980): 198–221.

Covell, Lemuel. "Visit of Rev. Lemuel Covell to Western New York and Canada, 1803." Buffalo Historical Society *Publications* 6. Buffalo: Buffalo Historical Society, 1903. 207–217.

Cumming, John, ed. "A Missionary Among the Senecas: The Journal of Abel Bingham, 1822–1828." *New York History* 60 (April 1979): 157–193.

Deardorff, Merle, and George Snyderman. "A Nineteenth-Century Journal of a Visit to the Indians of New York." *Proceedings of the American Philosophical Society* 100 (December 1956): 582–612.

Densmore, Christopher. "More on Red Jacket's Reply." *New York Folklore* 13 (1986): 121–122.

Elkinton, Joseph. "The Quaker Mission Among the Indians in New York State." In: Buffalo Historical Society *Publications* 18. Buffalo: Buffalo Historical Society, 1914. 169–189.

Fenton, William N., ed. "A Further Note on Jacob Jameson's Answers to the Lewis Cass Questionnaire." *Ethnohistory* 17 (1970): 91–92.

Fenton, William N., ed. "Answers to Governor Cass's Questions by Jacob Jameson, a Seneca (ca. 1821–1825)." *Ethnohistory* 16 (1969): 113–139.

Fenton, William N. "Locality as a Basic Factor in the Development of Iroquois Social Structure." *Bureau of American Ethnology Bulletin* 149 (1951): 35–54.

Fenton, William N., ed. "Seneca Indians by Asher Wright (1859)." *Ethnohistory* 4 (1957): 302–321.

Fenton, William N. "Toward the Gradual Civilization of the Indian Natives: The Missionary and Linguistic Work of Asher Wright (1803–1875) Among the Senecas of Western New York." *Proceedings of the American Philosophical Society* 100 (1956): 567–581.

Ganter, Granville. "Red Jacket and the Decolonization of Republican Virtue." *American Indian Quarterly* 31 (Fall 2007): 559–581.

Graymont, Barbara. "New York State Indian Policy After the Revolution." *New York History* 58 (October 1976): 438–474.

Gunther, Gerald. "Governmental Power and New York Indian Lands—A Reassessment of a Persistent Problem of Federal-State Relations." *Buffalo Law Review* 7 (Fall 1958): 1–14.

Harris, George H. "The Life of Horatio Jones." Buffalo Historical Society *Publications* 6. Buffalo: Buffalo Historical Society, 1903. 381–514.

Harris, Thompson S. "Journals of Rev. Thompson S. Harris, Missionary to the Senecas, 1821–1828." In: Buffalo Historical Society *Publications* 6. Frank Severance, ed. Buffalo: Buffalo Historical Society, 1903. 281–380.

Hauptman, Laurence M. "Ditches, Defense, and Dispossession: The Iroquois and the Rise of the Empire State." *New York History* 79 (October 1998): 325–358.

Hauptman, Laurence M. "Four Eastern New Yorkers and Seneca Lands: A Study in Treaty-Making." *Hudson Valley Regional Review* 13 (March 1996): 1–19, 4–22.

Hauptman, Laurence M. "State's Men, Salvation Seekers and the Senecas: The Supplemental Treaty of Buffalo Creek, 1842." *New York History* 78 (January 1997): 51–82.

Hauptman, Laurence M. "Who Owns Grand Island (Erie County, New York)?" *Oklahoma City University Law Review* 23 (Spring/Summer 1998): 151–174.

Holmes, Elkanah. "Letters of Rev. Elkanah Holmes from Fort Niagara." Buffalo Historical Society *Publications* 6. Buffalo: Buffalo Historical Society, 1903. 187–206.

Hopkins, Gerald T. "Visit of Gerald T. Hopkins, 1804." Buffalo Historical Society *Publications* 6. Buffalo Historical Society, 1903. 217–222.

Hopkins, Vivian C. "DeWitt Clinton and the Iroquois." *Ethnohistory* 8 (Spring 1961): 113–143, (Summer 1961): 213–241.

Howland, Henry R. "The Seneca Mission at Buffalo Creek." In: Buffalo Historical Society *Publications* 6. Frank Severance, ed. Buffalo: Buffalo Historical Society, 1903.

Hyde, Jabez Backus. "A Teacher Among the Senecas: A Narrative of Rev. Jabez Backus Hyde, 1811–1820." In: Buffalo Historical Society *Publications* 6. Frank Severance, ed. Buffalo: Buffalo Historical Society, 1903. 239–274.

Ingraham, Duncan [?]. "Extract from a Letter from a Gentleman Upon His Return from Niagara, 1792." In: Studies on the Niagara Frontier, Buffalo Historical Society *Publications* 15. Frank Severance, ed. Buffalo: Buffalo Historical Society, 1911. 390391.

Jackson, Halliday. "Halliday Jackson's Journal to the Seneca Indians, 1798–1800." Anthony F. C. Wallace, ed. *Pennsylvania History* 9 (April & July 1952): 117–147, 325–449.

Kent, Donald H. "Historical Report on the Niagara River and the Niagara River Strip to 1759." In: *Iroquois Indians II: Indian Claims Commission*. New York: Garland Publishing Co., 1974.

Kent, Donald H., and Merle H. Deardorff, ed. "John Adlun on the Allegany: Memoirs for the Year 1794." *Pennsylvania Magazine of History and Biography* 84 (1960): 265–324, 435–480.

Lerch, Richard. "The Rediscovery of Samuel Nelson." *New York History* 34 (1953): 64–71.

Lindley, Jacob. "Jacob Lindley's Journal, 1797." Buffalo Historical Society *Publications* 6. Buffalo: Buffalo Historical Society, 1903. 165–168.

Low, Esther Rutgers. "Narrative of Esther Rutgers Low, 1819–1820." Buffalo Historical Society *Publications* 6. Buffalo: Buffalo Historical Society, 1903. 275–280.

Manley, Henry S. "Buying Buffalo from the Indians." *New York History* 27 (July 1947): 313–329.

Manley, Henry S. "Indian Reservation Ownership in New York." *New York State Bar Bulletin* 32 (April 1960): 134–138.

Manley, Henry S. "Red Jacket's Last Campaign." *New York History* 31 (April 1950): 149–168.

Miller, Nathan. "Private Enterprise in Inland Navigation: The Mohawk Route Prior to the Erie Canal." *New York History* 31 (October 1950): 398–413. Review.

Niemcewicz, Julian Ursyn. "Journey to Niagara, 1805." Metchie J. E. Budka, ed. *New-York Historical Society Quarterly* 74 (January 1961): 72–113.

Parker, Arthur C. "The Senecas in the War of 1812." *Proceedings of the New York State Historical Association* 15 (1916): 78–90.

Parrish, Jasper. "The Story of Jasper Parrish, Captive, Interpreter and United States Sub-Agent to the Six Nations Indians." Frank Severance, ed. Buffalo Historical Society *Publications* 6. Buffalo: Buffalo Historical Society, 1903. 527–538.

Parrish, Stephen, comp. "The Story of Jasper Parrish . . ." Buffalo Historical Society *Publications* 6. Buffalo: Buffalo Historical Society, 1903. 527–538.

Pound, Cuthbert W. "Nationals Without a Nation: The New York State Tribal Indians." *Columbia Law Review* 22 (February 1922): 97–102.

Robie, Harry. "Red Jacket's Reply: Problems in the Verification of Native American Speech Text." *New York Folklore* 12 (1986): 99–117.

Rothenberg, Diane. "The Mothers of the Nation: Seneca Resistance to Quaker Intervention." In: *Women and Colonization: Anthropological Perspectives.* Mona Etienne and Eleanor Leacock, eds. New York: Praeger, 1980.

Severance, Frank H. "The Quakers Among the Senecas." In: Buffalo Historical Society *Publications* 6. Buffalo: Buffalo Historical Society, 1903. 165–168.

Shoemaker, Nancy. "The Rise and Fall of Iroquois Women." *Journal of Women's History* 2 (Winter 1991): 39–57.

Snyderman, George, ed. "Halliday Jackson's Journal of a Visit Paid to the Indians of New York (1806)." *Proceedings of the American Philosophical Society* 101 (December 1957): 565–588.

Tooker, Elisabeth. "Isaac Hurd's Ethnographic Studies of the Iroquois: Their Significance and Ethnographic Value." *Ethnohistory* 27 (Autumn 1980): 363–369.

Tooker, Elisabeth. "On the Development of the Handsome Lake Religion." *Proceedings of the American Philosophical Society* 133 (1989): 35–50.

Tooker, Elisabeth. "On the New Religion of Handsome Lake." *Anthropological Quarterly* 41 (1968): 187–200.

Tooker, Elizabeth. "The League of the Iroquois: Its History, Politics, and Ritual." In: *Handbook of North American Indians*. Vol. 15: *The Northeast*. Bruce G. Trigger and William C. Sturtevant eds. Washington, D.C.: Smithsonian Institution, 1978. 107–134.

Tooker, Elisabeth. "The Structure of the Iroquois League: Lewis H. Morgan's Research and Observations." *Ethnohistory* 30 (Summer 1983): 141–154.

Vallone, Stephen J. "William Seward, Whig Politics, and the Compromised Indian Removal Policy in New York State, 1838–1843." *New York History* 82 (Spring 2001): 107–134.

Vernon, Howard. "Maris Bryant Pierce." In: *Indian Lives: Essays on Nineteenth- and Twentieth-Century Native American Leaders*. Raymond Wilson and L. George Moses, eds. Albuquerque: University of New Mexico, 1985.

Wallace, Anthony F. C., ed., "Halliday Jackson's Journal to the Seneca Indians, 1798–1800." *Pennsylvania History* 19 (1952): 117–146, 325–349.

Wallace, Anthony F. C., and Deborah Holler. "Reviving the Peace Queen: Revelations from Lewis Henry Morgan's Field Notes." *Histories of Anthropology Annual* 5 (2009): 9–109.

White, Marian. "A Reexamination of the Historic Van Son Cemetery on Grand Island." Buffalo Society of Natural Sciences, Anthropology Contributions, *Bulletin* 24 (1968): 1–48.

White, Marian. "Neutral and Wenro." In: *Handbook of North American Indians*. Vol. 15: *The Northeast*. Bruce G. Trigger and William C. Sturtevant, eds. Washington, D.C.: Smithsonian Institution, 1978. 407–415.

Wilkinson, Norman B. "Robert Morris and the Treaty of Big Tree." *Mississippi Valley Historical Review* 40 (September 1953): 257–278.

Whiteley, Peter M. "Why Anthropology Needs More History." *Journal of Anthropological Research* 60 (2004): 487–514

V. Periodicals

Albany Argus
Buffalo Commercial Advertiser
Buffalo Emporium
Eastern Argus [Maine]
Farmers' Cabinet [New Hampshire]
The Friend [Philadelphia]
Ithaca Republican Chronicle
The Mental Elevator [Cattaraugus Reservation]
Monroe Republican [Rochester]
National Aegis [Massachusetts]
New York Daily Advertiser
New York Gazette
New York Herald
New York Times
New York Tribune
Niles Register [Baltimore]
Philadelphia General Advertiser
Republican Advocate [Batavia]
Rochester American
Rochester Daily Advertiser
Rochester Daily Democrat
Watchtower [Cooperstown]

VI. Dissertations and Theses

Abler, Thomas S. "Factional Dispute and Party Conflict in the Political System of the Seneca Nation (1845–1895): An Ethnohistorical Analysis." PhD dissertation. Toronto: University of Toronto, 1969.

Brown, Dorcas R. "The Reservation Log Houses." MA thesis. Cooperstown: State University of New York, Oneonta/New York State Historical Association, 2000.

Conable, Mary. "A Steady Enemy: The Ogden Land Company and the Seneca Indians." PhD dissertation. Rochester: University of Rochester, 1995.

Doxtater, Deborah. "What Happened to Iroquois Clans?: A Study of Clans in Three Nineteenth-Century Rotinonhsyonni Communities." PhD dissertation. London, Ontario: University of Western Ontario, 1996.

Evaneshko, Veronica. "Tonawanda Seneca Ethnic Identity: Functional and Processual Analysis." PhD dissertation. Tucson, Arizona: University of Arizona, 1974.

Haigh, Elizabeth B. "New York Antimasons, 1820–1833." PhD dissertation. Rochester: University of Rochester, 1980.

Karas, Faith E. "Material Culture on the Buffalo Creek Reservation, 1780–1842." MA thesis. Buffalo: State University of New York at Buffalo, 1963.

McClurkin, James M. "We Wish to Be Civilized: Ottawa-American Political Contests on the Michigan Frontier." MA thesis. East Lansing, Michigan: Michigan State University, 1988.

Mt. Pleasant, Alyssa. "After the Whirlwind: Maintaining a Haudenosaunee Place at Buffalo Creek, 1780–1825." PhD dissertation. Ithaca: Cornell University, 2007.

Patrick, Christine. "Samuel Kirkland: Missionary to the Oneida Indians." PhD dissertation. Buffalo: State University of New York at Buffalo, 1992.

Rapp, Marvin A. "The Port of Buffalo, 1825–1880." PhD dissertation. Durham, N.C.: Duke University, 1947.

Rothenberg, Diane B. "Friends Like These: An Ethnohistorical Analysis of the Interaction Between Allegany Senecas and Quakers, 1798–1823." PhD dissertation. New York: CUNY, 1976.

Tiro, Karim. "The People of the Standing Stone: The Oneida Indian Nation From Revolution Through Removal, 1765–1840." PhD dissertation. Philadelphia: University of Pennsylvania, 1998.

Tripp, Wendell E., Jr. "Robert Troup: A Quest for Security in a Turbulent Nation." PhD dissertation. New York: Columbia University, 1973.

Van Hoeven, James W. "Salvation and Indian Removal: The Career Biography of Rev. John Freeman Schermerhorn, Indian Commissioner." PhD dissertation. Nashville, Tennessee: Vanderbilt University, 1972.

Index

187